Mailboats of the Bahamas

Mailboats of the Bahamas

200 Years of Maritime History

Eric Wiberg

Island Books

by the same author:

Bahamas in World War II
U-Boats in the Bahamas
U-Boats off Bermuda
U-Boats in New England
Swan Sinks
Drifting to the Duchess
Drifting (script, with Paolo Pilladi)
Boston Harbor
Round the World in the Wrong Season
Tanker Disasters
Tankers East of Suez
Sea Stories & Scars
Yacht Voyages
Travel Diaries
First Fifty in Fifty
Napoleon's Battles (with Felix Wiberg)
Åke Wiberg, Bahamas Wibergs (with Mats Larsson)
Published Writing & Juvenilia

Published by Island Books, Boston, MA, USA
Copyright © Eric Troels Wiberg, 2021, ericwiberg.com

All rights reserved. No part of this publication may be reproduced in any manner or by any means without the prior written permission of the publisher except in the case of brief quotations embodied in articles or reviews. To contact the author email eric@ericwiberg.com.

ISBN ebook: # 978-0-9983759-0-8,0-9983759-0-X
ISBN Paperback: # 978-1-7356324-0-7,1-7356324-0-6
ISBN Hardback: # 978-0-9843998-9-5,0-9843998-9-5

Library of Congress Control Number: 2016919390

Printed in the United States of America

First Edition, Island Books, 2021

Dedicated to

- R. Craig Symonette,
- Kendal S. Butler,
- Ronald G. Lightbourn, &
- Capt. Paul C. Aranha.

Their combined encyclopedic knowledge of historical watercraft of the Bahamas is a national treasure.

Forewords

Mr. Butler:

When the subject of a book is Mailboats of The Bahamas, then those who know and love this archipelago would have a sense of heightened interest.

Over eight years ago, I met Eric Wiberg through a mutual friend. At that time, Eric's interests intersected mine, and we were aware of our mutual passion for the marine history of The Bahamas. He sought, and received, from me information and opinions on a number of Bahamian-built vessels and outstanding Bahamians in the marine professions. Additionally, he received information on international shipping and The Bahamas, including ship incidents in and near this country during WWII.

When a proper understanding and appreciation of The Bahamas is to be developed, then its marine historical narrative must be understood. Eric's treatment of this subject shows due diligence in research, sensitivity for details, and an understanding of the importance of vessels (Bahamian and foreign) to The Bahamas. His accessing official and non-official documentation as well as oral history of the various islands where shipping incidents occurred, enriches this publication.

The foregoing make this book a "must read" for all who wish to appreciate The Bahamas in its totality.

Kendal S. Butler
Historian of wooden boats of the Bahamas
Nassau, N.P.

Mr. Symonette:

Congratulations to Eric Wiberg on undertaking the research and due diligence to present the wonderful and rich history of our Bahamian mailboats.

These commercial craft have played an integral role in the development of all of our family islands. Many a Bahamian and visitor alike will always have fond memories of their first mailboat voyage to their favorite island. Most of the building materials and supplies were transported to these communities onboard these wonderful craft.

It is especially interesting to note that many of these craft were built within the Bahamas. This is a great tribute to the skilled craftsmen of Harbour Island, Abaco, Nassau, Andros, and Ragged Island.

I sincerely hope that Eric's book becomes standard reading for our younger generations, s it is a great way to better understand the rich nautical history of our country.

                                                        Craig Symonette
                                                        Ship owner, son of ship builder
                                                        Nassau, N.P.

Mr. Forbes:

In this book Mr. Wiberg a Swedish-American expat with a Bahamian soul, has managed to do something remarkable: he has managed to put down the history of his extensive travels on the mail boats of the Bahamas. In so doing, he has ultimately put down the history of any Bahamian who has had the good fortune to traverse the *baja mar*, or the Atlantic Ocean of this archipelagic country.

The Bahamas is indeed an archipelago, and by virtue of that fact, until very recently *il est* the last 40 years of its 528-years of new-world history, as well its pre-European Lucayan history, unless one were a fish or bird, to get from island to island one went by boat. Like travelling anywhere in the world, the vastness, or the quaintness, the riches or the poverty of a place and its significance is lost on local and foreigner alike until one ventures into its domain. In the case of the Bahamas, this could not be more true, especially as it relates to the wealth of its beauty; the cornucopia of its marine life; the variety of its foliage, the diversity of its wildlife and the uniqueness of the anthropological nature of its human inhabitants.

Unless one is a politician campaigning, or perhaps a wholesale distributor, or an avid sea-traveler, as the author is, very few Bahamians and-or foreigners for that matter, have traversed the four quadrants of the archipelago of the Bahamas. Indeed, It is in the traversing of these islands that one discovers why it is called the *isle of June* or the land of the pink pearl. It is said that "if the good lord never went on holiday tell me why did he make the Bahamas, and if his angels never like a sunny day, tell me why did he make the Bahamas?"

Some of my earliest memories as a child come from travelling on the mail boat: I could not have been more than three years old when I and my two elder siblings, who were no more than six, had to step of Potter's Cay Dock onto the deck of the bobbing *Captain Moxey*, which serviced south Andros. It was the *Captain Moxey* that took me to Pleasant Bay, South Andros, where I lived for the next few years, until I was about six years old. There at Pleasant Bay, I would go crabbing; walk barefoot on sharp rocks and develop a sole to rival any shoe, watch my grandmother cook real-peas soup and dumpling with that old salt beef, watch her kneed bread, leave it outside in the sun to rise, fry fresh fish seasoned with pepper and limes grown in her yard, and all cooked on three rocks outside over an open fire of dried wood.

I would walk to the beach, a stone's throw across the road from her house, and catch bonefish with a hand line, avoid stepping on the stingrays which, for some reason camouflaged themselves under the sand a few feet from the shore, walk along the rocks of the shore hunting for delicious red whelks, and draw water from the fresh-water well behind her house. We also watched her kill a large fowl snake that had deposited itself in the beams of the roof of her house by scalding it with hot water.

When my brother's elbow had been accidentally chopped with a cutlass by my cousin, we watched our grandmother grate coconut and bandage it with some cloth around it; today he has fully functioning arm, albeit with a smooth inch-and-a-half scar, never having had a single stitch. We saw her grow corn and grind it with her own mill, thus making her own grits; and we watched her plait straw and teach me how to plait it to send to market. We would walk what must have been a mile to buy her tobacco and a half-pint, drink tamarind punch with fire ash, and last, but not least, discover the tamarind switch. The mailboat, in short, took me to survival school via my grand-mother's house on Andros.

The straw went on the mailboat, the salt beef and Mahatma rice and Robin Hood flour came on the mailboat, the tobacco and the rum; everything came and went on the mailboat, *including the mail*. Unless you had a boat and the time to sail yourself, which the majority of people did not, then it was going on "the mail"

Kudos to Mr. Wiberg for writing a book on a vital part of our Bahamian history, and kudos to him again to him for simply writing a book on Bahamian history and taking an anthropological look at Bahamians, which is a rare thing found mostly only in Bahamian folk songs by Blind Blake, Eddie Minnis, Patrick Rahming, Ronnie Butler, and others.

Otis Forbes
Polymath
Nassau, N.P.

Acknowledgements

Many individuals – most of whom I have only met online, from around the world but sharing a common interest in nautical history and the compelling stories of little work boats, have helped with this project, which started as a web log in 2012. Originally, I fished around for a professional photographer to capture the colours and life at Potter's Cay, aboard moving mailboats, and in various ports, however this duty was relegated to me. I was able to cover Potter's Cay with about 20 visits over five years and leave it to the reader to judge my amateurish efforts at photography. My journalistic training helped me to scoop a number of sea stories and verify them online. I thank Jim Pennypacker of *Powerships* magazine (sshsa.org) for publishing my debut article on this topic across the US and beyond.

And around the globe, from New York City to the American Southwest and Delhi, India, I have been supported along the way by an able team, foremost among them Abdul Rehman Qureshi of Writing Panacea in Quetta, who leads a pre-publication, layout, editing and publishing team who get the job done, at the frenetic pace of a book a month. Abdul converts my work into the product you are holding, enabling me to focus on bringing you the best stories possible. Going back nearly a decade, Aditi Rae as editor and copy editor, as well as meticulous spreadsheet and credit assembly, Monica LoCascio, a New York-based publishing consultant and producer who ably pushed the envelope by editing, laying out, and colouring over 250 photographs, charts, illustrations. Finally, Sanchit Goel and his team at Pepperscript and Onomatopo has again pulled through with a unique and challenging assignment to prepare for publication as well as design a cover.

The most helpful folks have been those to whom I dedicated the book. Eddie Spargur and his alumni of AUTEC (US Navy's Atlantic Underwater Testing and Evaluation Centre) in Andros filled in a lot of missing holes in my research, as did the volunteers at Wyannie Malone Museum in Hope Town and the Albert Lowe Museum in the Abaco Cays. More specifically, Mr. Kendal Butler, a retired Nassau civil servant who has an encyclopaedic knowledge of all wooden boats built in the Bahamas and Turks & Caicos.

Ronald Lightbourn, the Nassuvian boat owner, photographer, and author who has carefully chronicled the architecture and history of the colony and then country's capital in at least one book. And my long-time friend and mentor, Captain Paul Aranha, an aviator, author, and an outstanding sleuth and organizer of history. He has played the patient job to my myriad requests to substantiate factoids ranging from a British yacht (*Tai Mo Shan*) aground in Acklins in the 1920s to an abandoned Royal Navy hospital and everything in between. His patience and acumen never cease to gratify me.

Finally, Craig Symonette, the son of Sir Roland and brother of Bobby, remembers in painstaking detail the history of each vessel and those that it related to his knowledge is immeasurable and unless someone jots it down, as I have tried to piecemeal, the country will have lost a national treasure. Mr. Symonette does more than talk, though – like his father he has been a visionary and with business partners he has reinvigorated, if not completely re-invented inter-island travel by starting and expanding the wildly popular Bahamas Ferries.

Rather than replace, this combination of cargo and passenger service supplements and compliments the existing mail infrastructure, providing a middle way between traditional mailboats and air delivery. And – for the record – even the ultra-modern Bahamas Ferries vessels can occasionally be espied with that tell-tale sign that they are still Bahamian – a small boat being towed astern as a way to earn a little extra freight or return a favour.

Eric Wiberg
Boston
April, 2021

Mailboat Routes

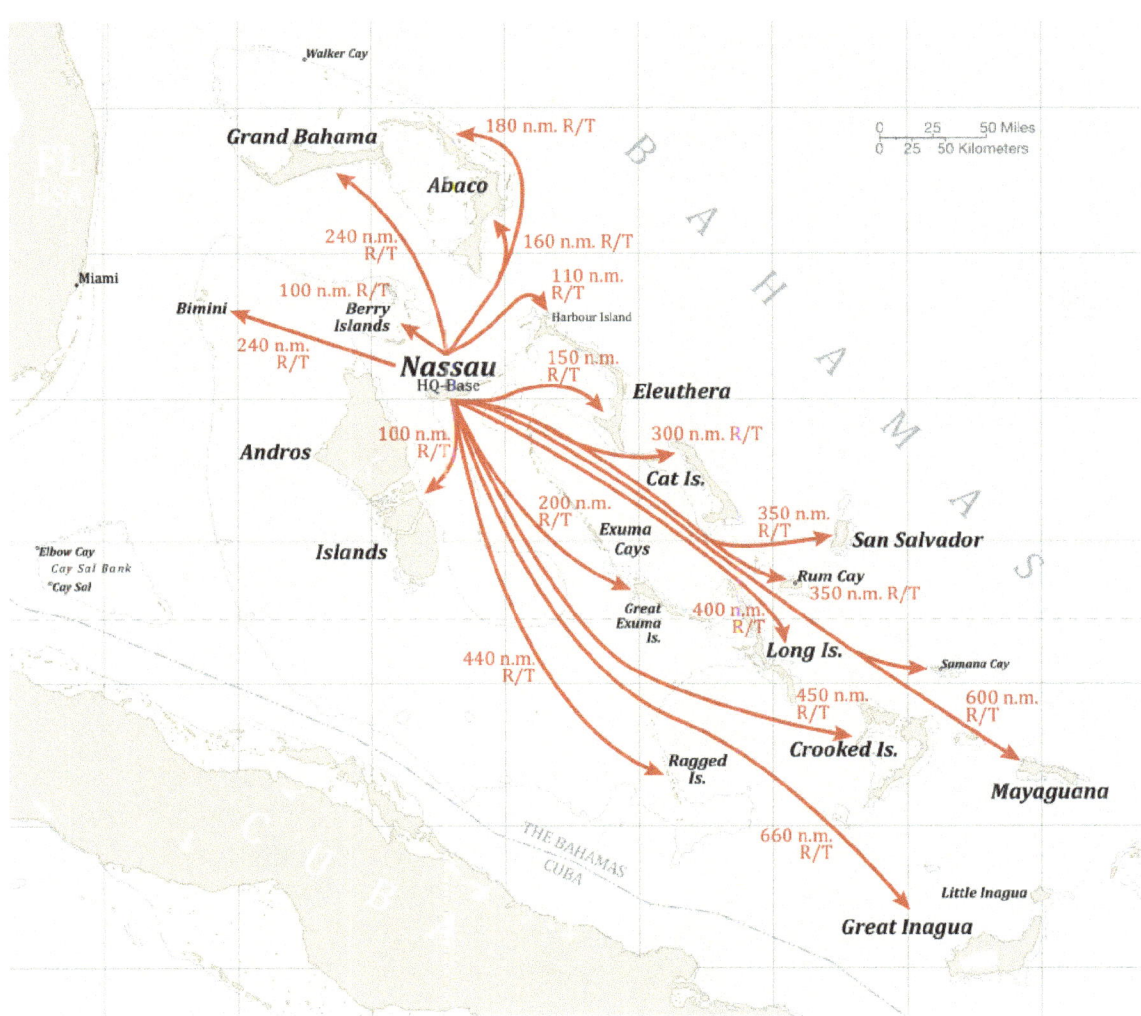

Mailboat routes mileage: round-trip and in nautical miles; over 7,000 miles a week.

Mailboat Ports 1800s to Present

- Abrahams Bay
- Arthurs Town
- Bennetts Harbour
- Bight (The, Cat Island North)
- Black Point
- Bluff (The)
- Bullocks Harbour
- Cherokee Sound (Abaco South)
- Chubb Cay
- Clarence Town (Long Island)
- Cockburn Town (San Salvador)
- Crossing Rocks
- Current (The)
- Current Island
- Deadmans Cay
- Driggs Hill
- Duncan Town (Ragged Island)
- Eight Mile Rock (Grand Bahama)
- Freeport
- Fresh Creek
- George Town (Exuma South)
- Governors Harbour (Eleuthera South)
- Great Harbour (Long Island)
- Great Isaac Island (Bimini Islands)
- Great Sturrup Cay (Berry Islands)
- Green Turtle Cay (Abaco North)
- Gregory Town (Eleuthera South)
- Harbour Island (Eluthera North)
- Hard Bargain (Moores Island)
- Hatchet Bay
- Highbourne Cay
- Hope Town (Great Harbour, Abaco North)
- Kemps Bay
- Little Exuma
- Long Bay Cays
- Long Cay (Fortune Island, Crooked Island District)
- Mangrove Cay (Andros South)
- Marsh Harbour (Abaco North)
- Matthew Town (Inagua)
- Morgans Bluff
- Nicholls Town (Andros North)
- Port Nelson (Rum Cay)
- Rock Sound (Eleuthera South)
- Salt Pond
- Sandy Point
- Savannah Sound (Eleuthera South)
- Simms (Long Island)
- Smiths Bay
- Spanish Wells (Eleuthera North)
- Staniel Cay
- Tarpum Bay (Eleuthera South)
- Treasure Cay

Table of Contents

Forewords	vii
Acknowledgements	xi
Mailboat Routes	xiii
Mailboat Ports 1800s to Present	*xiv*
Table of Contents	xv
130 Mailboat Portraits, by Year Entered Service	1
Bahamas Captains	17
Crew and Mates	23
Mailboats, A Personal Introduction	24
Mailboat Diary Entry, Age 16	29
Nassau Docks, Potter's Cay	33
Economic and Social Overview of Mailboats	36
Economics	*37*
Domestic Impact	*42*
Tourism	*46*
History of Mailboats in the Bahamas Since 1804	50
Abaco Islands	*58*
Eleuthera and Islands	*68*
Grand Bahama and Freeport	*78*
Bimini Islands	*82*
Berry Islands	*85*
Andros Islands	*88*
Exuma Islands	*97*

Ragged Island	*101*
Long Island	*103*
San Salvador and Rum Cay	*106*
Cat Island	*111*
Mayaguana	*113*
Crooked Island, Acklins Island, Long Cay (Fortune Island)	*118*
Inagua	*122*
Family-Owned Mailboat Dynasties	**125**
Roberts Family Dynasty	*126*
Taylor Family Dynasty	*130*
Dean Family Dynasty	*135*
Hanna Family Dynasty	*139*
Mailboat Photographs	**143**
Mailboats in Art	*175*
Shipwrecks	*180*
Mailboat Interiors	*187*
Wooden Boats, to the Present	**222**
European Boats, to the 1990's	**229**
Modern Boats, 1990's to the Present	**236**
Roundup: Mailboats as a Living Bahamian Tradition	**240**
Potter's Cay Dock and the Future	**246**
Historic Post Offices, by Edward B. Proud	**251**
Ports	**254**
Cargo	**256**
Portraits	**257**
Photos of Mailboat Voyages, 1984 – 2019	**259**

Mailboat Voyages Over 40 Years   **267**
   Fleet Overview, Over 200 Years   *268*
   Mailboats by Dates of Service Entry, by Decade   *269*
   Mailboat Names   *271*
   Owners, Part-Owners   *273*
   Other Participants and Contributors   *274*
   Builders, Bahamian   *275*
   Builders, Overseas   *275*
   Yards Large Enough to Both Build and Repair   *276*
   Mailboat Captains, 1804 to 2020   *276*
   Crew, Mates, Cooks, Engineers   *277*
   Charts   *278*

Further Reading   **280**
   Magazines, Booklets, & Pamphlets   *288*
   Newspaper Articles   *290*
   Online Resources   *293*
   Government Resources   *296*
   Filmography   *297*
   Interviews   *298*

Illustration Credits   **299**

About the Author   **304**

130 Mailboat Portraits, by Year Entered Service

Abilin, 1984

Air Pheasant, 1948

Air Swift, 1948

Albertine Adoue, 1898

Alicada, 1933

Alma B., 1995

Almeta Queen, 1957

Arena, 1940

Bahamas Daybreak II, 1962

Bahamas Daybreak III, 1982

Bahamian, 1932

Beluga, 1942

Betty Ann, 1947

Bimini Gal, 1965

Bimini Mack, 1981

Cape Mail, 2017

Captain C., 1990

Captain Dean, 1951

Captain Dean II, 1963

Captain Dean III, 1969

Captain Dean IV, 1974

Captain Dean V, 1977

Captain Emmett, 2019

Captain Gurth Dean, 1999

Captain Moxey 1st, 1975

Captain Moxey 2nd, 1998

Captain Roberts, 1945

Champion II, 1986

Church Bay, 1952

City of Nassau, 1922

Commonwealth, 1975

Content S., 1936

Current Pride, 1980

Current Queen, 1965

Dart, 1878

Daybreak 1st, 1962

Daybreak 2nd, 2018

Deborah K., 1970

Deborah K. II, 1985

Delmar L., 1972

Drake, Bahamas Drake, 1956

East Wind, 2007

Ego, 1943

Eleuthera Express 1st, 1979

Eleuthera Express 2nd, 1997

Emmett Cephas, 1998

Endion, 1920

Ettienne Cephas, 1975

Exuma Pride, 1978

Fiesta Mail, 2002

Frecil, 1950

Gary Roberts, 1957

Gleaner Express, 1972

Grand Master, 1993

Grand Master II, 2020

Harley & Charley, 1969

Inagua Spray, 2016

Island Link, 2014

Jeleta, 1990

Johnette Walker, 1972

K.C.T., 2012

Lady Blanche, 1973

Lady D., 1983

Lady Dundas, 1960

Lady Eddina, 1995

Lady Emerald, 2003

Lady Eula, 1978

Lady Frances, 1989

Lady Gloria, 1985

Lady Kathreina, 2005

Lady Margo II, 1995

Lady Mathilda 1st, 1989

Lady Mathilda 2nd, 1998

Lady Moore, 1974

Lady Rosalind 1st, 1987

Lady Rosalind I, 2002

Lady Rosalind II, 2006

Lady Tasha, 1971

Legacy, 2002

Legend, 2006

Legend II, 2006

Liberty, 1943

Lisa J. 1st, 1973

Lisa J. II, 1985

Madam Elizabeth Rolle, 1958

Mal Jack, 1989

Mangrove Cay Express, 1988

Marcella 1st, 1985

Marcella III, 1981

Maxine, 1989

Mia Dean, 1990

Miranda, 1978

Miss Andros, 1972

Miss BJ, 1990

ML 371, 1946

Monarch of Nassau, 1930

Nassau, 1950s

Nassau Moonglow, 1972

Nay Dean, 1985

New Day, 1972

New G., 2015

Noel Roberts, 1943

North Andros Princess I, 1984

North Cat Island Special, 1986

North Cat Island Special II, 2003

Passing Jack, 1950

Priscilla, 1924

Patricia K., 1930

Queen, Athelqueen lifeboat, 1942

Richard Campbell, 1937

President Taylor, 2017

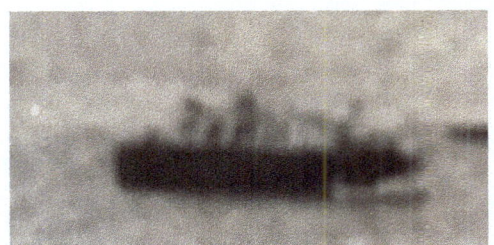

Princess Montagu, 1920

San Cristobal, c.1940

Sea Hauler, 1989

Sea Salvor, 1947

Sea Spirit II, 1999

Sealink, 2000

Seawind, 2003

Sherice M., 1995

South Andros Express, 1950

Stede Bonnett, 1942

Tolyn, 2016

Trans Cargo II, 2014

United Spirit, 1999

Treasure Lady, 1981

United Star, 1999

VI Nais, 2007

Willaurie, 1980

Windward Express, 1995 *Zelma Rose,* 1947

Bahamas Captains

Albury, Ancil, aka Spotty

Archer, John Spurgeon

Armbrister, Charles Napier

Albury, Harry

Archer, Robert Sherwin, Hon.

Bain, Frederick

Archer, Garnett

Archer, Tyrone

Barnett, Richard, aka Ricky

Brozozog, Lance

Carroll, Clifford, aka Cliff

Culmer, Leland, aka Blue Boy

Davis, Nigel

Dean, Ernest A., Jr.

Dean, Ernest Alexander

Dean, Jonathan

Farquharson, Arlington E.

Gray, Frederick

Gray, Rolly

Heath, Cecil

Kelly, David Austin

Lockhart, Edward

Higgs, Edison, aka Captain Bird

Knowles, Christopher

Lockhart, Roy Oral

Hyde, David

Lockhart, Anton

Lockhart, Vernon

Lockhart, Victor

Maycock, Etienne

Moxey, Edgar O.

Lowe, William Roy

Miller, Luther

Moxey, Henry Uriah

Miller, Rodney

Moxey, Hezron

Maycock, Cephas, Sr.

Moxey, Boycel, Jr.

Moxey, Kevin

Moxey, *Seawind*

Neilly, Patrick

Pinder, Reginald Elon, aka Reggie

Munroe, Emmett

Patton, Leviticus

Roberts, Ancil

Munroe, Jed

Pinder, Gurney Elon

Roberts, Hartley

Roberts, Leland

Taylor, Elvin

Turnquest, Harrod Audley

Roberts, Roland

Taylor, Limas

Wallace, Leonard

Roberts, William A., aka Augustus

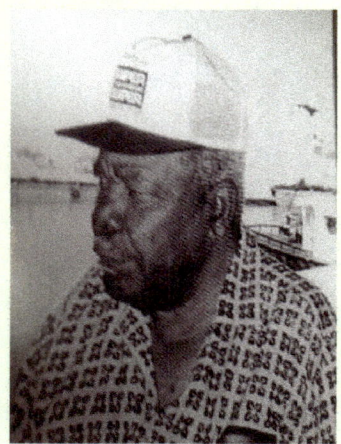

Taylor, Nathaniel Bruce

Weech, William Ferris

Taylor, Eddins Bruce

Crew and Mates

Armbrister, Anicka, Cook

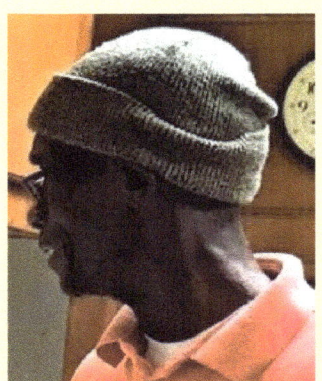
New G. Cook

Maycock, Cephas, Mate

Maycock, Jared, Seaman

Maycock, Tiaro, Cook

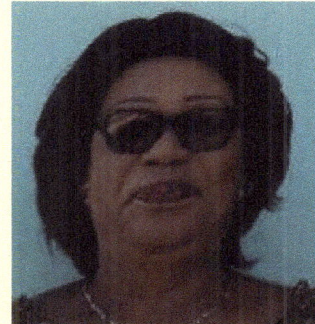
Forbes-Berry, Delores, Potter's Cay Dockmasters

Mailboats, A Personal Introduction

"Sir, since we are dealing with the topic of our nation's history and heritage, it is important that we are both continuously aware of the seriousness of this undertaking."

When I suggested to a fellow Bahamian historian that, after half a decade of close collaboration, we consider addressing each other by our first names, this was his reply. I was moved to tears by it, and still am. So I – we – approach this topic with a dose of humility, for mailboats unify our country: they are the sinews, the arteries, the highways and runways all in one, and while to many they seem colorful (they are), they are conducting serious business and with constant risk to life and limb of their officers and crew and those like the RBDF and BASRA; one the government defense force, the other volunteer captains and pilots. And yes, a decade on, he and I still address one another as *Mister* or *Captain*.

Why write about mailboats? It is a question I have often been asked, and most recently so by a group of yachtsmen visiting from the States. When I describe my passion for these slow-plodding beasts of burden to the folks on the docks at Potter's Cay or to friends and family members, they seem to understand, but not everyone does. And not every reader will.

In the early 1980s, when I was not yet a teenager, my parents – both expatriates who had lived several decades in the islands and honeymooned in Treasure Cay – took my three siblings and me on a mailboat voyage to Abaco. The voyage left quite an impression on us – being able to bring as many belongings as we wanted, to roam freely over the vessel, and to enjoy the fresh sea breeze the entire way was a thrill unmatched by air travel. It was also an unusual way for an expatriate family to travel at the time, though by no means unique, it was perhaps bohemian of us, or at least we thought so. Once my brothers, sister, and I figured out that we could get from Nassau to Harbour Island each way for about the cost of entry into Club Waterloo, we were hooked.

From the late 1980s onwards, Captain Moss of the *Bahamas Daybreak III* came to know us – the family that preferred to ride the mailboat. A resort owner on Briland, once challenged me as to why I would possibly take the mailboat. I hadn't really thought of the reasons – for some reason the idea of going to the airport and paying what I believed would be a lot more money seemed preposterous; something that rich people did. Ironically the prospect of flying seemed to me to cheapen the experience, as though stopping for a few minutes at Spanish Wells and then navigating the Devil's Backbone with its hairpin turns, skimming the wreck of a sunken locomotive, and brushing along the beach was a way of somehow earning the way to decadence on the island. Then again, we stayed mostly at the modest Royal Palm rather than the Pink Sands!

Somehow, over the years, Potter's Cay dock worked its way into the family lore. Like the time our mother waved us off on the *Daybreak* she realized she was locked out of her car – we had the keys – and in her Pajamas on Potter's cay at dawn. A kindly cab driver looked after her. For a midnight departure I left a group drinking at Big Daddy's at 11 pm to tell the captain we would be back before midnight. We were, but the ship was leaving! He thought we had boarded already at 11. However, he misunderstood me, thought we were aboard, and cast off just as we ran up the dock to do a pier-head leap, just in time! Or the time when we turned back to the dock late at night because the captain's nephew, who was serving as crew, forgot his radio – outstretched arms, handed it to us – in those days before iPhones, from another mailboat, by understanding sailors.

Have I taken more mailboat trips than other Bahamians? Not by a long shot. Half a dozen voyages to and from Harbour Island, a few more perhaps on the modern Bo Hengy and *Bo Hengy II*. A longer cruise on the *United Star* to Acklins Island, on which, we shared the voyage with the new doctor-in-residence from the Philippines. I asked him his specialty – he replied that he was a veterinarian! There was a voyage from Nassau to Black Point Exuma, San Salvador, and Rum Cay, which didn't end so well when the boat ran aground off Port Nelson and I received a cold reception when I was rowed ashore, as I was (correctly) taken for a real estate speculator. Perhaps the happiest mailboat trip was the one that ended in Potter's Cay at dawn.

The aforementioned girlfriend and I boarded about midnight, the day after Christmas Junkanoo, and voyaged to Bullock's Harbour, Berry Islands. From there we set off for Moore's Island's only settlement – Hard Bargain. But halfway there we were startled to wake up to commotion and see a sheer wall of white steel looming out of our porthole. In all the excitement of loading and unloading the cargo, our otherwise earnest skipper had forgotten to deliver the mail to the Berry Islands and was having a cruise ship divert to complete the errand for him. We spent a night in Hard Bargain, alongside a vessel named Jesus Saviour Pilot Me, listening to the tales of old timers, on an island where strains of Yoruba were recorded as recently as the 1970s. From there we voyaged to nearby Sandy Point and the mailboat lay over for a few days. But we were eager to get back to Nassau and accepted a graciously offered ride aboard the Sea Star, arriving in time to celebrate New Year's Junkanoo in the capital. A memorable trip indeed!

Nowadays, one has the added convenience of bringing a vehicle, as we have done, to Abaco and North Eleuthera. And I once brought a bicycle to Mastic Point, Andros. But, as many readers will know, renting a vehicle in the family islands can be as simple as asking around, finding the car, and leaving the agreed daily rate in cash, along with the keys, behind the visor. My brother and I once went camping in Eleuthera to be met with the same kind of queries: why not stay in a hotel? For the same reason that one takes the mailboat, to get that little bit closer to nature, or at least to think you are. To get that little bit closer to the people who populate these wonderful islands, to hear and feel the breeze, not see it through an airplane portal at 3,000 feet.

Why take a mailboat? If I had to be entirely honest, the motivations were mostly selfish. In my teens and twenties, when I was single and came back home from school and later from college, during Christmas vacations, it was to get away from Nassau and all those married people after the crescendo of Christmas and New Year's. Later it was to look at land to invest in by being able to see several islands on one trip, always moving forward, rather than to fly to one island, return to Nassau, fly to another island, go back to Nassau, and so on. Partly I was escaping work at the family business – playing hooky as it were. Partly there were romantic aspirations – find a companion and head off together into the unknown for a few days, by picking the first mailboat to leave, wherever it would take you.

Pack a cooler full of sodas, beer, and sandwiches and you never know what daybreak, or the next wave, will bring you. Perhaps to an island that wasn't even on the itinerary, but where the captain needs to visit his sweetheart du jour. It's happened more than once. Besides, when the crew catches or buys fresh conch or fish, they are just as likely to share it, perhaps in exchange for a cold beer – a fair trade. That line trailing behind the ship may produce a fearsome barracuda, or it might just be trailing a pair of trousers being naturally washed by the wake. On a mailboat, you just never know for sure, and I guess that is the mystique – along with necessity, transport, trade, friends, and family and a host of other rational reasons – that drives people like me back to mailboats. And I hope – as my parents did – that my son catches the bug as well. He is, after all, named after one of the communities dear to our hearts and accessed by the *Bahamas Daybreak* those decades ago – Dunmore Town.

Simple map of the Bahamian archipelago showing the main island groups, but not ports. All of these major sixteen islands are served by mailboats, as well as smaller islands such as Harbour Island, Spanish Wells, Hope Town, numerous islands in the Exuma, Berry, and Bimini chains as well as off Abaco, and Rum Cay, to name a few. Little Inagua, Plana Cays, Little San Salvador, and many others, being uninhabited, are not served. In the Exuma chain, for example, every inhabited island has its own boat or boats which are used to voyage to nearby islands to collect supplies, fuel, food, mail, etc. So, each port that a mailboat calls is also a hub, or transportation node for the distribution of goods between manufacturers, consumers, producers, and markets.

Liberty in Spanish Wells, North Eleuthera, c.1950s. She was a 45-foot long wooden mailboat built by brothers Earl and Gerald Johnson in Harbour Island, probably in the mid- 1940s. This duo built at least four other mailboats, including the *Gary Roberts* and *Captain Roberts*. She plied mostly between Spanish Wells, North Eleuthera, Nassau, and, in the 1980s, Fresh Creek and southern Andros. Note that if you compare the photos, the narrow stern/transom, the 4 X 4 or so wooden rails, the single deck, and the large prominent cross-trees above the wheel-house, you will likely conclude that they are the same vessel. Even the tyres are hung from the same stanchions, if you look closely!

Liberty entering Fresh Creek, Andros in the early 1980s. The gentleman who submitted this photograph lived at the AUTEC base in Andros at the time and joked that at that time the crew of wooden mailboats didn't repair leaks, they just added another bilge pump.

Mailboat Diary Entry, Age 16

Thursday, 1 July, 1987 at 9:38 a.m., on board the mail boat Bahama Daybreak *heading from Nassau, to Harbour Island. Weather: Sunny and beautiful although it rained heavily last week. Writing from the top deck of this grand old mailboat, and I feel at peace with myself. I appreciate travel as a source of motivation. We woke up at 4:45 a.m. and my brother and two guests from overseas were aboard by 6 a.m. We cast off for Eleuthera by 6:10 a.m., and after stops in Spanish Wells and The Bluff, we hope to arrive in Harbour Island by 2 p.m.*

This boat is strong and slow, the Bahamian flag flutters at the bow, the sky is sunny + cloudless, the seas with a mild chop, winds from the East-South East. We took the cut north between Paradise Island and Atoll Cay, past Spruce Cays and the old quarantine station as we left Nassau Harbour. We came upon the north side of Rose Island, past Salt Cay and the Blue Lagoon, Booby Rocks, Chub Rocks, Green Cay and Honeymoon Cay. Right now, we are heading east past Current Island for Current Cut Eleuthera and on to St. George Island and Spanish Wells....

While I attempt to cover the logistics and larger picture of the mailboat story, at the end of the day for most of us, our experience with a mailboat is a personal one; the anticipation and planning, waiting for departure, the buzz of last-minute activity, the serenity of being out of touch, and the transition between missing those we've left, enjoying those we are with, and anticipating those we are about to be with, perhaps in a developing storm. In putting together the personal side of the story it has been necessary not to skim a phone book and dial, but rather to get down to the docks one more time and see who, and what you bump into there. Growing up, my siblings and I were able to see Stan Waterman, Jacques Cousteau, and others give presentations about the Bahamas at the Dundas Theater.

The best role models I had growing up for getting out and embracing the Bahamas and engaging fellow Bahamians one-on-one were the Popov Brothers of Love Beach; Dragan and Nicolas. I grew up in awe of them; our parents took us to their presentations and sponsored their trips, and hosted events at the family business for them. Most of all it was so tantalizing to see these young people zip around the bend into Old Fort Bay on their high-speed inflatable expedition boats which they operated like extra appendages, beaching them effortlessly. In 1995 I has the privilege to participate in an expedition, collecting charitable supplies, writing short articles, and then meeting the team on two sailboats in the Turks & Caicos before spending nearly a month in places like Hogsty Reef, Fortune Island, and in the Exumas.

The ethos of the Popov's Island Expeditions is that their multicultural members pride themselves on being unimposing, arriving in small boats, camping, fishing, and speaking with residents at eye-level, as fellow-mariners. I learned a lot from that modest and highly effective approach. I learned to recognize that locals, particularly those who are older, are the center of the attention and deserve to be heard. Whereas there are excellent written records and genealogies for some communities, for example, in Abaco, North Eleuthera, and New Providence, and many locally built boats made it into the index of the British Mercantile Navy, others did not.

The author keeping a record aboard the *Bahamas Daybreak* on the way from Nassau to Harbour Island, c.1988. Note that he is sitting in church pews. The names of *Bahamas Daybreak*, whilst apparently the same vessel, have gone from being the third (III) to having no number and simply *Bahama Daybreak*, reversing the usual trend. The vessel is 110 feet long and can carry 24 passengers in comfort on short passages. Her captain in the 1980s was named Moss, but he moved over to the Bahamas Ferries. Other captains have included Quincy Sawyer and Capt. Ashok. Her owner is listed as Captain Theophilus Stuart of North Eleuthera. Her route has always – since at least the mid-1980s – been from Nassau to Eleuthera, including Governors Harbour, Hatchet Bay, the Bluff, Spanish Wells, and Harbour Island, each round trip taking roughly half the week.

Having interviewed persons in Andros, Mayaguana, Turks and Caicos, Moore's Island and Sandy Point, and been welcomed into homes in Harbour Island to interview a retired, elderly mariner and his wife as they reposed in their beds, I came to recognize the strength and value of oral history, and it's accuracy. Every single time

I've gone to Potter's Cay over more than 40 years I have learned something, even just from looking from a car window on the way to pick up another weekly schedule. Of course, there were visits to archives and purchases of dozens of books, and scheduled interviews, as well as phone calls and emails too. Mrs. Susan Roberts met me for an interview with mailboat namesake *Richard Campbell* Roberts, her brother-in-law, with a car trunk full of paintings of Sir George Robert's mailboat fleet from she and her husband Noel Robert, for me to photograph. In April of 2020, artist Bill Johnson sent photos of his mailboat paintings and drawings from Lubber's Quarters, Abaco.

As part of due diligence, I also wrote to every government representative of each island, the AMMC, or Antiquities, Monuments, and Museums Corporation, the Bahamas National Archives, Turks and Caicos Museum, the Bahamas Ministry of Transport and Aviation, the Bahamas Maritime Authority, and visited the International Development Bank, or IDB, in Nassau. I also combed the news databases on microfiche in the Bahamas, digitally in Florida, the *Kingston Gleaner* in Jamaica and, others, 100 of which are listed at the end.

Just please remember that as you read an account of another port and another mailboat, that there is a 30% chance that the writer rode aboard the boat in question, if modern, and if the boat has called at Potter's Cay in recent decades it's quite certain he's seen it. When you see a description of an island or port (sadly, not Long Island and Ragged Island yet), it is probable that the writer has been there, and maybe even shot a game of pool, downed a beverage, and told sea stories there as well! He's climbed to the tops of the lighthouse at Hope Town, Hole in the Wall, Paradise Island, Castle Island and Great Inagua, camped under the Hogsty Reef light and helped light the small light at Fortune or Long Cay off Crooked. Cay Lobos and Cay Sal remain elusive.

It may be seem difficult to grasp, but for most of the Bahamas' history mailboats were about the ONLY means of public transport. Bahamas Airways was founded in 1936, yes, but the war intervened and many folks could not afford round-trip flights until the 1950s – and later. Even the government hasn't always been able to afford getting flights to every community every few days. Only 40% of the timespan of mailboats has there been an air option, so 60% of the time it was mailboat or nothing. Like the tortoise to the hare the faithful mailboats have plodded through all the crises, as they do in the spring of 2021.

Here's to hoping that you find this story about mailboats both informative and enjoyable, and that it inspires you to head down to Potter's Cay, or the nearest dock, bring family and friends, and watch the magic first hand; even the best mailboats eventually must be replaced, perhaps moving into the diving attraction market, carrying the gospel in Africa, as one boat is doing in Tanzania, as the third *Marcella* is believed to have done under the name *Our Lady of Mercy*, or simply becoming tens of thousands or razor blades or rebar.

Voyage companions aboard the *North Cat Island Special*, on one of its first voyages to several ports in Cat Island. The two men sitting are brothers going to see family; the man standing is on the crew. The gentleman in the blue trousers was a security guard at Lyford Cay Club. Taken on the way to Bennett's Harbour, March, 1987. The *North Cat Island Special* was built in the US – probably the US Gulf – in the mid-1980s. Her tonnage was 98 and length 80 feet. She served Bennett's Harbour, Orange Creek, Dumfries, and North and South Bight of Cat Island between roughly 1986 up to about 2010. One of her masters was Captain Roy Oral Lockhart (1927–2002), who was awarded the Queen's Certificate of Honour on 23 October, 2001.

Nassau Docks, Potter's Cay

Potter's Cay with three mailboats barely visible under bridge spans at top of cay, and two behind sheds to right. The one to the right appears to be of military build and may be *Air Swift*. Those to the left are likely controlled by the Dean family, which dominate that area.

Eastern Nassau, New Providence, 1936 showing wharves mailboats called before Potter's Cay.

Western end of Potter's Cay Dock when it was a sewerage treatment plant.

Modern Potter's Cay Dock, with the second bridge to Paradise Island showing, in 2016. The insides of the "T" to the right are taken by fishing craft and vendors, and Haitian trading craft and other small miscellaneous vessels occupy the north side, between the bridges. Aside from the southwest tip being used by Bahamas Ferries, the entire rest of the waterfront is utilized for – and available to – mailboats.

A wide-angle view of Potter's Cay from the eastern tip, in 2016, showing the causeway to the island at left, the Taylor Corporation's dock-side offices in blue in the foreground, and Atlantis resort in the background right, accessible by both bridges to Paradise Island, which are shown. This is the command centre and headquarters of all mailboat activity from which the manager of the government mailboat office (right behind the photographer, who sits on an historic fort) can replace one mailboat with another and reorganize the fleet to ensure service commitments are met. He or she also disseminates a weekly list of arrivals, departures, and destinations to be picked up in person.

Economic and Social Overview of Mailboats

If there is a discernable pattern to mailboats, it is that the communities themselves start by helping themselves: by financing or building their own boats, due to a need for reliable supply chains and affordable passenger flow both ways, with the government largely reacting and keeping up with the dual motives of keeping the system running with subsidies, and keeping themselves elected. It wasn't always that way; originally the government owned and controlled all mailboat service, and chartered in tonnage where not, making it the second-largest mailboat operator in Bahamian history. The opposite of that centralized control took place in the 1970s and 1980s, when the fleet blossomed as a result of widespread government expenditure, allowing new participants to invest in the sector. Since then many of the boats which didn't succeed foreclosed, were sold out of the market, sank, or were scrapped.

Today the main challenges are removing derelicts from usable dock space on Potter's Cay, watching that too few owners not control too great a percentage of the fleet (or at least not leverage that advantage too greatly), and, as always, government subsidies being able to keep up with economic realities and owners being able to balance debt load with profits, fuel costs with freight revenues. No one doubts that mailboats will survive the jet as well as the internet ages; they are thriving. Here is a good one-paragraph overview of the whole system my prolific historian Michael Craton:

From the 1920s the scattered islands were more firmly roped together by a heterogeneous flotilla of small motor vessels. Many of them were wooden-hulled converted sailboats, seemingly rickety and top-heavy, but still capable of negotiating the shoals and storms of Bahamian waters in the hands of their sea-hardened and expert captains and crews. Named after their owners' wife, children or girlfriend, the owner or captain himself or in one case, even and 18th-century pirate the *Stede Bonnet*. Each vessel had its own character. Along with their captains and crew, they became respected even loved by the islanders who they served year after year. Though most of the boats were owned by Bay Street merchants, some were still captained by their owners, and all captains, whether white, brown, or black, were very important personages indeed in the islands which they served. Typically, one of them owned shops, and kept separate families in Nassau and Long Island." (Craton, *A-Z of Bahamian History*, p.240).

Economics

Regarding economic aspects of the establishment and maintenance of the mail boat service in the Bahamas, the National Archives retains an extract from the Privy Council minutes of 25 June, 1819, in the Governor's Dispatches, 1818 to 1825. Mr. McKinney, member House Assembly, proposed to direct the mail establishment to the Bahama Islands. "The purpose was to transport and deliver mails by boat from Crooked Island, the main depot, to the other islands; hence the term "mail boat." The cost of running the mail boat service was GB pounds sterling 700 per annum."

Since 1980 the BDB, or Bahamas Development Bank has subsidized the mailboat fleet to the tune of about $2 mm per year, or $80 mm since then. Part of their reasoning is explained thus: "Though dedicated to making it as much self-sustaining private enterprise as possible, in order to maintain a reliable general service and sustain some of the less prosperous Family Islands, the government has been constrained to pump up to $20 million to operators through the Bahamas development bank since 1980," in a 1992 *Bahamas Handbook* article published by Dupuch Publications (p.241). According to the same article, subsidies amounted in 1992 to between $750 to $6,864 weekly.

Included in the exchange is a promise of reliable service; "mail boat operators are bound by contract not only to carry postal mail, but they are also required to carry, free of charge, cargo assigned to other government ministries and departments. For example, a lighthouse keeper and his family travelling from one island to another in the line of duty, are exempt from paying." The same is also true for Family Island Commissioners. The Ministry of Transport uses the Inter-Island Mail Shipping Rates Rules. A random check in 1991 showed that foodstuffs are the least costly to ship. A case of eggs is $2. Household appliances cost more to ship. Refrigerators $25, gas stove $10 to transport (still less than for a person). Concrete blocks are 50 cents per, bundle of shingles $5. There are freezers, but live sheep are $2. Japanese cars $100, with an American Chevrolet 9-passnger wagon costing $150 (1992 *Bahamas Handbook*, p.412). A simple but adequate bunk in a cabin with up to three meals a day can be had for, depending on the length of the voyage, less than $50.

Not only the vessels, but the public docks they require to transact business, land and load cargoes and passengers require funding and maintenance. Potter's Cay, the indisputed hub for all things mailboats, cost the government £487,000 (roughly USD $11 mm today) from the Out Island and Freight Terminal Loan Act of May 23, 1962, "to construct an Out Island Passenger and terminal at Potter's Cay ,with a causeway and bridge leading therefrom, and certain transit sheds and other buildings thereon." Additionally but unrelated, Kelly Island was to be turned into Arawak Cay on the western end, under the Nassau Harbour Development Scheme. Included in this mega-project was the Frederick Snare Corporation of New York. Four years later another loan from the Bahamas Development Bank, this one for USD $14 mm, was secured by a legislative act of 1966.

What does all the money go towards, and how do citizens accrue the benefits of these far-sighted investments. Naturally those who rely on mailboats the most will benefit the most, and since tourists and a different market utilize air and cruise nodes of transport more, the trade allows more artisanal farmers and craft-persons and those who rely on the mailboat for transport to benefit the most, with the least competition. Furthermore, the government regulates the sector to ensure deliverables are met, starting with inspecting vessels and crew. Their agent, dockmaster, eyes the dock pretty much constantly from the highest perch on Potter's Cay, as though an air-traffic-control tower. The 1992 *Bahamas Handbook* notes that "mailboat captains must be experienced seamen with good general knowledge of the Bahamas before a captain's license is issued. In most cases, a written examination is conducted by the Port Authority, an organization which also sets rules regarding the safety of mail-boat passengers. (p.415).

In 2020 a fleet of roughly 18 primary and 3 to 5 substitute mailboats cover up to 7,280 nautical miles each week. That is an average of 315 nautical miles per mailboat per week, according to distances between ports (see chart) and recent schedules published by the Potter's Cay Dockmaster's office. That's an average of 45 nautical miles per day, which although most can cover 250 a day, is impressive given the many nights a week they must lay over in port and keep schedules. In order to keep subsidies they must wait for the customer and adhere to published schedules. The government subsidizes between 25 and 30 mailboats at a time, some of which rotate duties due to repairs and fulfilment of duties such as rush fuel or medical shipments, or substitutions.

The number of official post offices per island and port is assumed to be fairly static, and each will have a Post Master or postal agent. An annual government report in 1966 (Appendix 1), shows a total of 88 post offices on 18 major island, as follows: Abaco, 9, Acklins, 4, Andros, 9, Berry Islands, 1 (variously given as Bullock's Harbour, Lignumvitae Cay, and Great Harbour), Bimini, 2, Cat Island 8, Exuma, 9, Grand Bahama, 3, North Eleuthera, 7, Inagua, 1, Long Cay, 1 Long Island, 7, Mayaguana 2, New Providence 5, Ragged Island 1, Rum Cay 1, San Salvador 1. This equates to 11,000 miles is if you sailed to each of the 52 ports for 5,535 nm, and then back; most boats call various ports along a string rather than each one and back. In 1991 and 1992; 20 mailboats made more than 30 trips per week.

The *Bahamas Handbook* and other economic studies estimate the annual subsidization of the mailboat fleet at roughly $2 million Bahamian dollars since the 1980 time-frame, when significant funds were expended to centralize mailboat, commercial fishing, and industrial freight operations between Potter's Cay and Arawak Cay, and away from the docks owned by traditional industrialist families downtown. That would mean that roughly $60 million has been spent, with probably much more in the form of loans from the likes of International Development Bank (IDB, with offices adorned with mailboat photos, overlooking Potter's Cay), and the Bahamas Development Bank. As one economist observed in the early 1990s, "the market for marine transportation in the Bahamas is estimated to be close to $100 million, and is growing in line with the population and economic activity in the family islands."

Since the primary recipients of these funds are the owners of mailboats, a closer look at their composition is called for. To start with, out of 168 vessels with identifiable owners, when the government is removed, and all those without some kind of family connection to each other, only 20 boats are eliminated, our 12%. In other words, 88% of known mailboat owners, even those with just two boats, have some relationship through kindred with each other (though not, of course to other owners necessarily). So right away we can divine that this is an industry where close bonds of trust are a foundation for long-term, multi-generational business. That can be reassuring to customers, as well. (*Important qualifier*: a data dump of 150 boats which mostly plied in the 1800s arrived after this analysis was run: because of the highly individual and fragmented ownership structures of 100 years ago, most boats were chartered by H.M. Government and most boats were owned by one person, or at most a small handful by one person. So that data is simply not included here, as it distracts).

Out of 197 vessels going back 200 years, there are 60 identifiable owners. Put another way, only less than 17% of the total fleet (33 out of 197) has been owned by single owners, and even those may mask a fleet owner. There are 10 owners with just 2 boats, and 26 owners control 74 mailboats. The top 3 by fleet numbers are the Taylors with 23, the British government, with 16, and the Deans have 14. Hanna and the Roberts dynasties are tied at fleets of 9 vessels. At some point data can become a blur, so perhaps this simplifies the concept of economies of scale benefiting existing owners and creating barriers to entry with industries like cruise shipping and hotels as well: 70 owners split 197 boats. But 26 of those owners (control 38% of the boats.

Let's study the relative influence of the top owners; Taylors own 23 ships, and we should discount H. M. Government, so next ae the Deans with 14, followed by Hanna and Roberts, each tied for 9 vessels and 18 together. So, in aggregate these four families control 55 boats out of the 168. I am removing the government as that was mostly 100 years ago, and including both Hanna and Roberts, Roberts not being in the market today, so the data is skewed, but the point remains; the top 3 owners control 33% of the fleet, or 55 boats out of 168, even though they represent only 5% of the total ownership pool, which is 32 single-boat owners, 10 double-boat owners, and 4 to 5 "whales" with 9, 9, 14, 16, and 23 vessels respectively. If ownership was distributed not per-boat (that would require 168 owners, or 197), each owner would have 3 boats. In reality, 16 owners control an average of 7.25 boats each, and the 32 single-boat owners control just 19% of the fleet, with two-boat owners controlling 12% of the boats, although they represent 17.25% of the ownership pool.

This is completely common to shipping fleets globally and will probably remain so. For example, the top three cruise line owner globally control an eye-watering 72% of the world fleet, with Carnival Corporation having 47% of the passengers and 39% of the revenue, Royal Caribbean Cruises (RCCL) holding 20% of persons and 23% of the income, and Norwegian Cruise Lines (NCL) controlling 9.5% of the passengers and 13% of the revenue, with MSC Cruises in fourth. Fragmentation and inefficiencies are limited, as larger fleets can substitute tonnage and survive crises better and more cost effectively, ultimately benefiting the consumer and gaining their confidence, however the opportunity for price gauging, monopolistic behaviour, and other flip sides of the economic equation exist per human nature and failings. I was aboard a large vessel delivering an emergency shipment of gasoline to an island for the government. When I offered my hosts to pay to fill their truck with gas, they all assured me that such an offer was ludicrous and that I could not afford it, and they were right.

Lest this seem like a hopeless, and calcifying oligarchy, increasingly vertically integrated as owners branch into trades with the US, and going for larger portions of the passenger market, or bleeding from the passenger into the mail sector without carrying mail, just freight and rolling stock, we must remember that the government keeps the doors of this market open for public bidding. Certainly in theory. In 2007 national and other newspapers declared, in a piece headlined: "The Ministry of Lands and Local Government invites tenders for its 20 inter-insular Mailboat routes." Continuing, the public notice declares that "persons interested in participating in the bidding process [for mailboat contracts] may visit the office of the Ministry of Lands and Local Government at Dockendale House, West Bay Street, or the former National Insurance Building on Robinson Road, from 9.30 am to 4.30 pm. Tenders are due by 4.30 pm on Friday, September 21, 2007," which was roughly two weeks after the advertisement ran, on 6 September, 2007. So, while it is not a closed market in theory, in practice economies of scale are at play.

As we have seen, in practice a majority of the mailboat fleet is owned by multi-vessel owners, who have clawed their way over generations into that position of dominance, weathering many storms. One exception to the tight control of tonnage was in the late 1970s into the early 1990s when loans seem to have been bountiful and plentiful; as the expression goes "money seemed cheap" to fund expansion, enabling newcomers from mom-and-pop family-run ventures to financial forays by well-heeled politicians to have a hand at the mailboat system. "Since the beginning of the 1980s, the mail-boat business has become an important venture for the small Bahamian businessmen. The Bahamas Development Bank, an organization set up in

1978, provides loans for small business operators in ...transportation.... up to 1991, loans totaling more than $8 million have been made to more than 21 mail-boat operators," (1992 *Bahamas Handbook*).

This approach of going to a money trough is all rather different from Captain Ernest Alexander Dean taking an adze to a tree to build a boat to sail from Sandy Point to Nassau for milk for his family. Sadly, many of the exuberant plays in the market ended on stilts and the scrapping torch at the likes of Bradford Marine in Freeport, when the loans came due and the revenues weren't there in the late 1990's. It's a tough, scrappy business. As co-owner, operator and captain Eddins Bruce Taylor put it in the early 1990s, "the mail-boat service is almost indispensable... in the early 1960s, a group of businessmen attempted to operate a hovercraft service between Nassau and Eleuthera, but it failed. The hovercraft might be faster, but it cannot carry a lot of freight. Family Islanders must get their produce to Nassau, and Nassau merchants must get their heavy cargo to the islands. Only the mail-boat can do it. Mail boats, as I see it, will be around for a long time."

The focus remains, as it did with pacquet boats and falluccas, on the delivery of mail node to node. "Without the freight services provided by the mail-boats, people on the Family Islands could not exist, Transportation Officer Chris Francis, Ministry of Transport, said. Everything has to be shipped from Nassau, groceries in particular. Mail is first to go aboard, then freight then passengers." The carrying of mail from the central Post office in Nassau to a dock in a family island does not mean an end to the responsibility of the mail-boat operator, Francis said. He is then left with the responsibility of getting the mail as soon as possible to settlements where postal facilities exist. The task is normally assigned to persons known as mail-boat agents. These agents must be reliable persons hired by the mail-boat operator to perform this task (1992 *Bahamas Handbook*, p.412). Craig Symonette corroborates this, describing how a captain hired by his father Sir Roland's company, had a daughter deemed very reliable, who is now an agent for a modern shipping line in the same area. It is an important position, on whose shoulders persons' business and personal well-being might depend.

Describing the arrival of the *Air Swift* and other boats *Air Swift*, *Passing Jack*, and *Liberty* at the Government Dock in Dunmore Town, Harbour Island, it's hard not to detect a bit of irony in narrator Richard Malcolm's tone: "When *The Mail*, or *Air Swift* docked at Harbour Island on Friday afternoons, carrying the "Royal Mail," the police blocked off the western portion of the dock with a rope, and stood guard over the disembarking mail. No one, except essential persons, was allowed near the boat until the Royal Mail, so marked in large lettered canvas bags, carried by horse-drawn dray, left the dock under the watchful eye of a police constable. Very serious ceremonial procedure."

Domestic Impact

As recently as the early 1990s the comings and goings of mailboats were so important that in the capital "broadcast the departure times of mailboats 3 X a day. Delays and postponements then become known quickly" (1992 *Bahamas Handbook*, Dupuch). A British transportation expert named Hagety hired by the IDB concluded that "The Bahamian mailboat system is the only one of its kind in the Western Hemisphere, and for years was the only link between the Out Islands and the rest of the market." A French volunteer aboard a 1980s-era Popov Island Expedition noted that "the mailboat is a vital organ to the life in the islands. It brings supplies, news, cars, medicine as well as carries passengers at a cheaper rate. It is also, for a lot of older Bahamian, who cannot get used to the idea of flying in the air, a much safer way to travel! (Pascale, aboard the *Nay Dean* to Long Island, p.87).

In a classic 1930s-era study of the Bahamas named of *Isles of June* the author marvels at the grandfather of the future first black-Bahamian Prime Minister, Lyndon Oscar Pindling, writing "I found the *Alisada*'s coloured master, a huge six-footer, Bain [Frederick] by name, poring over [Greek classic mathematician] Euclid when off watch. Alternating with this hobby came his studies in navigation. An aid came to him on this trip from an aged Church of Scotland minister, who was making a tour. The curling grey locks of the son of the hills, and the black crown of the skipper where close together when I went to sleep. Now and then I would wake up and overhear the rich burr of the Highlander interlaced with the soft speech of the Bahamas, and two pencils would be scribbling and marking copies of Euclid (*Isles of June*, p.51) Later British naval officers stranded in Acklins aboard their yacht from Hong Kong, *Tai Mo Shan*, corroborated Bain's captaincy, as has Craton in *A-Z Bahamas* and others. Craton amplifies that "...typical of these [mailboat captain] heroes was Frederick Bain, the towering grandfather of the future prime minister, Lyndon Pindling, captain of the sawyer's *Alisada*, who owned shops and kept separate families in Nassau and Long Island," (p.240) Ronald G. Lightbourn has photographs of the *Alicada* with Bain in them during a luncheon on deck and underway).

Obviously the impact on mailboats varies from that of a weekend outing to a nearby island or the delivery of financial sustenance. An interviewer with the *Bahamas Handbook* found a crab vendor on Potter's Cay named Lolita Rolle of Calabash Bay, Andros. Lolita explained that she prefers the mailboat: "I'm not in a rush to get where I am going. And furthermore, I prefer to travel with my crabs. That way I can keep an eye on them and see that they reach Nassau safely. (1992 *Bahamas Handbook*, p.415). In July of 2018 the author was able to help catch land crabs at night near Drigg's Hill Andros and share a ride back on the *Captain Moxey* with many carefully tended crab cages. An elderly woman interviewed for an oral history book named *Bahamian Memories* recalled how, growing up on West End, the mailboat came "twice a month. That's how we got the news from Nassau and everything else" (*Bahamian Memories*, p.10)

Mailboats have been empowering in other ways as well, with a direct descendant of Sir Milo Butler explaining that "there were four additional female boat builders on Sweetings Cay, eastern Grand Bahama, from 1848." Among the women boat-builders of Sweeting's Cay are Adeline Cooper and A. Sweeting, the wife of political leader Neville Wisdom (emails to author). Sometimes large concepts like fleet acquisition and ownership can be manifested in small tokens. After a trip to Europe to survey and purchase the coastal trader *Jade*, Captain Eddins Bruce Taylor, was given a Dutch hat from the seller, a kindred maritime soul. In 1981 the *Jade* became *Marcella III* and her coloring remained green.

Dave Gale, *Ready About* memoir, p.45 "That's why they are called the out (now Family) islands, - they are out from Nassau, in many cases really "out" there, and until recently they were 'lef out,' politically, socially, and economically."Author, sailor, marina owner Dave Gale has been on Parrot Cay, Abaco for over half a century. In his highly readable and informative book *Ready About* he devotes an entire chapter mailboats and what they have accomplished. "The government subsidized small freighters to carry the sacks of Her Majesty's Bahamas mail between the post offices of the Out Island settlements and Nassau. A freighter with a government mail contract was known as a "mail," and each island, or group of islands, in this seafaring nation had its own mail. The mails also carried people and freight at fares and rates that were set by the government as part of the mail contract. This government control kept the rates low for the poorer people of the Out Islands, and while the boats and crew and rates have changed over the years, the Bahamas mailboat stystem is still very much intact today." (*Ready About*, p.44). It is a hub and spoke system, in that it is quite centralized: planes or cargo needing to go from one island to another which is not the capital, generally go through Nassau again.

Being closer to Nassau, with a spine of narrow islands enabling captains to choose a lee, or sheltered side much of the time, North Eleuthera has had its share of mailboats and ferries. Speaking about the 1940's time-frame, when the *Ego* was calling at Three Island and Captain Austin Kelly ensured that the mail to Upper Bogue and Lower Bogue and Bluff and Currents went onwards by horse, a writer noted how "The people have been enterprising enough to run their own mailboat, the *Ego*, a tiny craft, which serves both the island, the Current, and Upper and Lower Bogue, to Nassau one time a week" (p.158). The author Everild admired how "in The Current, everybody rushes down to the jetty with wheelbarrows to collect their freight, and it is astonishing to see how much their tiny craft can carry," (Everild, *Eleuthera, an Island Called Freedom*).

Mayaguana is an interesting and in many ways contradictory place to study in the context of national transportation infrastructure, largely because it defies standardization. Within the past decade the population has been 277 persons, in the three settlements, Abraham's Bay, Pirate's Well, and Betsy Bay. One gas station. A lovely hotel. Was to have been a US Navy base from 1940, in World War II, but it was just a dock for high speed rescue and reconnaissance boats. Was a Cold War tracking station and the population boomed with massive airstrip and even a deep-water dock. The income from that? Local inflation flattened the curve and led to a depression when the base closed. Recently a major US developer bought half the island and set about improving the runway; result? Local resentment that only non-locals were given title, and when the developer shut off the runway lights for upgrades and locals parked out of line for an emergency, a horrible accident killed inhabitants, meaning the developer packed up and left, selling the heavy equipment to Turks and Caicos and leaving just abandoned smuggler planes. Amazingly, however, a few stalwart families, going back to 1805, have been building and buying mailboats and other freighters, from Europe to the US Gulf, and built by far the largest mailboat fleet in the country, from a tiny base. Those are the Taylors, Blacks, and Williamsons, and I've sat at Mr. Higgins' knee in Pirate's Well to learn the story.

Why does this matter? Because Mayaguana can show the transformative power of mailboats on an economy and a populace, and that even an island with some of the biggest runways in the world can lose them twice in decades and still rely upon mailboats. The port destroyed by a storm? The Taylors blasted a notch in the rocks and at high tide wedge their flat-bottomed steel boats into it and lay on their bottoms when the tide goes down. That is ingenuity. The local situation has appeared grim. In "Settlements and Demographics," an anthropological study of Mayaguana in the 1950s the authors wrote that "Until 1955, the only safe means of transportation between Abraham's Bay and the settlement of Betsy Bay and Pirate's Well was by government mailboat. Even today, many inhabitants of the island – especially women – have not been to another settlement in years, because of continued poor transportation. During my field work I met with individuals who had not visited another settlement in 15 to 20 years. Inhabitants of the three settlements often see each other more frequently when they visit Nassau, than during their residency on the island." Then in 1956, a road was constructed Betsy Bay to Pirate's Well, but not Abrahams Bay, even though the distances are comparatively not so great.

Here is an article about the bad old days, which seems patronizing from a modern perspective, yet some of the observations were, in fact, on point, per the above study. The 1940 US article reads in part: "The US has found one of their hemisphere defense bases in the remote Bahamian island of Mayaguana selected recently by a military commission. They US will use to create a $60 mm defense chain. 700 to 800 persons live there now. Meanwhile, they are "depending for their scheduled contact with civilization upon a sailing sloop that brings mail once a month."

When [President] FDR used a US Navy cruiser to escort the presidential yacht in order to go bone-fishing, the Mayaguana Justice of the Peace went out in a row-boat, and tapped on the hull of the cruiser, but the vessels paid him scant attention. The island has no electricity, no roads, no telephones, and no vehicles of any sort. Money is virtually unknown and ... barter [is commonplace]. The government [supplies a] small radio station, and locals grow their own food. At 700 miles from Miami and 400 from Nassau, Mayaguana will be the closest base to USA of the chain" (Fred Strozier, Somerset, PA, Dec. 4, 1940). Thanks to the tenacity of the Taylors and the resourcefulness of locals, as well as the US Navy personnel, and the developers and the government, Mayaguana has blossomed into an extraordinary place which has outstripped all other communities in the Bahamas on a mailboat-per capita basis, with roughly one mailboat over time for every 12 inhabitants; a ratio of 277 persons to 23 mailboats.

Hagarty, the consultant, observed in the 1970s how "transportation is vital to the development of the Bahamas. Airplanes and the government-subsidized mailboats are the two main transportation systems." That is inarguable, just as the reality of said transportation can sometimes require flexibility. A travel writer wryly noted that "the Bahama Out Islands Association [catering to non-Nassuvians] publishes a handy brochure listing sailing schedules and fares with the following notation: 'The Mailboats are primarily for transporting freight... if no agents is shown, passenger must go to dock to find captain. On-board accommodation are Spartan, to say the least, but many island-hops can be made in a few hours... Schedules are flexible ("ship sails, weather and captain permitting"). Mailboats ... reflect a casual way of life that has persisted for centuries away from the bustling centres of Nassau and Freeport.... Many Goombay folk tunes have been written about their voyages." (article on the *Spanish Rose* in the US paper *Selkirk Enterprise*, 3 Sept 1975, p.7).

Closer to home, a Floridian travel writer wrote, nearly 50 years ago, that on mailboats, "the food is included in the fare. Not that it's gourmet cuisine what the crew eats... cracked conch (usually delicious) and rice and beans." *Naples Daily News*, February 11, 1973 *Out Island Hopping is Fun, Reasonable*, by Tony Weitzel, *Daily News* travel editor. A traveler to northern Long Island in the 1980s was pleased to note that "when the boats ran by sail, a trip took 8 days, now the ships take 15 hours to the north end of Long Island, and 23 hours to the south end." Observing that three trucks outside Mrs. Gibson's Lunch Room at Landrail Point, Crooked Island constituted a traffic jam, a writer recited a local's very detailed assessment of what made the mailboat *Lady Mathilda* on time or not. "If she runnin' on 2 engine, she might reach by midnight, but if she runnin' on one she pass the night in the Bight," meaning the vast bay between Crooked and Acklins Island" (*Conde Nast Traveler*, 1996).

Tourism

For many non-Bahamians traveling by mailboat, there is generally scant up-to-date information. What one finds in print are glossy travel magazine articles detailing how a world-wizened author from a major cosmopolitan city managed to outsmart the rest of us, and with an often very photogenic companion "escape" onto a rustic mailboat for a few weeks' sojourn where they invariably 1) heard music 2) ate lots of fruit and conch 3) were regaled by a one-legged captain and 4) survived some kind of calamity, usually of a four-legged hooved variety, or chickens, or a grounding. These are often richly illustrated and very readable stories. Some authors like the *Lonely Planet* (the closest guide to getting the origins of mailboats right) tell it "like it is" and give an unvarnished glimpse filled with real-world sights, smells, delays and disappointments.

Then there are more generic serialized stories in US newspaper Sunday travel sections, mostly from the 1940s to 1970's, about how risky but rewarding a trip was, and finally, more recently, one has more down-to-earthy travel blogs, often by mariners who had to take a mailboat to get supplies, or wait on one for supplies for their Family Island home or yacht, with photos and fun recitations of adventures and mis-adventures. One example of the genre is Captain Fred Braman, US Navy retired, who has taken his sailboat throughout the Bahamas for decades and fallen in love with seeing the Bahamas via mailboat, contributing dozens of articles and even a book about his adventures with friends to all corners of the archipelago, where they are always welcomed warmly by mailboat owners and all they encounter.

What is interesting is one important observation: The Bahamians for whom the mailboat system was constructed for the most part do not "break ranks" and "tell tales" about the boats and the experience. Overall they are modest, unassuming, and not ones to work themselves into the central narratives. What that means is a corpus of literature bereft of the lead character's perspective! The telling of the tale has largely been, and continues to be, left to outsiders, including this author, and everyone seems alright with that. And for the most part, foreign tourism accounts for such a small part of the overall industry, particularly to farther-flung islands, that it hardly seems to matter and foreigners are just adjusted to as a pleasant surprise (except for a trip where our group took all the bunks, down and back....).

Before it was sneaker-chic to throw bourgeoise concerns to the wind, in a colony where class – and race – were taken very seriously, it is clear that writers were declaring that travel on a usual mailboat, barring to and from one's own communities, was simply not done, and crossing the color bar was akin in the author's mind to crossing the harbour bar in a rage, or storm. Take for example this guide to Nassau in the 1960s. Mrs. Higg's chapter on *The Out Islands* from her Nassau guide reads "While many of the Bahama Islands, other than New Providence, are both interesting and attractive, they are difficult to visit, owing to the lack of comfortable vessels in which to reach them. The only boats which regularly visit the larger of the islands are manned by native coloured crews, and do not offer the conveniences usually associated with pleasant ocean travel."

By equating non-white with unpleasant, what today we would consider the author's jaundiced, racially and class-prejudiced views are reflected in many, if not most writers who describe mailboats from the perspective of middle-class Nassuvians and visitors from the American mainland. These perspectives tended towards racial (locally and from the US) and class distinctions on the European side. Even in more modern accounts readers can pick up on subtle digs using only slightly less discreet words like "quaint," rustic, local, third-world, throw-back, easy-going, possessing a certain rhythm, with Floridians and others in yachting magazines referring to the Bahamas as their "backyard" or "playground."

Those accounts, whether intended to be dismissive, judgmental, rude, or otherwise, have had the perhaps beneficial side-effect of making it less likely that mass-tourists in high volumes will alter the proportionality of passengers aboard mail boats. While a huge proliferation of airplanes and landing strips on or near virtually all inhabited islands gave all passengers options over the mailboats going back to the 1950s, nowadays there are non-mail, high-speed passenger services on offer by the likes of Bahamas Ferries, some of them even with VIP sections, WiFi, air conditioning, and food and beverage service, meaning that mailboats remain the steady option they have always been, with a fleet still including a wooden boat – the *Current Pride* – if not any sailboats any more. And the less negative publicity the better as far as owners and captains are concerned, though large groups of visitors taking up several cabins do at time displace islanders looking for a berth for a potentially long passage home; particularly if the out-of-towners remain on the boat the entire way, out and back, whereas normally passengers would disembark at either end.

In contrast to Higgs (who, one suspects, never actually rode on a mailboat for fun), is an extraordinary account by Amelia Dorothy Defries, in her 1916 account published by the *Nassau Guardian* entitled *In A Forgotten Colony, Being Some Studies in Nassau and at Grand Bahama During 1916*. What makes this account quite entertaining is its tongue-in-cheek nature; she plays the shocked upper-class white woman, well, but is actually a much better sport about it than she lets on.

Here is a passage in which she encounters a mailboat named the *Hazel Dell*, built and owned in Bimini: "what looked like a week's washing was hanging from the boom, and from the yards; heaps of onions, bananas, and coconuts were piled up, and a basin full of limes. Many kegs of flour and barrels of hominy weighed the boat down, and dried fish was scattered about, smelling horribly, while a pile of conchs made matters even worse." She is also rather specific, in a way to make any maritime historian appreciative, describing how "by the wharf lay a small, two-masted vessel, a 28-ton open boat, just 50-feet long and only 18 feet wide, built at Bimini in 1901, and with a hold 6 feet deep." Later she switches to a private vessel named the Income, expecting a major upgrade, only to be upstaged by a bovine passenger and taking it in stride: "The captain of the *Income* sent word; a cow went on board *Income* before her; a schooner built in 1888, Musgrove...." (pp.16-17). So the narrator proves that even though she might seem a prig, in fact she shows great aplomb and that essential ingredient to any happy trip; a sense of humor.

Amelia Defries also showed what seems surprisingly blunt and wide-eyed racial and class views, observing about the crew: "The lowest of the low they were said to be, but, except for the indescribably filthy condition of the Government mailboat, I did not find them any lower than people of a similar class (or occupation) in other lands. If we are to judge white sailors by the writings of Masefield and Kipling, indeed these were lambs in comparison, for all on board were gentle to each other and kind; kind and courteous to us; and we two women were as safe among them as among our own kind – perhaps safer" (p.24). While by today's standards this may not seem enlightened, at the time they were probably taken as radical. If nothing else, Ms. Defries' view show the wide range of reaction to mailboat travel in the Bahamas across a span of a century, gender, race and class.

There is also a bit of mirth to be derived from exotic claims made, such as "a mailboat can take you to endless islands," referring to the *Current Pride*. The irony is that the many islands it could take you were basically Current, the island just off Eleuthera, or The Current, the community on North Eleuthera separated by a few hundred yards. Of course a reader in Des Moines or Wolverhampton reading that article over coffee in the 1970s would not have known that. For every example – except Father Jerome Hawes in Cat Island – of idealists being dropped off for a long-term change of life on Inagua or similar (*Monarch of Nassau* dropped a commune off there in the 1930s), there is a return trip to retrieve the bedraggled remnants. In 1994 the *Lonely Planet* gave it's brass-tacks version; "all the vessels are slow and notoriously unreliable. Most are small general-cargo freighters, long on durability and short on luxury and, sometimes, seaworthiness, steered by a cheroot-smoking skipper surrounded by bales of bananas and sacks of letters." One cannot blame the publication for lack of fair warning!

None of us are immune from a sales pitch, with this author arguing that mailboats can "enable one to escape to the real Bahamas; the Family Islands: they are not dangerous, and you may find rest and local food, new friends, and music;" extraordinary what a deadline and payout can do to writers. A few years later one finds a diary entry for a trip to Inagua which never left the planning stage (at least not for 24 more years): "Family trip to Inagua on the planning board. Fly down on Friday, fly out on Monday. The mailboat is the MV *Lady Mathilda*."

For my first article on mailboats I jotted down these student-friendly prices in December, 1992:

- *Lisa J. II*, cabin bunk, USD$10 on deck, USD$25 for a bunk in a cabin.
- *Bahamas Daybreak III*, Captain Stuart, has large freezers for crawfish tails and frozen fish and meals on back decks.

Mailboats have a yellow cinderblock office east of the bridge on Potter's Cay, with a white door. The harbor master, or dock master's office is there, with staff, and they produce a weekly program showing boats, times, days, departures and arrivals. Meals are provided, cabins cost extra. The Andros-owned, family-run *Lisa J. II* brings fish to and from North Andros, and the owners support visitors traveling by mailboat.

I bundled what I knew into a few sentences for prospective travelers; "a fleet of 25 mailboats service some 50 islands and almost 100 settlements. Mailboats are still as rustic and alive with local colour as ever, while retaining a very live-able and comfortable shipboard environment. Cabins with cleaned bunks are customary on overnight voyages, and often three hot meals per day are served to all passengers. Go to Potter's Cay Dock. You may want to familiarize yourself with the boat and captain you choose. They are often accessible, friendly, and informative. There is nothing like leaning over the bow of a vessel laden with bricks, boat, cars, fruit, goats, and mail, gazing at starfish or plankton, to the sound of gospel hymns being sung!" Seems like any author can fall for the charm and allure of mailboat travel.

It is a lovely thing to be in a country where you are able to roll out bed after some holiday or reunion had ended and you have a couple day's free – or for any or no reason at all – and head down to Potter's Cay Dock with comparatively little money and take a ride of several days to new places, bunk, room, meals and pleasant company included! That's what a new friend and I did after Boxing Day Junkanoo during student days, and I have done several times. After a visit to Potter's Cay I made these quick notes, shared them with a friend, discussed them and and set off!

- 5 ½ hours, to Fresh Creek, Andros
- 8 ½ hours, to Rock Sound and Davis Point, Eleuthera
- 7 hours, to Sandy Point and Moore's Island, Abaco on the *Champion II*, Tuesday, midnight
- 15 hours, to Georgetown, Exuma, on Tuesday at 2 pm, returning Friday 8 am

Decision: We are to take the MV *Champion II* to Sandy Point via Bullock's Harbour, Berry Islands and Moore's Island, Abaco, departing Nassau at midnight on Tuesday January 7, and ideally returning the morning of Friday, January 10, 1992.

History of Mailboats in the Bahamas Since 1804

For over 1,000 years vessels have been carrying both people and goods between the islands of the Bahamas – right since the time of the Lucayans. Indeed, the Bahamian archipelago – like those of Greece, the Philippines, and Indonesia – is reliant on workhorses, like its mailboats, to ply between the islands carrying everything from people to pincushions, tractors to pickaxes. Pinning down which years such trade has been government subsidized becomes a challenge, but not an insurmountable one. The quest is as relevant as ever, as presently there are 18 mailboats based at Potter's Cay in Nassau serving over 45 communities on 14 of the family islands, from Bimini to Inagua.

Though what we know as mailboats will carry everything from church pews to livestock, sodas and beer, passengers, nails, mattresses, vehicles, and pretty much everything in between, the focus of early inter-island service was concerned primarily with the mails, as upon that cargo the subsidies relied. Initially the offices of the *Bahamas Gazette* served as the post office, and then in 1761 came the "earliest known record of a letter being sent from the Bahamas." In 1788, "an act for the establishment and regulation of a post office was passed." In 1858, British postage stamps were introduced but only a year later "the Bahamian post office became independent of London and issued its own stamps."

As for the origins of the service, one detailed source is the book *Bahamas Early Mail Service and Postal Markings*, by Morris Hoadley Ludington (Alpha Philatelic Printing & Publishing Co., Washington DC, 1982). He cites the *Bahamas Gazette* from 1784, the Bahamas Royal Gazette from 1804, and numerous other sources that he read from the originals in the public library that used to be the goal. He notes that "a vessel called the *Nassau Packet* sailed a number of times during 1799 between Nassau and Charleston," but this was not inter-island mail service. In 1802, Henry Moss of Crooked Island was made Acting Postmaster (p.8), followed by a Mr. Leitch in Nassau.

According to Ludington " . . . the first mention found in the Bahamas newspapers of Crooked Island and of a mailboat being sent from Nassau to meet the Packet there," was of the *Mary and Susan*, Captain Fisher, dated Friday, 21 September, 1804. The vessel is described as an "armed Government schooner," as during the Napoleonic Wars "many privateers were active throughout the West Indies." (p.9). Soon other vessels – like the *John Bull*, Captain Fulford, a Government felucca, and the schooner *Nassau*, Captain Gibson, appear, along with the Packet *Lord Spencer*, on the route to and from Jamaica and England.

As obvious as it may seem, in order to understand the origins of mailboats in the Bahamas one is best served studying philately; the postal systems, its offices, officers, stamps, regulations, and above its ships. Many before have focused more on regulations and fleets, however the postage world tends to be fanatical about details and facts, which is immensely helpful and allows us to add over a decade to the history of intra-insular mail in the Bahamas. There are four authors of primary books on the topic of Bahamian philately: Harold Gisburn, Edward B. Proud, and Raymond Gale. Of these the most prolific, was Ludington, from Connecticut, who due to a health condition as a child was forced to voyage to Bermuda, Bahamas and beyond, who turned a fascination with stamps and postal systems into a series of excellent books on the topic, two of them devoted exclusively to the Bahamas. After him, and using Ludington's tireless research into originals of the *Bahamas Gazette* came Edward B. Proud, and his extensive *The Postal History of The Bahamas* (Proud-Bailey, UK, 2000), which adds nearly 200 intra-insular mailboats was well as critiques of them by Commissioners, and details of contracts, owners, even photos of postmasters.

Originally mail was distributed not just from Nassau to outlying islands, but originated in the colony's faraway capital in London, stopped Fortune Cay off Crooked Island, and then was shipped on smaller vessels to Nassau, where the problem became how to reliably distribute it from there. Ludington notes that war and peace modulated the need protect, and how to man, the ships. By the early 1800s "The British ships were again heavily armed. The islands of the West Indies, including the lonely "out-islands" of the Bahamas, were favorite haunts of the enemy ships, and many mails were in consequence lost in this area. Up to the year 1818, the packets were under the direct control of the Post Office, who hired the crew (mainly ex-naval men), but in that year, the [British] Admiralty took over the manning of the ship, principally as a training-ground for seamen...." from merchant, or non-military sailors.

Between *Mary & Susan* under Fisher in 1804 and the *Rising Sun* in 1835 there were four other mail boats serving the Bahamas; the *Nassau* under James Edgecombe Gibson in 1805 to Cat Island, Long Cay (Albert Town, Fortune Island) up to 1812, then the *John Bull* under William G. Fulford, to about 1820, *Dash* from 1821 to the 1830s, and *Paragon*, short-lived in 1821. By 1821, the schooners *Dash* and *Paragon* are described as plying the same route, connecting islands within the Bahamas with mail coming from outside the colony. All were wooden and sailboats.

A letter which is seen as creating mailboats in the Bahamas, an 1832 dispatch from Smith in Bahamas to Goderich, in London, on 5 June, 1832 regarding the sailing vessel *Dart* and mail to Harbour Island reads: "the principal service of the mail boat was the transport of the mail packets coming from England and America through the Bahama Islands using Crooked Island as the chief mailing station;" from a 1981 National Archives exhibit, this is framed and hangs in the lobby of The Mailboat Company in Nassau. Ludington notes that after a decade or so with wrecks and high ownership costs, chartered schooners began to replace those owned by the mail lines on the St. Thomas to Nassau route in the 1850s. Also, from 1840 aboard fleets including the

Royal Mail Line and West Indies Packet services started to chafe, as military and civilian postal services clashed.

In a description of mailboat services dated 5 June, 1832, Smyth relates to Goodrich that mail packets came "from England and America through the Bahama Islands using Crooked Island as the chief mailing station." This was extended to Kingston, Jamaica. This was referred to as intra-island mail service. Ludington informs us that Royal West India Mail Steam Packet Company was founded by James McQueen, a Scotsman, living Grenada since 1789. In 1839 he and British merchants built a mail line from Falmouth, England, which began sailing to the Bahamas, Caribbean, and US ports like Charleston starting in March, 1840. In 1852 "the mail service to Nassau was radically changed. It no longer was a branch line from St. Thomas, but became instead part of a much larger branch route connecting Chagres and Jamaica to Nassau and Savannah." Voyage times out were 24 days, or basically a month each way. Mail from the United Kingdom to the Bahamas left Southampton on second day of each month

Truly inter-island mail service is believed to have begun with the 35-foot-long schooner *Dart*, which was enlarged at its mid-ships twice over its career. Built about 1867, in Harbour Island, it was owned by John Saunders Harris of that island. One of its captains was William James Harris, born in 1848. The boat served Harbour Island and Spanish Wells Eleuthera from Nassau for over 50 years until about 1922, when it was lost in a hurricane. Accommodation aboard was segregated. Michael Craton and Dr. Gail Saunders, in their seminal work *Islanders in the Stream*, Volume II, write about Abaco that " . . . sailboats had been replaced by government-subsidized motor mailboat services to most other islands by 1929." As we shall see, 23 other vessels are listed as having initiated intra-island mail service before the venerated *Dart*; the reason may lie in their being under government contract. In an event, these discoveries by postal historians make a rich story richer.

Ludington lists 25 mail vessels plying the inter-island routes of the Bahamas between 1849 and 1885. Chronologically, these were the *Palestine, Experiment, Union, President, Electric, Eugenie, Georgina, Amelia Ann, Brothers, Mary Jane* (named for mary jane black of Pirate's Well, Mayaguana), *Jane, Arabella, Quick, Jimmie, Admired, Dart, Cicero, Charlton, Rebecca, Osborne, Argosy, Attic,* and *Arctic* in 1884. By 1849, the following Bahamian ports were being served by mail on a regular basis: East end of Eleuthera, Port Howe, San Salvador, Little Exuma Harbour, North end of Long Island, Port Nelson, Rum Cay, Sandy Point, Watling's Island, Great Harbour, Long Island, Long Cay, Crooked Island, and Inagua. *Palestine* was listed as government-owned and began service in 1849, under captains Cunningham & Bain in 1850, and Williams in 1851.

In March, 1865, the government sought to "provide for more frequent communication between certain islands of the Bahamas and the Seat of the Government." This may have been an indirect response to the recommendations of

Thomas C. Harvey to the Colonial Secretary, C. R. Nesbitt, in 1858 in which he reported "The great variety of productions in the Bahamas would . . . if there existed an inter-insular steam communication, become available to all, and the cultivation of the land and development of many valuable resources, would speedily follow the power of obtaining a sure market. At present some cays are, at times, absolutely destitute.' The resultant act (Inter-Insular Communication, 28 Vic. C. 18) found that the previous act for a single vessel was inadequate. Therefore, the new act empowered the Governor, on the advice of the Executive Council, to " . . . hire by the year, or otherwise, for the service . . . a good and sufficient vessel and pay therefor the sum of money as the same can, by public tender, be procured for not exceeding in the whole sum of five hundred pounds per annum." The act was good for five years.

In May, 1867 (30 Vic. C.18), the government specifically enabled subsidized mail service between Nassau and "the inhabitants of the districts of Eleuthera, Harbour Island, and Abaco." The government was authorized to procure " . . . fast-sailing vessels of not less than 20-tons burthen, each to be employed in the conveyance of fortnightly mails." The act authorized the procurement of three different vessels. Interestingly, this act confirms the existence of service to Inagua, instructing the postmaster in Nassau to "make up mails . . . as he now makes up and dispatches mails by the mail vessel running between Nassau and Inagua." The act sets out a tariff for the carriage of freight and passengers – capping the amounts by law. It even governs luggage. The receipts were to go into the public treasury. There were nine ports covered under this act: Gregory Town, Governor's Harbour, Tarpum Bay, Rock Sound, Spanish Wells, Dunmore Town (Harbour Island), Cherokee Sound, Great Harbour, and Green Turtle Cay, Abaco.

The *Kate Sturrup* joined the fleet in 1890, servicing Harbour Island for Arnold Ingraham, the *Hattie Darling* in 1894 to Exuma, and *Hattie H. Roberts* the same year to Abaco, followed by the *Pelican* to Long Cay off Crooked Island, *Star of the Sea* to Andros, and *Trackless* to Eleuthera. In 1895 *Eastern Queen* set off for Inagua, *Experience* to Ragged Island for John Samuel Pintard, *Raven* to Grand Bahama, return to Long Cay, and *Sappho* to Andros. Both *Antila* and *Tropic* served Andros starting in 1896, with the re-built *Albertine Adoue* going to Abaco for the Roberts of Abaco, the *Glynn* went into service for Eleuthera, *Siren* to Inagua and *M.E.B.* to Andros in 1898, and *Pilgrim* the last of the 1800's boats began mail and passenger service in 1899.

Within a few decades there were acts passed to fill in the gaps between Inagua to the far south and Abaco to the north. For example, "Act (No. 7 of 1907) establish[ed] an Inter-Insular Mail Service in the Bahamas. It empower[ed] the Governor in Council to establish a Mail Service between Nassau and the Out Islands, and to cause contracts to be made for this purpose." This 1907 act was further amended and expanded by "An Act to Establish an Improved Inter-Insular Mail Service" passed in August, 1948. Through it, the "Governor establish[ed] mail service between Nassau and the Out

Islands." Its geographic scope is broad, as it covers trade " . . . between one Out Island and another Out Island and between settlements in any Out Island district." It also states that vessels propelled by sail, steam, or "other mechanical power" such as motors may perform the service.

The act is granular in its coverage, making allowance for the "sufficient supply of life-saving apparatus and boats, the employment of a competent master and crew, over-crowding, cabin accommodation" and so on. It also calls for the periodic examination of mail vessels and their life-saving equipment. The list of island groups covered is extensive, from Inagua and Crooked Island to the Biminis. There are over 50 communities listed – 10 in Andros alone. The prescribed tonnage of the vessels ranged from 20 to 150 – the largest for the longest routes and only 20 tons for the comparatively short passages from Nassau to the Current in Eleuthera. The act includes specific costs to carry items ranging from "half firkins and kegs, jars and demi-johns" to "tierces, hogsheads, and other vessels not exceeding thirty gallons." It includes "Madeira, horseflesh wood, yellow wood, and other timber . . . Potatoes, yams, and other roots . . . mares, mules, and cattle, lignum vitae and braziletto [wood] . . ."

During the interwar years, postmaster Stephen Dillett informed the public that "letters handed to any master of an Out-Island Mail Vessel for transmission by post, instead of being posted at the Post Office, shall in addition to the ordinary rate of postage be subject to an additional rate of one penny to be prepaid in stamps." Cancellations are the seals which postal officials use to certify that the postage paid has been redeemed, in other words is recognized but can no longer be used. They are artistic within boundaries, as collectors are avid about them.

Another philatelist informs that of rare cases of floating stamp cancelations in Bahamas ,such as underwater Post Office and M/V *Ena K.*, a highly active converted schooner in the Trevor Kelly fleet which plied between Miami and Nassau mostly. One Bahamian vessel that possesses what is called a ship cancellation, as in from a floating post office, was "the M/V *Ena K* plying between Miami and Nassau. It is a straight 3-line marking inscribed "SEAPOST MAIL – BRITISH M.V. *ENA K* – NASSAU BAHAMAS" Fig. 29 illustrations. The simple word "paquet-bot" may also be found on occasion." *Paquetbot* is simply a French spelling for packet boat, or mid-sized, fast sailing ship, later steam, often with sail auxiliary, crossing the Atlantic with the mails at the time.

The next overhaul of the Mailboat Act, as it is known less formally, came in 1966, and again the rules were tweaked in 1974 and 1987. Interestingly, mailboat owners with dual roles in government, such as Sir Roland Symonette and Sir George Roberts, had hands in shaping legislation. Then in 1995 and 1996 the Rates for Carriage of Freight rules were amended again, basically updated and modernized to keep the investors, entrepreneurs and mailboat owners in their livelihood. The latest version on the Official Website of the Government of the Bahamas is from October, 1966 – an amended version of the 1948 act. On the site is the agreement, which mailboat owners can enter into with the government. This requires the service provider to subject their official logs twice yearly for inspection, and to keep up the ship's Registration Certificate, Business License, and Inter Insular Mail Shipping Rates. If the vessel and its officers and crew and the service provided are deemed not up to government standard, then the government can revoke the license and with it the agreement.

In 2008, it was reported in March that the government had signed a three-year contract with mailboat owners and operators, "in response to complaints by mailboat owners and operators that the tariff does not take into account that the cost of doing business has escalated and the cost of fuel has also increased exponentially." The tariff they amended was drafted in 1996. In a contemporary article from *The Eleutheran*, the Honourable Sidney Collie wrote, "My Ministry is aware and very concerned about the price of diesel fuel and the impact that it is having on the mailboat industry and the economy as a whole." The article continued, observing, " . . . the Family Island residents depend heavily on the mailboat for transportation of goods and other essential services." In short, the Mailboat Act and its amendments remain a vibrant, to some degree flexible document, enabling mailboat operators to continue to serve remote communities with affordable, reliable access to the capital across the decades and centuries.

It is noteworthy that government subsidy of the mails has enabled at least one mariner and entrepreneur, Captain Ernest Dean of Sandy Point Abaco, to make his career, motivated at first by the need to obtain regular supplies of milk for he and his wife's infant children. Starting in 1949 when he constructed the mailboat *Captain Dean* in Sandy Point by hand, without electricity (it took over two years to build), he went on to commission and ply six vessels under the same name and numerous others owned and operated by his family before his recent death. His life, boats, and career are chronicled in the book *Island Captain*. In March, 2015, the Minister of Transport and Aviation announced that the government had allocated $3.1 million towards wreck removal, refurbishment, the expansion of warehousing, the repair of the causeway and installation of bathrooms at Potter's Cay. Despite attrition, like the sinking of the Andros mailboat, *Lady D.*, in July, 2014, whose wreck obstructed dock frontage until 2017, it would appear that the inter-island freight and mail service can, with help, remain as vibrant a part of the Bahamian islands' fabric as it has been for at least 200 years.

The *Dart* on a voyage to or from Harbour Island and North Eleuthera. This woodcut image is one of the first purely inter-island mailboats in the Bahamas. It hangs in the office of Elvin Taylor and his brothers, Eddins and Limas, at the headquarters of The Mailboat Company in Nassau.

Dart was originally a 35-foot fast pilot boat, taking pilots to ships over the Nassau Harbour Bar, however she was lengthened amidships twice in her career. Able to make the trip to Harbour Island in the fast time of eight hours, she won in a number of regattas in the Bahamas. She was apparently lost in a hurricane – probably that of 1926. *Dart* was likely built in Harbour Island around 1867 by the Albury family. Her dedicated route was between Spanish Wells, Harbour Island, and Nassau. Her owner was John Saunders Harris and her captains were William G. Harris and William James Harris. She served for over 50 years, from 1870 to 1920. The photo and caption appears in several history books, including Harvey Oppmann's *Harbour Island: Yesterday and Today, a Memoir* (2009).

The original *City of Nassau* under its previous name in Europe. This ship was not strictly an inter-island mail steamer, though she is believed to have run to and from Harbour Island, Nassau, and Florida. She represents the transition for wood and sail to steel and steam. It is also emblematic of the trend to import large vessels from Europe, which were not necessarily ideally suited to the shallow Bahamas, which lacked coaling stations. Before being sold to the Bahamas in 1927 this steamer, built in Scotland in 1885, was a passenger freighter serving the Channel Islands as the *Laura*. Then the Florida Inter-Island Steamship Co. of Nassau purchased her and ran it for a decade. Its fate is murky – she was either broken up for scrap or lost during bootlegging. Another source has her lasting until 1957.

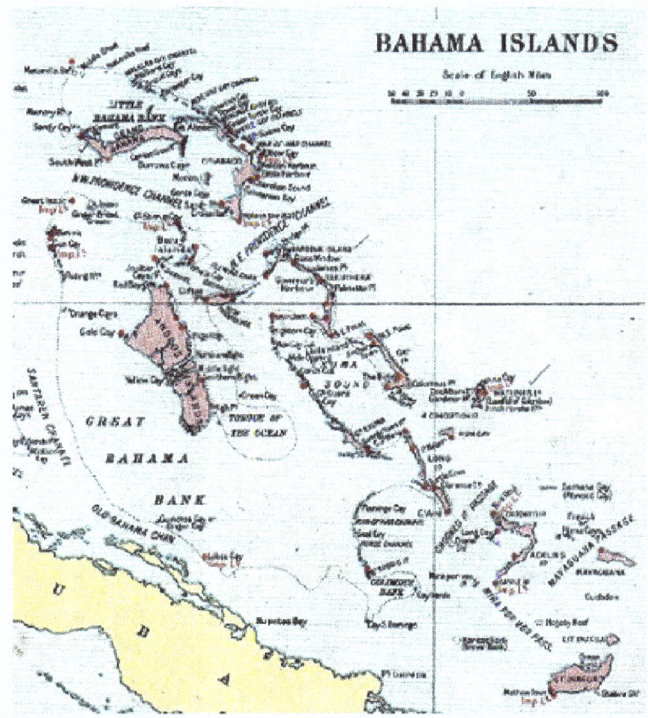

A 1926 chart of Bahamas showing ports and settlements still relevant today.

Abaco Islands

Mailboat service to Abaco and the Abaco cays began as early as 1894 with the remnants of a salvaged vessel and continue to this day. Though the primary port is Marsh Harbour, mailboats have, over the years, also served Sandy Point, Cherokee Sound, Hope Town, Man-O-War Cay, Green Turtle Cay, Great Guana Cay, Little Harbour, and other settlements. As an illustration of how adaptive Abaconians are, there is even a daily high-speed passenger boat connecting eastern Grand Bahama with Little Abaco Island instituted this century. There are also numerous freighters, which serve Abaco directly from eastern Florida and Nassau, however in this article we will focus on those vessels that carried mail – as well as passengers and cargo – between the islands, principally Nassau, and Abaco and its islands.

Many vessels have connected Abaco with the capital, its markets, services, and people. Until the 1950s these boats were often the only connection to the largest city in what was then still a colony. Writing in 1983, Steve Dodge, in his book *Abaco, The History of an Out Island and its Cays*, observed that "Despite the advent of airplane service to Abaco during the past thirty-five years, Marsh Harbour as well as other Abaco communities are still dependent on the mailboat for freight service, as anyone viewing the empty supermarket shelves on a Tuesday or a Wednesday can testify – 'no milk until the mailboat comes in' is a common refrain." Although this author doubts that a delayed mailboat would cause such shortages today, still, the importance of these vessels to the survival of businesses, communities, and even individuals in days of yore would be too easily overlooked. Captain Ernest Dean of Sandy Point for example, was inspired to spend 2.5 years building his first mailboat because he and his wife, Eula, would run out of milk waiting for the mailboat to come in from Nassau. One of the family's later mailboats was of course named *Lady Eula*.

There have been at least 33 mailboats serving the many cays and ports of Abaco, form Sandy Point and Cornwall to South and West to Cooper's Town to the North and West. They are, in order of appearance, the sailing lighthouse tender *Georgina*, which in 1865 began serving Hope Town, Marsh Harbour, Green Turtle Cay, for a year. Built of wood in 1861, she was 224 gross tons and owned by Felix MacCarthy of Nassau, who chartered it to the government. The sailing vessel *Brothers* followed in 1868, serving the Abaco Cays until 1875. She was built by William H. Albury (aka Uncle Will) on Man-O-War Cay, of wood and weighed 37 tons. One of her captains was R. Russell of Great Harbour Abaco. *Brothers* was replaced by the schooner *Quick* in 1875, built of wood in 1867, was 20 tons and chartered by the government. *Admired* took the Abaco route from *Quick* in 1878 up to 1883. Built in 1869 of wood, she was 27 tons and also on government charter.

In 1884 the wooden schooner *Arctic*, of 75 tons and 70 feet long, which was owned by Hilton C. Albury of Nassau replaced *Admired* after for roughly a year. In 1894 the schooner *Hattie H. Roberts* owned by Ellis H. Burnside of Nassau began some 20 years of service from Cherokee Sound and Man O' War Cay in 1898 to the long run to Inagua in 1908. Built in Abaco of wood in 1882 and of 67 tons, this indefatigable ship was still in the 1920 registry 38 years later. The *Albertine Adoue* represents a chapter in ingenuity. From 1897 she served Pointed Rock Channel, Man-O-War, Abaco Cays, Marsh Harbour, then Inagua from 1898-1926, Abaco, and Long Island from 1908-1909, then Inagua from again 1927 to 1930. Owned by William Augustus Roberts, the first hull was built in Bath, Maine, wrecked and rebuilt in Abaco in 1894. The new ship was 69 tons, wood, and over 100 feet. Other owners include R. J. Anderson Farrington, in 1926, Hartley Roberts, Osbourne Roberts and Roland Roberts. In 1920 the schooner was replaced by *Edna M. R.*, then *Priscilla* in 1923. She was thought lost with 40 passengers in the 1926 hurricane, went aground in North Carolina with liquor, and was lost in 1930.

The sloop *Sea Witch* in 1918 served from Spencer's Point (Little Harbour), Old Place, and Great Guana Cay, Abaco; the wooden boat substituted in for *Albertine Adoue*. *Edna M. R.* brought mail to Abaco from 1920 to 1924, owned by Johnie Albury of Marsh Harbour. She was built in 1916, 32 tons, wood and 50 feet long. Owners include William A. Weeks, from 1916 to 1920, William Augustus Roberts, 1920, and sons, 1924. It was a converted sponger. In 1924 mails had to go overland, even up to 1932, to get to Cooper's Town, Old Place, Great Guano Cay, sometimes using two other, unnamed sailboat (*Two Sloops*).

Then from 1923 to 1946 the *Alice Mabel* carried mails to Abaco, then Moore's Island, and Grand Bahama, and eventually the Exumas and Long Island from 1927, even to Sal Salvador. Built of wood of 27 tons and 51 for Sir George William Kelly Roberts of Harbour Island and named for his daughter, her captains included Wilson Roberts, Maury brothers, Green Turtle Cay, John Morrell Carey, Claudius E. Storr, and crew Berke Rolle.

By 1947 the two post offices in the Long Island district had mail taken overland from Simms and Burnt Ground. In 1955 the vessel was perhaps peaked, with a commissioner commenting that she was: "much too small, very old, becoming less and less sea-worthy. Captain and crew been very courteous and accommodating." Photographer and author Ruth Rodriguez in 1947 called her the "condemned, substitute mailboat" (*Out Island Portraits*).

The *Priscilla*, which had a steel hull and motor, joined the Abaco run in 1923, then added Eleuthera in 1932 and Bimini and the Berry Islands in 1936. A busy ship, she also called at Eleuthera in 1921, Inagua in 1936, and San Salvador in 1938. *Priscilla* was built of iron in Wilmington, Delaware in 1885, was 151 tons and 87 feet long. Her owners included Reginald, aka Reggie, Farrington, Richard W. Sawyer, Interinsular Mails, Ltd. of Nassau, Leland Albury, Sherwin Archer, Bobby Archer, Osbourne Roberts, Roland Roberts, Hartley Roberts, Howard Lowe, and mate C. Curry, mate. In

1932 she was converted from sail and replaced the *Albertine Adoue*, which sustained structural damage in the hurricane of 1929, and was destroyed by the hurricane of August, 1932. By 1937 the 52-year-old ship was considered by commissioners to be "unsuited for the Windward Islands route, top-heavy, unsafe, and the passengers are afraid to go on her."

In 1926 the motor vessel *Halcyon* began the Abaco route, and following a battering by three hurricanes that year, she was the government relief ship from Nassau to the Exumas, Long Island, and Long Cay (Wayne Neely, *Greatest and Deadliest*). Her route expanded to Eleuthera, then in 1927 to the Exumas & Long Island, and even as far away as Inagua. The large elegant *Alisada*, owned by Jack Farrington of Nassau and skippered by Frederick, Bain, reported to be the grandfather of Prime Minister Linden Pindling, entered the Abaco mail route in 1927, later that year adding Eleuthera, then Inagua. Later on *Alisada* served Acklins, Inagua, and Crooked, from 1932-1936. It was during that period that the 86-ton wood sailing ship and captain were written about; historian Michael Craton says the Sawyers owned it; author Ronald Lightbourn says Jack Farrington. Frederick Bain was described by a travel writer as 6' tall and studying the Greek mathematician Euclid, and Martyn Sherwood of the stranded yacht *Tai Mo Shan* received help from the vessel, which in November, 1936 was destroyed by fire at Long Cay.

Wisely named for a governor's spouse (think *Lady Dundas*, or *Sir Charles Orr*, whose owner's skipped the spouse) *Lady Cordeaux* began carrying the mail to Abaco in 1927. She was built of steel in Milford, Delaware in 1922, weighed 116 tons and was 153 feet long. Her primary duty appear to have been to make a voyage for the government to bring relief to Abaco following the hurricane of 1932; otherwise she was a government supply tender. The motor vessel *Patricia K.* served Abaco, the Berry Islands, and Bimini from 1930, including Cat Cay, Lignum Vitae Cay, and Whale Cay. The route expanded in 1931 to include Exuma and Long Island, and Eleuthera between 1930 to beyond 1956. In about 1930 a vessel with the fishy name of *Old Horse Eye* (like the type of jack fish), which had been built by T. Berlin Albury at Harbour Island and was 97 tons, wood hull, and 74 feet long, entered the Abaco route. She was owned by Percy Sweeting and John P. Sweeting in 1956, per a 1960 article by Dave Gale.

The former motor yacht *Content S.* was to revolutionize passenger comfort, and did so, however at the expense of cargo-carrying capacity. She began serving Abaco in 1932 and rotated south to central-south Eleuthera up to 1946. The yacht was built for Percy Hance as *Percianna II* by J. M. Densmore and Co. in Quincy, outside Boston in 1920, of wood and weighed 123 tons, and was 110 feet long. In the Bahamas, investor Carl Sawyer saw an opportunity in Florida where the boat was laid up after a career between the New York Yacht Club and an owner from almost land-locked Vermont, who named her *Content* but left it for years. R. W. Sawyer Co. of Nassau, hired Stanley Weatherford, of the Abaco cays then Roland Roberts of Eleuthera as captains. In March, 1942 she rescued crew from several torpedoed ships off Hope Town and Cornwall, at Cross Harbour; *O. A. Knudsen*, *Daytonian*, and *Athelqueen*. She replaced *Priscilla* after 1932, however was not reliably profitable and was only occasionally chartered, including to the government. After intermittent use to the mid-1940's, *Content S.* was rammed and sunk by the Canadian tug *Foundation Aranmore* off Cuba, in 1946.

The schooner *Lillian & Brothers* joined the Abaco run in 1934 for two years. She was built of wood in Abaco in 1931, and was 34 tons, being owned by Shadrack Cox of Sandy Point. She was small enough to reach the numerous temporary saw mills in south great Abaco at the time: the several Cornwall's, Norman's Castle, and so on, most of which had their own post offices which needed mailboats. The motor vessel *Marmaduke* served the mail circuit of Abaco starting in 1936, also serving South Eleuthera that year, and Exuma, Long Island since 1931, adding Inagua in 1937 and San Salvador in 1938. *Marmaduke* was built of wood in the Cayman Islands in 1922, was 59 tons and 62 feet. The owners were David A. M. Smith and Roland T. Symonette of Nassau. Her first trip was as a substitute was 1936, and the following year a commissioner reported "only four first-class passengers, absurdity of having her on the run."

The motor boat *Midwest* joined the fleet to Abaco in 1936, adding Bimini and Berry Islands 1937, and South Eleuthera as well. *Midwest* substituted for *Priscilla* which broke down on October 15, 1936. *Monarch of Nassau* began serving Abaco and South Eleuthera in 1936, then Inagua a year later, and San Salvador in 1938. Originally named *Sir Charles Orr*, she was built by J. Crighton and Co., Ltd. in Cheshire, England in 1930 of steel and weighed 214 tons with 116 feet length. Her owners as a mailboat were Sir George Roberts Co., also the Monarch Line, Carl Sawyer, and one captain was Roland Roberts. The boat delivered Father Jerome Hawes to Cat Island, and rescued 30 Greeks merchant sailors from the *Cygnet* when their ship was sunk by an Italian submarine named *Enrico Tazzolli* off San Salvador in March, 1942.

The sailing sloop *Arena* under charismatic entrepreneur Senator Sherwin Archer began serving Abaco around 1940. Built in 1910, the wooden boat had been a sponging sloop of 70 feet. Sherwin Archer was captain and his son Bobby Archer and nephew Garnet Archer supported him as captains and mates to 1955. Needing an engine to compete with post-war air service, the boat was replaced by *Tropical Trader II*. A quirky local mailboat was named *Beluga*, after the word for whale, because it was in fact a whale-bottomed lifeboat from torpedoed Norwegian tanker *O. A. Knudsen* built by Deutsche Werft AG of Hamburg, Germany in 1938 and sunk in March, 1942 east of Abaco. Her salvor was Granville Bethel of Cherokee Sound and did brief service assisting neighboring Crossing Rocks, also cut off with barely any road access.

New Plymouth was a wooden motor vessel of 37 tons that served Abaco in 1942, and was a substitute boat to Inagua. She was built in 1932 by Charles R. Hodgkins and Richard Hodgkins of Green Turtle Cay and registered by at least 1936. Named for a pirate, the *Stede Bonnet* was built as the 1942 as a Royal Navy minesweeper HMS *MM 194* to a Jenkins Roberts design at Symonette Shipyards in Nassau. She served both Abaco Cays and Eleuthera from 1942 to 1970. An impressive 148 tons, her wood hull was 119 feet long. Masters included Sherwin Archer, his son Bobby Archer, Ancil Albury, Lionel Albury, and Lloyd Albury, Leland Roberts, Archie Bethel and Noel Bethel, and cook Ludd Lowe, cook. She appeared in the *Nassau Guardian* shipping list 1960 and 1965, and memoirist Dave Gale said she offered two cabin classes. *Stede Bonnet* sank in Hurricane Betsy in Marsh Harbour on the night of September 4 to 5, 1965, and is commemorated with a photograph in the Wyannie Malone Museum, in Hope Town.

The steel-hulled freighter *Betty K.* performed only substitute mailboat between 1944 to 1989 at various Bahamian ports. This *Betty K* (there were two others, one of which was built in 1938) United Concrete Pipe Company Los Angeles, California, 1943, of 579 tons and 126 feet; in the Bahamas she was owned by Trevor C. Kelly of Nassau. The Kelly companies have owned eight (8) vessels plying between Miami and Nassau since the 1920s – a century. Her captains included Howard Sweeting, Mait Lowe, and Anthony Lowe. She was sold as the *Lady K.* to Columbia from 1984 to 1991. The *Tropical Trader II* served Marsh Harbour and the Abaco Cays from 1950-1957. Built of wood in the 1930, she was 250 tons and 120 feet and owned by Senator Sherwin Archer, supported by captains Bobby Archer (son), Garnet Archer, Donald Moss, and Joseph Moxey, engineer. Moxey said *Tropical Trader II* had a single Caterpillar engine, cargo derrick in old style block and tackle, and vessel was not long in trade. In 1957 Percy Archer said she was replaced by *Almeta Queen* on the Abaco run and became inactive (*Abaconian,* November, 1997, p.30)

The wooden motor vessel *Church Bay* served Abaco from 1952 to the 1970s, Cat Island up to 1973, and Grand Bahama at least during 1964. Along with the Stede Bonnet, *Church Bay* was built in Nassau to fill a need for British minesweepers. HMS *MMS 194* was laid down 18 August, 1941 and launched 4 June, 1942. Her pennant was J694, she was an MMS I class vessel and was decommissioned in March of 1946. In *A Salute to Friend and Foe*, Sir Etienne Dupuch noted that the "British Admiralty contracted for two trawlers to be built in Nassau, and they were launched in a ceremony by the Duke of Windsor." At 225 tons and 119 feet, her initial owners were J. W. Roberts for the Abaco Lumber Company, then Sir Roland Symonette's Three Bays Corporation, who used it in the 1950s for long haul voyages to Mexico and beyond from Miami.

Under her final owners (denied by him) Oscar Johnson, Member of Parliament for Cat Island, she suffered chronic engine trouble. The vessel's captains are said to have included Jenkins Roberts, Roy Oral Lockhart, and crew Herbert Stevens. On January 11, 1973 she was lost to fire on Potter's Cay; Mrs. Hannah Poitier and her three children were on board at the time but escaped injury. Interestingly the person said to be the vessel's owner denied being so, and the crew went on record stating the vessel had "no official Captain." The officers and men of the tug *Mako* put themselves in peril to push the burning hulk off the dock at Potter's Cay and away from people and vessels. (*Nassau Tribune*, 11 January, 1973, Front Page, George A. Smathers Libraries, University of Florida, Caribbean Newspaper Digital Library). *Church Bay* was replaced on the Cat Island run beginning in 1973 by the *Sea Salvor Express*.

The wooden 126-ton motor vessel *San Cristobal* served Abaco and its cays, in the 1950 to 1952 timeframe, Dave Gale's *Ready About*. She was still registered in 1956. The 120-ton, 81-foot wooden motor vessel *Almeta Queen* served Abaco and northern Bahamas between 1952 and 1972. She was built in Abaco in 1947 and carried crawfish in the 1940s. Her owners were Sherwin Archer from 1957 to 1968, for the Abaco Trading Company, then Benjamin Roberts, then David Lowe of Green Turtle Cay. Captains included Sherwin Archer (1950s and 1960s), Garnet Archer, from 1968 to 1972, with Joseph Moxey as engineer. She was sold in 1972 to David Lowe but when her portholes were left open on the voyage from Nassau to Abaco at night, she sank. *Almeta Queen* was replaced by *Deborah K.* from 1972, and it not to be confused with the sailboat *Almeta*, 49 tons, built before 1946 from Nassau.

What are known as the unnamed *Abaco Sloops* provided an important service to Cooper's Town, Cedar Harbour, Fox Town, and Crown Haven on Little Abaco, and beyond, in some cases as far was Walker's Cay, starting in 1962. Melvin Wells initiated this spur line, shuttling mail from larger mailboat which carried it to other communities, but no further. The *Miz Desa* took mail to Marsh Harbour, Treasure Cay, Green Turtle Cay, and Hope Town from 1971 to 2003 and beyond. Travel guides including *Adventure Guide to the Bahamas* feature her, aka *Mia Desa* offering passages to Abaco for $45 per person, from the 1990s to 2003. She was built of steel and delisted from 2012.

The 381-ton, 161-foot-long motor mailboat *Deborah K.* served the entire Abaco chain under Archer ownership from 1972 to 1982. She was originally the *Betty K. III*, built by New Jersey Shipbuilding with Dutz diesel engines in Barber, New Jersey as a wartime LCI(L), for Landing Craft Infantry in 1944, and sold out of the US Navy from 1946. C. Trevor Kelly, *Betty K.* Line, aka Kelly Lumber in Nassau owned her from 1946 to 1970, mostly on the Miami-Nassau run. Her new owner was Garnet Archer, with Archie Bethel, from 1970. Captains and crew included Garnet Archer, Fabian Archer, a Mr. Nixon, Donald Moss, mate from 1990, Hansel Bain, engineer, George, and Leo, an engineer, in 1985. Per the Archer family, May, 2020: "Garnet Archer obtained and captained a war supply ship named *Deborah K.*" Samuel Shelton Archer worked on her on school breaks 1975-1977 for his uncle Garnet Archer, and full-time 1978-

1982. On being replaced by *Deborah K. II*, *Deborah K* was taken to Man-O-War Cay, Abaco, then in 1983 her engines were stripped out, and the ship was taken to the deep water on the ocean side and scuttled, or sunk. She is cited in the book *Out Island Doctor*, by Evans Cottman.

The 348-ton, 180-foot long steel mailboat *Deborah K. II* entered the Abaco service to replace her namesake in 1982 and up until 1995. She was owned and operated by Garnet Archer, who served as captain, supported by mate Donald Moss, Fabian Archer, Samuel Archer, Wayne Archer, George, Leo engineer, and Joseph Moxey, supporting engineer and crew. Garnet Archer purchased *Deborah K. II* from owners in Germany in 1981, where it was known as *Windhund*, and delivered it across the Atlantic. In the summer of 1984 this writer voyaged with family aboard this large ship to Elbow Cay Abaco, Abaco, and in several communities it was necessary for the mothership to anchor and passengers and cargo and luggage to be passed down to smaller boats. Samuel Archer said Garnet Archer took pride in serving even the far-away small communities on Little Abaco out to Grand Cay, Walkers Cay; his motto was "52 trips per year." In the 1990s the ship was sold to Mr. Melltorp in Hope Town, and thereafter drops off the register.

The 485-ton steel Ro-Ro landing craft *Legacy* is 160 feet long and serves Abaco's mail needs since 2002. That year she was completed at Rodriguez Coden in Coden, Alabama and her owners Dean Shipping Company, under Ernest Dean Jr., delivered her to Potter's Cay. Her captains include Ricky Barnett, Michael Watkins, and the ship is still operating, with a deep green hull colour. On 9 November, 2011 the story might have taken a different turn, as The *Nassau Tribune* and others reported how "The M/V *Legacy* was pushed up on rocks as it tried to navigate its way through the North Bar Channel in Abaco. The seas were in full Rage conditions with swells running at 20-foot-plus. A US Coast Guard Helicopter was dispatched form Andros to rescue the Crew from the vessel."

The *Albertine Adoue* which was made from the scraps of a larger vessel into a 60-foot schooner to a 160-foot steel freighter, the *Legacy*, with a salvaged lifeboat, the *Beluga*, ferrying cargo between Cherokee Sound and Crossing Rocks. The *Content S.* was a converted yacht which, at one point, was registered to Lake Champlain in Vermont, and was tended to by *The Queen*, the lifeboat from the British tanker *Athelqueen* which was sunk by an Italian submarine off Hope Town in 1942 – the boat was a gift from her grateful officers and crew and was featured in a painting by renown Abaco artist Alton Lowe, whose Albert Lowe Museum is a fine repository of mailboat ephemera.

The original *Albertine Adoue* was named after the wife of prominent businessman, Bertrand Adoue, of Galveston, Texas. His partner, Jean Jacques Mistrot, and he invested in blockade running in the American Civil War – apparently profitably. While bound from Philadelphia to Galveston with a cargo of coal, the ship foundered near

Spanish Cay, off Little Abaco, on the 29 March, 1894. Enterprising locals built a schooner from the timbers, with the resulting craft being 60 feet on deck with two masts. She was to serve the Bahamas as a mailboat from Nassau for 29 years under the same name. The *Albertine Adoue* was not popular with the government Commissioner in Hope Town, who wrote, "It is impossible in these progressive days [1922] to expect a mail service to be satisfactorily performed by a sailing vessel. Apart from speed there is no comfort or privacy to be obtained for passengers." He further hoped that a motor vessel would "... take the place of this wind jammer." The vessel nominated to take the schooner's place was the *Priscilla*, a steel-hulled 100-footer propelled by a 115-horsepower Fairbanks Morse diesel engine. Rumoured to have been a racing sail yacht, her contribution to mail service "significantly reduced the degree of Abaco's isolation and made commerce more feasible."

With the implementation of wireless service to Nassau the same year, Dodge notes that what would have taken a fortnight before 1925 took just minutes in terms of transmission of information. According to Evan Loew, the cook on board was his relative Osgood Lowe; the mate was Howard Lowe, and the Captain, Hartley. Although the *Priscilla* could never be as fast as a telegram, and was "no panacea," her contribution to trade was considerable even if imperfect. Among the other settlements she called, Green Turtle Cay was included. In August, 1932, the vessel was "blown ashore and destroyed" during a hurricane. Another account, in Wayne Neely's book, *The Great Bahamian Hurricanes of 1899 and 1932*, more modestly states, "M/V *Priscilla* reported some damage to the structure of the boat."

The Queen was the affectionate term for the *Athelqueen*'s lifeboat, which was given to Hope Town citizens as a gift from survivors (three of whom drowned trying to make it to shore). According to Vernon Malone, *The Queen* was burned after its useful life shuttling people, mail, and cargo to and from mailboats was expended.

Stede Bonnet, named after a famous pirate, the other the *Church Bay*, which later burned in downtown Nassau. An online commentator added this colourful rendition of the coconut telegraph: "That omnipresent Short-Wave Radio played its part in announcing the arrival of the mailboat. The Captain would simply key his mike on the ship's radio and announce, '*Stede Bonnet* reporting; just left East Side Marsh Harbour on the way to Hopetown. Someone please tell Mr. Robley Russell to bring the tender out by Parrot Cay for freight and passengers. *Stede Bonnet* out.'"

In the book *Islanders in the Stream* Captain Russell and he were described as "a Conchy Joe captain and mate and all-black crew." The authors Saunders and Craton continue: "Cherokee Sound was only the first of the six Abaco settlements at which the *Richard Campbell* called, following a routine that, though tedious, greatly raised Jack Ford's admiration for the seamanship, efficiency, and toughness of Captain Russell and his crew." Cherokee Sound was shallow and required shuttling of small vessels to carry cargo and people ashore, Captain Granville Bethel devised an ingenious way to supply the similarly isolated community of Crossing Rocks to the south – he salvaged a lifeboat from a torpedoed Allied freighter which had washed up there. According to his son Patrick, the small craft was renamed *Beluga* and plied its route from 1945 or so into the 1950s fitted with a small engine.

The *Almeta Queen* was built for War Supply in Toronto in 1942 and converted to sail in 1946. Captain Ernest Dean speaks of utilizing her services to tow one of his new-built vessels (the *Captain Dean II*) from Marsh Harbour to Nassau around 1965. She carried crawfish between Abaco, Florida, and Nassau. In August, 2007, she was sighted in aerial photographs rotting on the River Platte of Argentina. *Legacy*, built by the same yard as *Captain Gurth Dean*, is capable of carrying 600 tons of cargo. Thoroughly modern and shallow draft, it was built in 2002 and still calls at Marsh Harbour, Guana Cay, Green Turtle Cay, and Nassau on a weekly basis. Commissioned by Dean's Shipping Limited of Nassau for the specific Bahamas trade, this vessel represents a new generation of service to the islands – continuing a long line of entrepreneurial-ship in shipbuilding and investing and calculated risk-taking that has covered a dozen decades, as many vessels, and everything from yachts to lifeboats to converted schooners and spongers to modern landing craft. It is worth noting that with the possible exception of the *Deborah K. II*, Abaco has avoided the trend of some other regions to purchase older ships from Europe and trade them until they become either dive sites or fodder for South American operators.

The extraordinary reconstructed sailing mailboat *Albertine Adoue* serving Abaco. This is a rare photo of the schooner mailboat *Albertine Adoue* in motion c.1922. She is laden with passengers and cargo – note the person on the port ratlines (rigging) aloft, as well as the stains of the sails (lower right) probably from traffic over them whilst they lay on the boom over the cockpit, from people grabbing the boom for support as they went below. She was originally built in Bath, Maine in 1890.Then, in 1894, she was wrecked in Spanish Cay, Abaco, partially salvaged, and re-built from timbers at Black Sound on Green Turtle Cay Abaco. Her captains included Hartley Roberts, Osbourne Roberts, and Roland Roberts. Her Bahamian owners were R. J. Anderson Farrington and William Augustus Roberts. Whilst running liquor past the blockade into North Carolina she grounded off Oak Island and foundered on Christmas Day in 1930. Owned by a prominent French-American merchant family in Texas, her namesake is said to have been the most prominent woman in Galveston. She traded throughout the entire Bahamas, from Inagua to the northernmost islands. Surely few countries could have produced such an ingenious hybrid of a vessel – literally a phoenix rising from a wreck.

Eleuthera and Islands

Dunmore Town, the furthest port in North Eleuthera from Nassau, is named for John Murray, the Fourth Earl of Dunmore, the last British governor of the American colonies and the Royal Governor of the Bahamas from 1787 to 1796. After tripling the colony's population with loyalists and slaves, the cotton crops failed and the economy crashed. He made Harbour Island, the oldest settlement, politically important by keeping a second home there. Though a claim of the town being the colony's capital is not historically supported, it certainly is vocally. As a result, given the proximity to Nassau and the option of choosing shelter behind a string of islands between Nassau and The Current, nearly 20 mailboats have served Harbour Island, going back to at least the 1860s, with mail, added to which nearly 40 served Eleuthera, which is 110 miles long.

The wooden sailing vessel *Mary Jane* first served North Eleutheran ports of Harbour Island and Spanish Wells from 1868 to 1878. She was built at Dunmore Town, Harbour Island, in 1853 and weighed 41 tons. Her owner was John Cleare of the same port, and in 1878 she was replaced by the resilient sloop *Dart*. The *Mary Jane* was broken up in Nassau in 1900. The schooner *Jimmie* carried the mails to Eleuthera between 1876 and 1878, on charter to Her Majesty's Government. Built of wood in 1867, she weighed 15 tons. *Jimmie*'s route was Eleuthera, excluding Harbour Island, which in 1878 the *Dart* took over.

The wooden schooner *Cicero* served Harbour Island from November, 1878 to about 1883, and was on the Abaco run from 1860. At 17 tons she was owned by George Higgs of Nassau, and D. Russell of New Plymouth, Abaco. Between 1883 and 1922 *Cicero* began competing with the *Dart* in the Harbour Island route and eventually enlarged to include others calls. The *Dart* covered Harbour Island, Spanish Wells, and North Eleuthera, starting in 1878 then expanding to cover more ports by 1882. Mail dropped at Three Islands, where the ferries to Harbour Island set off, was carried by horse to Bogue, Bluff, Current, and North Eleuthera 1878 to 1922, per Godfrey Kelly, grandson of Captain Austin Kelly.

The *Dart* was built on Harbour Island in 1867, weighed 32 tons, and her wooden deck was 35 or so feet long. Her initial owners were John Saunders Harris, and one of her captains was John Saunders, aka Run Joe, of Eleuthera, William James Harris, and Mr. McKie. According to philatelist Edward Bailey Proud, the *Dart* ran nonstop, with no named substitutes, for 27 years, from July 11, 1894 to December 30, 1921, with supplemental over-land mail delivery to Current. Usually critical commissioners' comments were mild, such as in 1919; "A little paint would do no harm." In November of 1878 *Dart* shared route with *Cicero* and they expanded the services on offer to 1883 and beyond. *Dart* was lost in a 1922 hurricane.

The wooden schooner *Rebecca* replaced the *Jimmie* in 1883 on the Eleuthera run, excluding Harbour Island, until 1885. She was built on Eleuthera in 1881 at 20 tons and owned by Sarah M. Bethel of Governor's Harbour, then Charles A. Bethel of the same port. She should not be confused with an 8-ton *Rebecca* owned by Moses Kemp of Nassau, nor the 46-tonner owned by George D. Harris of Nassau in the 1915 registry. The *Kate Sturrup* served North Eleuthera, including Harbour Island, from 1890 to the 1930s. this wooden vessel was 51 tons and crafted of wood, whose owners were Henry William F. Sturrup and Arnold Ingraham. *Kate Sturrup* departed for Jamaica by 1935, not to reappear.

The schooner *Trackless* carried the mails to central and southern Eleuthera from 1894, including Gregory Town, Governor's Harbour, Savannah Sound, Tarpum Bay, and Rock Sound, a route said to have been established in 1882. She was built in Hope Town in 1881 of wood and weighed 67 tons. Her owners was Thomas T. Bowles of Governor's Harbour. She appears in the 1915 registry, not thereafter. The schooner *Glynn* followed *Trackless*' route to southern-central Eleuthera from 1897. She was built in Noank, Connecticut, in the US, in 1884 of wood and weighed 58 tons. Her Bahamas owner was Edward Fraser Griffin of Governor's Harbour, and last appears in the 1910 registry. The schooner *Leon* joined the route from Gregory Town to Rock Sound in 1900.

The motor vessel *Endion* was brought in to upgrade the service to Harbour Island, Spanish Wells, The Bluff, and North Eleuthera from 1921 to 1939. She was constructed in 1898 by the Charles L. Seabury Company, aka the Gas Engine Power Company in Bronx, New York. The vessel was 61 tons, wooden hulled, and 100 feet long, and fitted with a 4-cylinder 60 ihp diesel, she could carry 17 passengers and needed 10 crew. She served in the US Navy out of Boston as USS *Endion*, SP-707 between 1 May, 1917 and 6 October, 1919. On 19 March, 1921 Bahamian investors (possibly Sweetings or Harris') bought the *Endion* at public auction in the US, and registered her to the Bahamas. The following year the Harbour Island Steamship Company, with Albert Sweeting, E. B. Sweeting, and William G. Harris, purchased her. William Harris was a captain and William Bethel a mate. The *Endion* was badly damaged at Harbour Island in the hurricane of October, 1926. Then the *Dart* substituted for her for one trip. In 1937 the commissioner commented that the *Endion*'s cabins needed improvement, and that her subsidy was too low. By 1939 she was replaced by *Lady Dundas*. The *Endion* helped usher a new era or more comfortable motor-driven mailboat to the region and the colony.

The schooner *Content* sailed to central-south Eleuthera, starting in 1921 and in to the 1940s. A commissioner's report of 1940 noted that fortnightly the *Content* shared the rouge with *Priscilla*, and that both were supplemented by the *Three Bays*, a 54-ton motor boat active from Eleuthera from the 1940s and part of the Arthur Vining Davis group of companies, a dairy component of which was in Rock Sound; he was a founder of ALCOA. The schooner *Indiana* entered service in 1921 to central-south Eleuthera. She was built in Abaco in 1900 at 31 tons, and of wood, and owned by George J. Bethel of Eleuthera; she last appears in the 1920 vessel registry, so probably did not continue past 1925.

Starting in 1921 the sailing vessel *Mayflower* dropped mail at Three Islands, North Eleuthera, where it was carried, Godfrey A. Kelly, on horseback. She was built of wood on Eleuthera in 1909 and weighed 26 tons. Her owner was John Albury, and Captain Robert Austin Kelly would take the ferry from Harbour Island, ride a horse to The Current in order to assume command of her. Shipwright Brother Henry, aka Bo Hengy and Robert A. Kelly lobbied their North Eleuthera representative, W. C. B. Johnson to get the mail contract for the smaller communities of North Eleuthera. In 1909 a tender was proffered for a three-year contract. Before carrying the mail, *Mayflower* would also drop supplies twice a month to the keepers of Egg Island Lighthouse, to the west of Spanish Wells and Royal Island, however it was destroyed by the hurricane of September 16, 1928.

The motor vessel *Maysie* served the communities of central-south Eleuthera from 1921, per commissioners and mail reports of the day. The steam ship SS *Ballymena* entered the Eleuthera route in 1922; well known in popular culture, the ship was built in 1888 of steel. Austin Ira Destoup, who lived from 1883 and 1956, was a constable, composer, and pianist. He composed, published, distributed and with Harry Belafonte popularized the song *Ballymena* in 1927. The ship was closed from the registry in 1926. Lyrics include "Put the *Belamena* on the dock, And paint the *Belamena* black, black, black, Paint the *Belamena* black, black; When she come back, she was white." During the Prohibition, in order to throw off the US Coast Guard and law enforcement in the US, ships would repaint themselves often.

The steamship SS *City of Nassau* steamed to and from Harbour Island and other Eleuthera ports between 1922 and 1937. The steel ship of 592 tons and 207 feet long was built by Laura, Granville Aitken and Mansel at Whiteinch, Glasgow in 1885. She replaced *Princess Montagu* on Miami-Nassau route in 1929. Broken up 1937, listed in 1940, another possibility being that she was lost in the bootlegging business. In 1926 the schooner *Hero* sailed for Governor's Harbour and continued all the way up into the 1960s. The boat's owners were either Thomas Demeritte, Uriah Saunders of Governor's Harbour, or both. She was believed to have been built in Abaco in 1900 out of wood and weighed 68 tons. *Hero* survived the 1926 hurricanes, and was de-listed by 1965.

The 46-ton gasoline-engine yacht *Quankey* began serving Current Island, and on North Eleuthera The Current, and Lower Bogue in 1927 and on into the 1950s. She was built in the US in 1927 and was approximately 45 feet long, with a consortium of owners including Burton Symonette and others. *Quankey* arrived in the trade before *Dollymae* or the *Ego*, according to Godfrey Kelly of Harbour Island, whose grandfather

Robert Austin Kelly was an active mariner at the time. Originally registered to the US, she was delisted by 1932. The sailing sloop converted with an auxiliary motor named *Olga* carried mails to North Eleuthera, not Harbour Island for one trip, substituting in for *Mayflower*, in 1929. Otherwise the 10-ton wooden boat served Staniard Creek, North Andros. She was built in 1899 and owned by William H. H. Maura of Nassau, and appears only in the 1920 vessel registry.

The motor vessel *Sir Charles Orr* sailed from the builder's yard in England for the Bahamas in order to carry mail and persons to and from central-south Eleuthera between 1930 and 1936. After being built by J. Crighton and Company in Cheshire, she crossed the Atlantic in just 19 days, arriving in July, 1930 bearing the name of the Governor. Her British-Bahamian investors included the Eleuthera Shipping Company and Major George R. Benson. Made of steel, *Sir Charles Orr* weighed 214 tons and was 116 feet long. The vessel was well outfitted to accommodate 16 first-class and 16 second-class passengers, with room for ventilation, cargo, and mail.

Arriving in Nassau from Miami on August 13, 1930, her owners had secured a three-year mail contract with the colonial government. Under either name, the ship sailed Father Jerome Hawes the Hermit of Cat Island, to Long Island and Cat Island. The *Monarch of Nassau* rescued remnants of a group of Californian Utopians from the Turks Caicos, and 30 torpedoed Greek mariners post-U-boat, from the *Cygnet*, from San Salvador in mid-March of 1942. From 1936 she became the *Monarch of Nassau* as part of the Monarch Line, controlled by Sir George Roberts, then Carl Sawyer. Captains included Roland Roberts.

The motor vessel *Ivy S* served North Eleuthera from 1930, then southwest Abaco, including the Cornwall lumber camps, from 1936. Built of wood she was small, and followed *Quankey* and *Mayflower*. The motor mailboat *Lelia* followed the *Ivy S.* to North Eleuthera in 1933, before *Dolly Mae*. In 1934 the motor vessel *Emmie* served North Eleuthera for four years, before the 1938 when the sloop *Merlin M.* covered Harbour Island, Spanish Wells, and the Bluff. The wooden *Merlin M.* was owned by John N. Albury of Nassau, and is not to be confused with *Merle*, a sloop with auxiliary motor at the same time. The motorboat *Dolly Mae* provided mail services to North Eleuthera and Andros from 1940.

From Three Islands, the mail still went by horse to Bogue, Bluff, and Current into the 1950s. Also called *Darling May, Dollymae,* and *Dollymae*, she was named for co-owner William Ferris Weech's wife Mae Elizabeth Symonette. Built in Eleuthera of wood about 1929, she was about 40 tons and owned in shares by Burton Symonette, William Ferris Weech and others. Captains included W. Ferris Weech, and a Captain Pinder. The boat appears in Chicago newspapers to 1984, but in 1985 she was described by commissioners as providing "irregular and far from satisfactory" service. *Dolly Mae*'s tenure lasted between other Current boats *Quanky* and *Ego*, per mailboat investor Godfrey Kelly. Ferris Weech is said to have owned her before reaching age 21.

The motor mailboat *Lady Dundas* began carrying the mails to Harbour Island and North Eleuthera in 1940, then southern Eleuthera, Cat Island, The Cave, Knowles, McQueen's, Cockburn Town, Sandy Point Creek, and Grahams Town, San Salvador. Between 1960 and 1974 her list of coverage grew to include Mayaguana and Grand Bahama. Her builders were Earl Johnson and Gerald Johnson, with design contributions by well-known Oyster Bay Long Island New York yacht designer Lawrence Huntington. She was built and launched in Dunmore Town in 1939, was 115 tons, made of wood and 92 feet long. Owners included Berlin T. Albury and Harry Albury, the Harbour Island Steamship Co. Ltd., with shares held by A. Johnson, W. Bethel, Albert Sweeting, and William Roy Lowe, KBE. Captains included William G. Harris, William Roy Lowe, Calvin Sawyer, engineer, A. Sweeting, mate and A. Johnson, in the 1970s. In the 1940s commissioners noted that *Lady Dundas* performed regular service, and that many visitors travelled on her. Richard Malcolm features her in his books on Harbour Island. She followed *Content S.* and *Priscilla*. *Lady Dundas* was last heard of under new owners, arrested in Haiti in 1974 for smuggling, and thereafter became inactive.

The motor vessel *Samana* served from Governors Harbour to Spanish Wells and beyond between 1940 and the 1960s. She was built by talented shipwright and Harbour Island resident Victor Percy Cleare at Hatchet Bay, Eleuthera in 1940. Made of wood, *Samana* weighed 119 tons, and was 96 feet long. The Rhode Island, US visionary and farmer Austin T. Levy d/b/a Hatchet Bay, Eleuthera Company, commissioned her; he lived from 1880 to 1951 and also owned *Arawak, Passing Jack,* and *52 Miles*. *Samana* last appears in 1946 registry, owned by Mervin and Mrs. Elvy Ferguson yet references to her appear up to 1965. The motor vessel *Three Bays* was serving Three Bays Farm from Rock Sound to Nassau from 1940. She made several trips to North Eleuthera as a mailboat in 1944, as a wooden substitute boat of 54 tons. Every two weeks she shared the route with *Priscilla*, and *Content S.*

The sloop *Merle* supplemented the Eleuthera route from 1940, covering from Harbour Island and North Eleuthera. She was built in Nassau in 1906 of wood and was 26 tons. Her owner was William J. Pinder of Nassau. There was a similar named sloop on the same route named *Merlin M; Merle* was in the 1911 ship registry. The sloop and auxiliary motor boat *Shamrock* served North Eleuthera from 1940, after already serving much of Andros from 1933 to 1938. The motorized mailboat *Noel Roberts* entered the North Eleuthera trade in 1943, then Grand Bahama to 1965. Her hull was built by Earl Johnson and Gerald Johnson in Harbour Island, then towed by the tug *BA 2* to Symonette Shipyards in Nassau for fitting out in 1943. At 180 tons, her wood decks measured 115 feet long. Her owner was Sir George Roberts, who named the ship and company after his son, *Noel Roberts* Ltd., d/b/a *Richard Campbell* Ltd.

One of her captains was Roy Oral Lockhart of Ragged Island, in 1965, thereafter *Noel Roberts* was wrecked in the Six Shilling Channel east of Nassau.

The 34-ton wooden motor vessel *Ego* was built at Symonette Shipyards in Nassau in 1943 and that year carried the mail to Harbour Island, Three Islands, and North Eleuthera until 1980. The 52-foot boat was owned by shares held by residents of The Current, including Arlie Symonette, Carlton Griffin, William Ferris Weech, and Julius Symonette. Her captains and crew included W. Ferris Weech, Maitland, crew Arlie Symonette, Donald Symonette, and Carlton Griffin. *Ego* was active to at least 1975, possibly 1980. Godfrey Kelly says she docked at the Moore's Wharf in Nassau and had a white hull.

The sleek motor merchant named *Liberty* was built of wood in 1938, 140 tons and 95 feet long. Her mail route from 1943 took her to North Eleuthera and Harbour Island, then Fresh Creek, Andros up until the 1980s. Her builders were Earl Johnson and Gerald Johnson in Harbour Island, and the owner was Albert Pinder, 1892 to 1960, of Spanish Wells. Conversations with Godfrey Kelly, and inclusion in Edward B. Proud's *Postal History* corroborate 1985 an image of her in a book by Richard Malcolm shows she is the same boat entering Fresh Creek, Andros in the early 1980s, as taken by US Navy sailors at AUTEC nearby. The motor yacht *Vergemere IV* went to Harbour Island and North Eleuthera from 1944. She was – uniquely for a mailboat – built for Marion B. Carstairs at her private shipyard on her private island, Whale Cay in the Berry Islands. It is named for Bostwick estate in Mamaroneck (which the author was able to tour), and there were at least four in the series. In August, 1942, *Vergemere IV* rescued 47 sailors from the American SS *Potlatch*'s lifeboat, off Crooked Island. She is in the 1940 registry.

In 1947 the schooner *Joyce Roberts* sailed for Rock Sound's Three Bays Farm, after traded between Miami, and Nassau. Constructed of wood at 100 tons and 86 feet long, her owners were the Sir George Roberts family's entity *Captain Roberts* Limited. Listed in the 1944 registry, already in 1940 *Joyce Roberts* was calling on sub-post offices at Tarpum Bay, Green Castle, Deep Creek , Weymss Bight, and Bannerman Town, Eleuthera, where residents used to walk six miles for the mail. The sloop *Mary and Elizabeth* in 1947 called at southern Eleuthera. The wooden boat was built in the Bahamas in 1925 and by going directly to smaller ports she and *Joyce Roberts* helped create a form of spur line.

The motor mailboat named *Rock Sound* served Rock Sound's Three Bays Farm and Nassau from 1947. She was a 68-ton, wooden boat which in 1940 bi-weekly shared mail runs with the *Priscilla* and *Content*, supplemented by the *Three Bays*. The tragic motor vessel *Zelma Rose* served North Eleuthera between 1947 and 1952, then Long Island, Rum Cay, Long Cay, Acklins, and Inagua. Build of wood to 34 tons, she was owned by Mr. Pinder in Spanish Wells, and captain Edison Higgs, aka Bird, from 1947 to 1952. She was subsidized at one point to carry tomatoes from Cat Island to Nassau.

In June of 1952 the *Zelma Rose* sank in the Fleeming Channel west of Current Island, killing six, including children. This inspired a mournful song named for the mailboat which entered the national conscience.

The heralded *Air Swift* began serving North Eleuthera and Harbour Island in 1948, and continued until 1977, later branching to central-south Eleuthera in 1957. She began as the US Navy's USS *SC-1340* from 1943 to 1945, then US Coast Guard Cutter *Air Swift, WAVR 471*, to 1948. She was built the Thomas Knutson Shipbuilding Corporation in Halesite, Long Island, New York, in 1943, of wood, at 134 tons and 111 feet long. Her Bahamas owner was Sir George Roberts in 1948, d/b/a *Richard Campbell* Limited. Later shares were owned by Carlysle Albury, David, aka Socks, Curry, Dr. Maloney, and Humphry Percentie. At different times captains and crew included Leonard Wallace, Kirkwood Campbell, P. Bastian, B. Bastian, D. Delancey, D. Grey, and F. Rahming, during a training cruise in 1977. The Harbour Island Percenties say *Air Swift* was badly damaged in Nassau during Hurricane David in 1979. In the *Abaconian* she was reported lost with fellow mailboat *Miss Beverly* in a severe storm on January 19, 1977, then scuttled on the Montagu Foreshore. One account has the government insisting on the boat's wreck being further destroyed and raked over.

The *Ena K.* served central-south Eleuthera from 1949, though her core route was Miami to Nassau, which she performed over 1,000 voyages on, connecting the Bahamas to USA in World War II. Wooden hull with motor auxiliary, she was owned by Trevor C. Kelly, and Kelly Lumber in Nassau. The *Passing Jack* motored to North Eleuthera and Abaco in the 1950s. She was built by Briland shipwright Victor Cleare for farm owner Austin T. Levy at Hatchet Bay, Eleuthera in 1939. The wood hull weighed 85 tons, and other vessels built by Clear for Levy included the *Arawak, Samana, Dairy Maid*, and *52 Miles*. *Passing Jack* substituted in for *Air Swift* to Harbour Island in the 1950s, per Godfrey Kelly and Richard Malcolm, though originally built as a yacht.

The motor mailboat the first *Bahamas Daybreak* was so named as it always set off at daybreak, whether from Eleuthera or Nassau. In 1955 it set off for North Eleuthera and Harbour Island, up to 1970. This vessel was wood, and about 80 tons, and was owned by the Stuarts of North Eleuthera up to the 1980s. A 1970 postcard depicts the MV *Daybreak*, offering "weekly freight and mail boat." In 1979 a passage cost $15 per day for two days. The motor boat *Current Queen* began its calls on the archipelago in 1965, adding Ragged Island, Spanish Wells, and The Current up to 1997.

The original *Spanish Rose*, from 1965 to 1977, was not a mailboat until it was sold as *Current Queen* and became one thereafter. She was built of wood in 1965, was 64 tons, and owned by Gurney Elon Pinder and Stephen Pinder, then William Ferris Weech. In 1977, this first *Spanish Rose* became the *Current Queen.* The second *Spanish Rose* began trading to the Current and Spanish Wells, and although cited in the press and schedules in 1975 and 1992 was inactive by the mid-1990s. She ultimately sank in daytime in 1997, with no loss of life.

The motor mailboat *Harley & Charley* sailed for mainland Eleuthera in 1969, then to South Andros up to the 1990s. She was 91 tons, made of wood, and 100 feet long. Her owner was Androsian Harley Simms, d/b/a Camp Bay Shipping; in 2016 Simms also owned *Abilin*. *Harley & Charley* is cited in 1988, 1989, and 1992, and de-listed by 2000. She was on the government list in 2016.

The *Nassau Moonglow* served Harbour Island and Spanish Wells from 1972 to 1975. Built of wood at 72 tons for the Spanish Wells Shipping Company. By 1985 she was owned by Sweeting, per Schmidt the owner of Remora Bay in about 1970. She is advertised in a 1975 Bahama Out Islands Association leaflet (*Selkirk Enterprise*) yet in the 1980s was out of service. The *Offshore* motored for Eleuthera in 1973 and continued for over a decade until 1984. This 78-ton steel ship was built in 1973, about 80 feet long, and owned by the Eleuthera Shipping Company, aka Eleuthera Limited. Her captains included Leonard Thompson and Willard Matthew Fox in 1984. *Offshore* is cited in the February 11, 1973 issue of the *Naples Daily News*, Dave Gale's book *Ready About*, and even photographs hanging on the walls of a bank lobby. Willard M. Fox in 2017 said her fate is unknown.

The steel motor vessel *Bahamas Daybreak II* covered Eleuthera from Davis Harbour to Harbour Island starting in 1978 and into the 1990s. Originally named the *Leamington*, the boat was built at S. G. Powell Shipyards, then lengthened in 1963 by Erieau Shipbuilding & Drydock in Erieau, Dunnville, Ontario, on the Great Lakes, in Canada for Hooper Motorships, Limited in 1957. The steel hulled boat is 102 tons and 81 feet. In 1978 she was purchased by Bahamian investors including Theophilus Stuart, Gerald Stuart, and Harvey Roberts. Her captains included Theophilus Stuart, with Joseph Moxey working the cranes. The Stuarts run the airport restaurant at North Eleuthera airport. Canadian maritime historian Kevin Griffin contributed.

The first *Eleuthera Express* served northern Eleuthera from 1979 to 1980. Her previous names included *Spiekeroog*, *Wischhafen*, and *Treasure Trader*, as she was built in Wilhelmshaven Germany in 1962 of 250 steel tons and 157 feet length. Her buyer was Junior Pinder. After 1980 she was renamed yet continued trading in the Bahamas, however in 1990 *Eleuthera Express* was sold to Miami. She sank *en route* from Haiti to Cuba in the early 1990s. The motor vessel *Current Pride* which began its North Eleuthera route in 1980 was built by Jerry Thompson at St. Augustine Trawlers in St. Augustine, Florida in 1980. Even though she was sheathed in fiberglass in 1988 (per Neal Sealy), she remains the only active mailboat in the Bahamas built of wood. Other owners include Gerald Elden, Derek Elden, and Reynold Elden of Elden Enterprises (Gerald and Reynold are nephews) and Patrick Neilly. Captains have included Patrick Neilly and William Ferris Weech.

The *Bahamas Daybreak III* joined its namesakes on the North Eleuthera service in 1982. She was built of steel of 110 tons around 1980, and her owners were Theophilus Stuart, Quincy Sawyer, and Bertram Sawyer. Captains have included Quincy Sawyer, Ashok, Captain Moss, and Jack Stuart. She is still operating, supplemented by *The Daybreak*, ex-*Tolyn*. The motor ship *Miss Juanita* took up bringing the mail to South Eleuthera in 1985 and continued doing so into the 1990s. She was built by the Stadium Boat Works of Cleveland, Ohio in 1944, and weighed 298 tons of steel. *Miss Juanita* was owned by the South Eleuthera Shipping Company, and appears in the 1998 and 1989 *Frommer's* guides, however was de-listed by the late 1990s.

The mailboat *Captain Fox* served Central Eleuthera from about 1995 to 2003 and beyond. The steel vessel was captained by Willard Matthew Fox and in 2000 was mentioned in an article by Blair Howard, and referenced in 2003 and 2009, yet inactive by 2000. Willard M. Fox also ran the *Offshore* from 1973 to 1984. The second *Eleuthera Express* hauled mail, cargo and passengers to Eleuthera from 1997 to 2018, and carries the same name as one built in 1962. This ship was constructed in Louisiana in 1996 and is 300 tons of steel and 132 feet long, owned by the *Eleuthera Express* Company. In February of 2018 she was sold to Nassau buyers, refitted for the tourism trade, repainted, and is now *Blackbeard's Revenge*. The motor mailboat *Daybreak* the second has had several identities for so new a vessel. She began serving Eleuthera in 2018. Before that, up to 2017, she was the Taylor-owned vessel *Lady Emerald*, and prior to that Tom Hanna's Ro-Ro landing craft the *Tolyn*, up to 2018. She is constructed of steel and 150 tons, and presently owned by Quincy Sawyer and in operation. Under Tom Hanna the *Daybreak* (aka *The Daybreak*) also motored to Rum Cay, San Salvador, and Long Island.

Although not strictly mailboats – they carry freight and passengers mostly – the *Bo Hengy and Bo Hengy II* have revolutionized sea travel – nay travel in general – between Nassau and North Eleuthera, providing a fast, efficient and affordable alternative to both conventional mailboats and aircraft. Built as Hull #5 by Pequot River Ship Works in New London, Connecticut the original *Bo Hengy* was named "after a Harbour Island shipwright Henry Sawyer, known as "Bro Henry" which then became *Bo Hengy*, who on top of wooden vessels made fish traps and tools for fishermen and spongers in the 1920s. Authors Anne and Jim Lawlor write in Harbour Island Story that in 1922 Sawyer " . . . built the first 5-horsepower motor boat in Harbour Island."

The modern *Bo Hengy II*'s impressive specifications include that she is 115 feet long, 27.5' beam, draft said to be 5', catamaran hull, 209 gross tons, capable of 177 passengers. Powered by MTU engines, 4,726 horsepower and flagged to the Bahamas; increasingly inter-island boats are flagged to Panama or other countries. Her owners are Bahamas Ferries Limited conveniently situated at Potter's Cay Docks. In May,

An image of the kindly Harbour Island craftsman Henry Sawyer, also known as Bro Henry, and Bo Hengy. The namesake of Bahamas Ferries' vessels *Bo Hengy* and *Bo Hengy II*.

2009, after ten years of service, she was sold to the Red Funnel Group of Southampton UK for service to Cowes, Isle of Wight, UK. This reverses the usual trend whereby many vessels were acquired second-hand from Europe and sold on to Latin America.

The *Bo Hengy II* was built in 2008 to replace her predecessor. She is 135 feet long, capable of 400 passengers (for harbour cruise, no luggage), and 394 passengers inter-island. Powered by Cummins engines, the vessel is capable of 25 knots. It features cold and dry storage, interior seating for passengers, weather-proof luggage stowage. She is 540 gross tons and capacity for 53 tons of cargo. Leaving by 8 a.m. the vessel makes the trip to Harbour Island in a few hours and permits visitors to take a day-trip to picturesque Dunmore Town – something unthinkable in the days of the *Mary Jane, Endion* and *Dart*.

The local mailboat, *Bimini Mack,* leaving Alice Town, North Bimini. Just shy of 100 feet, she was built of steel in 1981 at St. Augustine Marine in Florida. The mailboat is unique in the Bahamas in that is owned cooperatively, or communally by the Bimini Mack Association of Alice Town, or the Bimini Businessman's Association. The Ohio-based industrialist, Frederick C. Crawford, who had a home in Cat Cay, donated a church bell to South Bimini and the *Bimini Mack* carried it there. She is believed to have been trading as recently as 2015.

Grand Bahama and Freeport

There are at least 30 mail vessels serving the several ports of Grand Bahama, from West End to Sweetings Cay, since 1895. The island hosts the most industrialized sites in the Bahamas, with major shipyards, gantry cranes for container trans-shipment, the deepest port in the US east coast, one of the longest airstrips in the world, and much more including vast petroleum complexes. The communities have seen the boom of the Prohibition and the ravages of Hurricane Dorian in late 2019. The island is unique inasmuch as only the southern coast is used for deep-water movements, it has waterways cutting across it, is thinly populated to the east and north, is closer to Florida than Nassau, and holds two very large oil storage facilities, one of which failed during Hurricane Dorian.

Sweeting's Cay at the far east of Grand Bahama benefited from *Captain Dean*'s addition to the runs made by *Captain Deans* I to V and *Champion II*. There is now a high-speed passenger service, called Pinder's Ferry Service, between McLean's Town Grand Bahama and Crown Haven, Abaco. Bahamian historian Kendal Butler also confirms that there have been five female boat-builders in the islands since 1648, with Adeline Cooper of Sweeting's Cay being the most recent. The boats she built were prized by the Nassau elite.

The schooner *Raven* began serving Grand Bahama, Bimini and San Salvador in 1894 and continued for a decade, until 1904. She was built on Andros in 1880 of wood and weighed 16 tons. The boat's owners were W. J. Pinder in 1906, and Orlando F. Pritchard of Nassau in 1920. W. J. Pinder gained the mail contract to San Salvador in 1906, which *Raven* kept until 1908, then *Hazel Dell* took over. She left the ship registry by 1924. Another wooden schooner, the *Senela* began mail service to Grand Bahama and Bimini in 1903, followed by the schooner *Emma* in 1904, also calling at Alice Town and Grand Bahama. Emma was built of wood in Nassau in 1889 and was 13 tons. Her owner was George R. George, of Nassau, and there were two other schooners of the same name; in 1851 one of 9 tons owned by Benjamin Harris of Harbour Island, and the *Emma*, ex-*Ruby*, a schooner of 34 tons owned by Thomas Stead of Nassau.

The sailing schooner *Valiant* covered Grand Bahama and Bimini from 1905 to 1919. She was built in Abaco in 1868 and was wooden, of 15 tons. Her owners included W. D. Weech of Bimini in 1906, and Joseph Saunders, of Bimini in 1920. The April 1, 1906, tender for mail service was won by W. D. Weech for the *Valiant*, which last appeared in the 1920 registry. In 1907 the 25-ton wooden schooner *Ponce De Leon* served the mail needs of Alice Town, Cat Cay, and Grand Bahama. Her owners were Edward J. Wilkinson of North Bimini in 1911, and W. D. Weech of Bimini, who won the government mail tender of April 1, 1907 for *Ponce de Leon*, which he owned. She was built in 1876 on Bimini, which Spanish explorer Ponce de Leon left Puerto Rico in search of in 1513 with three ships; the *Santiago*, the *Santa María de la*

Consolación, and the *San Cristóbal*. They were looking for the Fountain of Youth, and though they never found it, or Bimini (they landed near St. Augustine, Florida); King Ferdinand of Spain made Ponce de Leon *adelantado*, or governor, of Bimini....

The wooden schooner *Mary Ella* began an ambitious mail route in 1909 which came to include High Rock, Golden Grove, Smith's Point, Eight Mile Rock, West End (after 1922), Settlement Point, Sweeting's Cay (home of women boat builders), Grand Bahama, and on Abaco Sandy Point and Moore's Island. She was built in the Bahamas in 1882 and was 15 tons, with Louis Isaacs of Nassau an owner. The 12-ton wooden schooner *Ghost* set out with the mail in 1910 to Whale Cay, Berry Islands, which it only served between April and July of that year. She was built in 1895 and owned by Thomas B. Hanna, of Acklins Harbour, and appears in the 1897 ship's registry.

The schooner *Charlotte* carried the mails to Bimini, the Berry Islands, and Grand Bahama starting in 1918, followed by the schooner *Julia* in 1919, which covered the same Grand Bahama and southwest Abaco communities as *Mary Ella* a decade earlier. *Julia* was constructed in the Bahamas in 1864 of wood and was 14 tons. Her owner was W. H. Curry of Nassau for whom she appears in the 1915 registry. Other vessels named *Julia* at the time were an 8-ton sloop owned by Azariah Curry of Abaco, then a 10-ton sloop built 1861, owned by William R. Saunders of Nassau, a schooner of 79 tons built in 1861 which was owned by Gustave Renouard of Nassau, and finally an 8-ton schooner which Thomas A. Hillier of Nassau owned.

The schooner *Amie* sailed laden with the mail for Grand Bahama and Abaco in 1920, adding at least one port in 1922. The schooner *Coraline* began the same route the same year, only added Alice Town and Cat Cay, Bimini as well as the Berry Islands. She was built by Symonette Shipyards of Nassau in 1917. Made of wood, it was 14 tons and 37 feet long. Her owners were Sir Roland Symonette of Nassau, who also built the motor vessels *Douglas Alexander*, *Ego*, *Vergemere III*, *Kenkora II*, *Mary Read*, and refit of *LCT 547*. This *Coraline* is not the sloop built in Bimini in 1907 of 10 tons and owned by Benjamin S. Brown. A wooden schooner named *Kim* set out with the mail in 1920 for Bimini, the Berry Islands and Grand Bahama.

The motor vessel *Princess Montagu* also covered Grand Bahama, Bimini, and the Berry Islands, from 1920 to 1929. Built of wood, she was beached in Nassau Harbour during the 1929 Hurricane, per hurricane historian Wayne Neely. Subsequently the *City of Nassau* took over the Miami-Nassau route. The schooner *Empress* served Grand Bahama and southwest Abaco from 1921. She was built in 1898 in Abaco of wood and was 19 tons. Owned by Mephaniah Wilchombe of Grand Bahama, she was on the registry in 1930. The schooner *Emerald* set sail for Grand Bahama and Abaco in 1924, having been built of wood on Man-O-War Cay, Abaco in 1900, and weighing 15 tons. Her owner was Roger Sweeting of Man-of-War-Cay. In 1926 the *Emerald* made 12 trips, or monthly. However the auxiliary motor sloop *Sydue* and motor vessel *Cruiser* and motor vessel *Christina* substituted for *Emerald*, because the commissioners found that the "captain and crew were very unreliable and discourteous," determining that the crew were far more interested in loading liquor for West End, which was much more profitable, than they were handling cargo, passengers and mail. The *Christina* served Grand Bahama and Abaco from 1926 onwards, followed by the wooden motor vessel *Cruiser* which went to Grand Bahama and Abaco starting in 1926, with the sloop *Sydue* following the same year; all of them picking up after the *Emerald*.

The wooden schooner named *Skipper Bill* joined the Grand Bahama and southwest Abaco mail run in 1928. Her owners may have included Robert Griffin of Current Island, per Briland mailboat investor Godfrey Kelly. The *Nellie* set out in 1929 Grand Bahama and Abaco with the mail. She was built in the Bahamas in 1883 out of wood and was 26 tons. Her owners included Benjamin P. Sturrup of Nassau. In 1945 services to lumber camps at Pine Ridge, then Water Cay was added by carrier service, as was Melville in Abaco in 1930. *Nellie* appears in the 1885 registry. The motor boat *Huron* also joined the Grand Bahama, southwest Abaco run in 1929, under the ownership of A. John Albury of Marsh Harbour. She also added Melville lumber camp in 1930. The route went in 1952 to the *Alice Mabel*, and over time several vessels joined the route, including the *Albury S., Paddy Halferty, Madam Queen, Castlerag, Marmaduke, Midwest, Madam,* and *Patricia K.*

Next the large steam ship SS *Bahamian* headed for the northern Bahamas from 1932 to the 1950s. This storied British vessel was also known by her first name, the Yacht *Candace*, HMS *Firequeen* (1920), and HM *Lighthouse Tender Firebird*. She was built in Leith England in 1882 of steel, was 446 tons, and 168 feet long. Her charterers were the Bahamas (Imperial) Lighthouse Service. One captain was W. Moxley, and other officers were Charles Munro, and Cleveland Malone on radio in 1935. Then, in 1953 she was wrecked off Blue Lagoon Island, northeast of Nassau, and is known as the *Mahoney Wreck*. In 1972 the Taylor-controlled vessel *Marcella II* voyaged with the mails to Freeport, Andros, and Eleuthera, mostly on a substitute basis up to 1988. She was named after the Taylor's grandmother.

The large steel coastal trader *Marcella II* was built as the *Corona* in Husumer Schiffswerft in Husum, Germany as hull 1096 in 1956, for German firm Ahlmann Transport, of Rendsburg. She was 298 tons, steel, 162 feet, and could carry 662 tons. In 1972 the Taylors bought, renamed and delivered her, and patriarch Nathaniel Bruce Taylor was captain from 1987 to 1988. Other captains included Eddins Taylor, Bob Garroway, and Limas Taylor, who is still the company skipper for Grand Bahama vessels. *Marcella II* was damaged in a storm in 1988 and ultimately wrecked 2 nm off Pirate's Well Mayaguana, then the hull was submerged. Next was *Marcella III*, which began service to Freeport in 1981, up to 2004. Her original name of *Jade* was changed to be the third *Marcella* named after the Taylor's grandmother. The ship was built of steel at 364 tons and 157 feet long by Neue Jadewerft in Wilhelmshaven Germany in 1959. Her owners in Bahamas were the Taylors of Pirate's Well Investments, and

Marcella Shipping Limited. Captains included Limas Taylor, Elvin Taylor, and Eddins Taylor. She has had a global career; from Germany to Bahamas, then Bolivia to Haiti, the other names being *Miss Eva I* in Bolivia from 2009, *Michelda* from 2011, and after that *Our Lady of Mercy*, to J. Merelus of Cap Haitien, but flagged to Tanzania.

The motor mailboat *Bahama Sky* sailed to Freeport and Abaco from 1985. She was built of steel to the Ro-Ro passenger design in 1970, and weighed 1,995 tons, being 259 feet long. She was on the official mailboat schedule for 1988, not thereafter. The Chinese-built steel Ro-Ro, passenger vessel *Fiesta Mail* started the Grand Bahama run in 2002, to Freeport and West End and is still active under veteran captain Limas Taylor. In 2002 Xinhe Shipbuilding on Tianjin, China built *Fiesta Mail* at 2,485 tons, and 228 feet long. She was commissioned by the largest mailboat corporation in the history of the Bahamas, the Taylors, of Pirate's Well Investments, under The MailBoat Company.

The *Seawind* has served Grand Bahama, Andros, Exuma, Long Island, Abaco, and Governor's Harbour from 2003. Weighing 485 tons of steel, she is 147 feet long and owned by Bahamas Ferries. *Seawind* is still operating as a Ro-Ro, capable of carrying 40 vehicles and 175 passengers in air-conditioned comfort. The bright blue and yellow-painted landing-craft-type ship *Inagua Spray* motored to Freeport then Abaco with mail and freight from 2016. Her previous names were *Costa IV*, *Caribe Sun*, up to 2015, and *Grindavik*, from 1966 to 1993. *Inagua Spray* was built in Jacksonville, Florida, at Bollinger Shipyard in 1966 or steel and weighs 1,297 tons, spread over 248 feet of length. Her owners are Bahamas Ferries and she is still operating.

The *Cape Mail* has been a substitute for *Fiesta Mail* since 2017, and serves Freeport, West End, Sweetings Cay, and when required, George Town, Exuma, and Smith's Bay, Cat Island as well. She was built in 1983, is 858 tons of steel, and 200 feet long. Her owners are the Taylors, as Pirate's Well Investments, and one of her captains is Limas Taylor, who is also skipper of the *Fiesta Mail*. *Inagua Spray* is still operating, like most Ro-Ro-type landing craft and larger mailboats and ferries, from the far western end of Potter's Cay.

Bimini Islands

There were fourteen boats serving Bimini as mailboats over the years, a fact more impressive when one considers both a population of fewer than 2,000 and proximity to Florida of just over 60 miles, meaning it is closer to Florida than Nassau, by roughly half. Captains in the past century have included William D. Weech, Jr., Neville Stuart, Sean Munroe, Emmett Munroe, Spence Brown, and Chris Knowles. Like Freeport, Bimini benefits from its close proximity and relatively easy access to Florida and the commercial opportunities to be had. It is closer to Miami than to Nassau. Nevertheless, the islands have a proud history of freighter and mail service – for example the vessel *Bailey Town* was built there in 1946, was 46.5 feet long and owned by Theodore R. Saunders, and the *F. A. Marie* of 57.7 feet, though built in the Cayman Islands in 1928 was owned by William D. Weech Jr. in Bimini in the 1950s, who also owned the 58.5-foot *Peloris* not known to have carried mail.

The schooner *Increase* set sail carrying the mail for Alice Town and Cat Cay, Bimini, and Whale Cay, in the Berry Islands, where post was collected from Frazier's Hog Cay, Bond's Cay, Little Harbour, and Bullock's Harbour, in 1908. She was built in Bimini in 1906 at 25 tons and made of wood. Owned by Edward Wilkinson of Bimini, he won the mail service tender on 1 October of 1907. The wooden schooner *Defense* sailed from Nassau to Bimini and Lignum Vitae Cay and Whale Cay, in the Berry Islands, from 1915 to 1926. Her builder was Walter H. Roberts of Hope Town, Abaco in 1905 and it was 22 tons. *Defense*'s owner was John A. Levarity of Bimini. Then, in 1926 the mail schooner was wrecked in Bimini Harbour by the 1926 hurricane. Per Wayne Neely, she was smashed and sank.

The 21-ton wooden schooner *Tryon* sallied forth with the mails to Bimini, Berry Islands, Grand Bahama, and Abaco, starting in 1920. Built in 1898, her owner was Thomas F. Malone of Hope Town, and she appears in the 1920 registry. The *F. A. Marie* covered Bimini and the Berry Islands from 1929. She was built in Georgetown, Cayman Islands, in 1915 of 58 tons, a wooden hull and 40 feet long. Her owner was William D. Weech, Jr., of Bimini, and she appears in the 1940 ship's registry. The motor vessel *Patsy* carried the mails to the Berries and Bimini starting in 1935. She was made of wood at 15 tons and appears in the 1923 ship's register. The schooner with an auxiliary motor named *Monarch* also covered mail needs for Bimini and the Berries from 1936. She was built in 1904 in Marsh Harbour, was wood, and 20 tons. *Monarch* was owned by Richard E. Roberts of Marsh Harbour, and others on run were *Priscilla*, *Marmaduke*, and *Richard Campbell*, which was in the 1920 registry.

The motor mailboat *Paddy Helferty* began covering Bimini and the Berry Islands in 1936, after Exuma and Long Island from 1934, and before Abaco and Mayaguana, from 1943. She was built of wood on Marsh Harbour, Abaco in 1928, of 55 tons, wooden hilled, and 51 feet long on deck, with a 5 hp engine. Her owner was Edmund

D. Knowles of Nassau in 1954. On January 21, 1943, in the midst of World War II, *Paddy Helferty* was reported overdue from the lumber camp at Cornwall, Abaco. A comprehensive search found her 30 miles west of Mayaguana, which is an astounding 600 miles off course. The Royal Air Force sent a bomber named B25 FL184 to search. The register closed on her after 1954. Other iterations of the name include *Betty and Billy*, and *Paddy Halfready*.

The 46-ton, 47-foot wooden mailboat *Gary William* started service in 1938 to Bimini and the Berry Islands in 1938. She was rebuilt in Nassau in 1938 after having been built in Marsh Harbour in 1922. Sir George Roberts named her for one of his sons, and owned it through the *Richard Campbell* Company of Nassau. She last appeared in the 1940 registry. *Bimini Gal* was recorded serving Ababo by Dave Gale (*Below Another Sky*, p.281).

Midinette was a sloop with an auxiliary motor which in 1938 sailed the post to Bimini and the Berry Islands. She was built in Marsh Harbour in 1922 and weighed 30 tons, and was owned by Sir George Roberts of the *Richard Campbell* Company in Nassau, last appearing in the 1911 registry. The steel motor boat *Bimini Gal* delivered mail, passengers and freight to Alice Town and Cat Cay, Bimini from 1965 to 1972. She was built in the US in the 1940s, owned and operated by Neville Stuart, founder of the Big Game Club in Bimini. After *Bimini Gal* sank in 1972, the *Staniel Cay Express* under Rolly Gray took over, per Bahamian columnist Larry Smith and philatelist Edward B. Proud.

The *Bimini Mack* assumed the mail route to Bimini and the Berry Islands, including Chubb Cay, then Rock Sound Eleuthera from 1981 to 2017. She was built of steel at St. Augustine Marine in St. Augustine Florida in 1981, was 207 tons and 100 feet long. Her owner was a cooperative named the *Bimini Mack* Association, aka The Bimini Businessman's Association. Joseph Moxey was an engineer. She was in operation to 2014, when the vessel was sold for scrap, with Bradford Marine, Grand Bahama informing that *Bimini Mack* was cut up or sold by 2018. The *Sherice M.* delivered mail to Bimini, Salt Pond, Deadman's Cay and Seymour's Long Island from 1995 to 2018. She was built of steel in the US in the 1980s and 126 feet long. *Sherice M.*'s owners were the Emmett Munroe and Shawn Munroe. A severe galley fire while the ship was berthed in Alice Town Bimini on 16 June, 2018, led to her total lost, and so she was replaced in 2019 by the *Captain Emmett* brought in from Polynesia.

The steel motor boat *Alma B.* served Bimini from both Nassau and Florida between at least 1998 and 2000. The 120-foot boat was owned by Spence Brown until it sank off Kitten Cay, south of Bimini in March of 2000, leaving two persons dead. The motor vessel *Legend II* started to serve Great Harbour Cay in the Berry Islands, then Harbour Island, Cat Cay Bimini, Driggs Hill, Andros, Eleuthera, and the Exumas, starting in 2006. She was built of steel by Rodriguez Coden in Coden, Alabama in 2006, weighs 488 tons, and is 181 feet. Her owners are Dean Shipping Company of Sandy

Point, Abaco, and one captain is Chris Knowles. Although put up for sale in April of 2015, *Legend II* is still operating with its dark green color scheme and Ro-Ro landing craft ramp.

    The *Captain Emmett* arrived at Potter's Cay from Polynesia via the Panama Canal in August, 2019. Replacing the burnt-out *Sherice M*, she calls at Cat Cay, Bimini starting in 2019. Previously known as *Layar Mas 291*, and having flown the flags of Moldova, Cook Islands, and Malaysia before the Bahamian ensign, *Captain Emmett* was built in 2009 of steel, weighs 499 tons, and is 154 feet long. The Munroe family; primarily Shawn Munroe and Emmett Munroe. She is still operational. The voyage took 45-day from Rarotonga, in the Cook Islands, starting on June 17, 2019. The author happened to be on Potter's Cay at their arrival, and also happened to have sailed from Panama (via Nassau) to Rarotonga back in 1993 to 1994.

Berry Islands

The Berry Islands have switched to and from different post offices, including Lignum Vitae, Great Harbour, Whale Cay, Chub Cay, and settled on the postal distribution point of Bullock, or Bullock's Harbour, on the west side of Great Harbour Cay, northeast Berry Islands, as the primary destination for mailboats. The fact is that with a handful of islands (Bonds, Little Harbour, Comfort, Fanny, Cistern, Great Stirrup, Ambergris, Devils, Sand Dollar, Hoffmann's, Bird, Crab, and two controlled by cruise ships at the north) and at least four landing strips (Chub, Whale, Little, Whale, and great Harbour), the Berry Islands probably owe their mailboat service less to their population (barely 800 in 2010) as to their central position between Nassau, Bimini, Grand Bahama, Sandy Point Abaco, and even Florida.

Much of the contractual traffic in the past half-century has been provided by the dynasty founded when Ernest A. Dean built his own boat at Sandy Point to fetch milk for his wife and their infant. As a consequence the route has been to Bullock's Harbour then Moore's Island (astride another cruise ship island named Castaway Cay), and Sandy Point, which supports a fishing fleet whose catch has to make it to market, and the road now connects all the way to Crown Haven, and a high-speed ferry to McLean's Town, Grand Bahama. The earliest record mail to the Berries was the *Frances E.* in 1913. with such a small population base and lacking significant agricultural output, the Berry Islands have had to forebear being the one "in the middle," largely making do with mail service whose primary nodes are either Alice Town to the West, Freeport to the northwest, or Sandy Point to the northeast. Thus, since at least the1950s, mailboats serving south Abaco, and Bimini boats have called at the Berries *en route*. People come from the other Berry Islands to Bullocks Harbour to collect the mail.

The Deans to some extent pioneered the route to the Berry Islands, which added to their responsibilities without forcing them into competition with northern Abaco, Grand Bahama, or Bimini; in doing so they carved out a niche market which had been underserved by road or air: the Berries, Hard Bargain, Moore's Island, Crossing Rocks and basically Great Abaco south of Cherokee Sound. (*Vignette*: the author was once startled awake by the sight of the rivets of a ship's hull through an open mailboat portal; a cruise ship had come alongside to pick up the sacks of mail which the *mail*boat had forgotten to leave in Bullock's Harbour.....).

The sloop *Frances E.* joined the mailboat service to Berry Islands via Lignum Vitae Cay Route in 1913, then Inagua, via Rum Cay, and Long Island in 1930, and Cat Island, Fortune Island, and Acklins also from 1913. She was built in Nassau in 1910 of wood and weighed 68 tons, across 74 feet of length. Her owner was Charles C. Saunders of Nassau and she appears in the 1920 ship's registry. The sloop *Caroline* sailed for the Berry Islands in 1922, followed in 1928 by the sloop *Sea Bird*, a wooden vessel of roughly 16 tons owned by Jonathan H. C Ogilvie of New York; though listed at 163 tons, that was unlikely (but not impossible) for a large for a sloop crossing Great Bahamas Banks or others. The schooner *Arrow* sailed in 1933 for Lignum Vitae Cay, Berries. She was built in *Castiret*, in the US in 1848 of wood and was 36 tons. Her owners were R. A. Menendry of Nassau, and she appears in the 1915 mercantile marine registry.

More recently, the motor vessel *Captain Dean* joined the service to Berry Islands in 1951, then motored towards Sweeting's Cay Grand Bahama, Moore's Island, and Sandy Point, Abaco all the way to 1980. She has been owned by Christine D. Dean and patriarch Ernest Alexander Dean of Sandy Point and was constructed of wood at 30 tons. Her captains have included Ernest Dean and James Dean in 1985, and the vessel appears in the *Christian Science Monitor* of 1979 covering Bimini, yet is not active after 1980. Another Deans-owned vessel, the 45-ton wooden boat *Margaret Rose* set sail from Nassau to Sandy Point in 1953, and called at Bimini and Hard Bargain, Moore's Island in an arc on the way up to roughly 1961. *Margaret Rose* was built in Nassau in 1951, commissioned by Abaconian captain Ernest A. Dean. From 1953 he was also a captain, until in 1961 she was replaced by *Clermont*, and sold. *Clermont* began the Abaco and Berry Islands route in 1962, having been built of wood in Nassau in the 1950 at 112 tons. Ernest A. Dean and family owned her, and he also commanded her. Sadly, it sank in 1962 off Hole-in-the-Wall Light, Abaco, the year it began service.

The *Captain Dean II* took over the route from *Clermont* in 1962 on the same route up to 1968. Her 1963 builders included Johny Albury and Walter Hatcher of Dundas Town Abaco; they crafted a 110-ton wood boat of 60 feet. Her captains included Ernest A. Dean and Sherwin Archer. *Captain Dean II* started service between January and December, 1962. Finally the larger *Captain Dean III* replaced on the run. *Captain Dean II* caught fire and sank between the Berry Islands and Abaco in 1968.

In 1969 the *Captain Dean III* hauled the mail from Bullock's to Hard Bargain, Sweetings Cay to Sandy Point, and did so for half a decade, up to 1974. She was constructed by John Petrudis of St. Augustine, Florida in 1969, weighed 137 tons, and her wood hull was 90 feet long. The Deans; Ernest A. Deans and sons, owned here, and the patriarch was on captain, until in 1974 disaster struck again, when *Captain Dean III* sank near the Mackey Shoal Buoy, roughly two thirds of the way across the Great Bahama Banks between Chubb Cay, Berry Islands, and Alice Town, Bimini. The *Captain Dean IV* then served the same route from 1973 up to 1977. She was built by Jerry Thompson of St. Augustine Trawlers in Florida in 1973, and her wooden hull was 110 tons and 90 feet long. The owners were Ernest A. Dean and sons. She was commanded by Ernest A. Dean and John Dean, who was in command when run *Captain Dean IV* had to be run aground intentionally in her home port of Sandy Point, with a US Coast Guard helicopter assisting in the rescue.

Captain Dean V joined the Dean fleet in 1977 heading first for Abaco, then Eleuthera up to 1986. She was built at 90 tons burthen of steel by Jerry Thompson of St. Augustine Trawler Company, aka St. Augustine Marine, in Florida in 1977. Her owners were Ernest A. Dean and sons, one of whom, John Dean, was captain, then Stanford Curry. In September of 1986 *Captain Dean V* caught fire in a dock-wide conflagration on the Frederick Street Dock in Nassau, and tragically Captain Curry was killed. What was left of her was thereafter sold to Haitian interests. This was a devastating blow to both the Curry and the Dean families.

In 1986 the smaller steel mailboat *Champion II* set off on the Berry Island circuit ending in Sandy Point, and continued up till 2012. She was built for the Deans by St. Augustine Marine Trawlers in Florida in1986, was 150 tons and 75 feet long; designed specifically to do a kind of limbo underneath US regulations which didn't require as rigorous arrival procedures of smaller boat. The Dean Shipping Company owner her and one captain was Ernest A. Dean. She could carry 60 passengers, in 1991 this writer being one of them, and was cited in publications and schedules in 1997 and 1999 yet was inactive by 2012.

The *Captain Gurth Dean* set out after many Dean footsteps to Sandy Point, Moore's Island, and Bullocks Harbour in1999 and is still operating. She was built of steel by Rodriguez Coden Alabama in 1999 and was 500 tons and 111 feet. Not part of Dean Shipping Company, her captains included owner Jonathan Dean and Cliff Carroll. The ship has been laid up, but was back active in 2020.

Andros Islands

Being the largest island in the archipelago with 2,300 square miles, with the freshest water and one the longest barrier reefs in the world at 124 miles, it is not surprising the Andros has provided employment to at least 54 mailboats in its history. That and that there is agriculture, are 8,000 residents, tourism, an important US Navy base named AUTEC, and exports from agricultural to timber to crafts and seafood, to name some. Depending on the status of reverse osmosis machines and the water lenses of New Providence, there have also been daily shipments of fresh water in motorized tankers from Mastic Point to Arawak Cay. From a mailboat perspective, two things make the Andros route different: its proximity to Nassau at less than 40 miles at closest, and the fact that, unlike all the other island groups, there are not "along the way" stops; Andros, like it's Greek namesake, may have three islands, but they are all part of Andros, and enough to keep most mailboat owners and officers busy.

Over more than 125 years here are some of the carriers of Andros' hopes and dreams. The schooner *Star of the Sea* held the contract for mail services to North Andros from 1894 to 1902, during which times she served Nicholl's Town, Mastic Point, Staniard Creek, Fresh Creek, Salvador Point, Mangrove Cay, and Long Bay Cays. The wooden boat was built in the Bahamas in 1880 and weighed 14 tons. Her owner was Robert Henry Sawyer of Nassau, and *Star of the Sea* appears in the 1915 register. The schooner *Attic* entered the mail trade for North Andros as early as 1894, and expanded south to Long Cay in 1901. She was built in Abaco in 1877 out of wood and weighed 44 tons. Her owner was Robert N. Musgrove of Nassau. In the following year the schooner *Sappho* began four years of mail delivery on the same route up until 1899. She was owned by Robert N. Musgrove of Nassau and is in the 1900 shipping register.

Next a schooner named *M.E.B.*, named for Mary Black, wife of Captain Frederick Black of Pirate's Well Mayaguana, covered the North Andros starting in 1899. Built of wood, she was owned by Frederick Black, who also commanded here. This vessel is listed in Edward B. Proud's *Postal History of the Bahamas*; however it might be conflated with a boat named *M.B.* The 13-ton wooden schooner *Right Arm* sailed for North Andros in 1902. She was built two years earlier, in 1900 for William Benjamin Smith of Andros, and appears in registries for 1902 and up until 1915. Next the schooner *J. G. Converse* arrived from Nicholl's Town to Long Bay Cays from 1903. *J. G. Converse* was built in the Bahamas in 1884, was 21 tons and made of wood. Her owner was Robert William Sawyer of Nassau, and the vessel appears in the official registry for 1915.

The schooner *Zephyr* added Kemp's Bay, Deep Creek Andros, and then San Salvador to its route from 1904. Furthermore, in Exuma it called on Rolle Ville,

Georgetown (from where mail went overland to Steventon), and even Simms, Long Island, thence via land to Clarence Town, in 1908. *Zephyr* was 20 tons and built of wood in the Bahamas in 1886 and owned by Robert Henry Sawyer of Nassau up to 1924. In 1907 both commissioners and resident justices insisted on adding ports to mailboat routes, hence the 1909 overland spur from Simms to Clarence Town, Kemp's Bay to Deep Creek, South Andros, and Rolleville to Steventon, Exuma. After 1924 the ambitious little ship was no longer registered.

Petrel was a 1901-built wooden schooner of 22 tons which in 1905 carried the mails from North Andros and also to Fresh Creek, Salvador Point, Mangrove Cay, Long Bay Cays, Bimini, the Berry Islands, and Grand Bahama from 1912 to 1918. Then *Petrel* set off to serve Exuma and Long Island in 1919. She was built in Nassau for Charles R. Arteaga of Nassau, and in February, 1932 substituted in for the routes to Bimini and Andros, last appearing in the 1940 registry. *Nellie Leonora* was a schooner with a busy mailboat life which met a tragic end. From 1909 she served North Andros to Deep Creek, then Exuma and Long Island up to 1916. She was built in Abaco in 1900 of wood and weighed 38 tons. Her owner was Edward Willis Bethel of Green Turtle Cay. In August of 1916 *Nellie Leonora* was wrecked off Rum Cay, as recorded by commissioners in both Mangrove Cay and The Bight, Cat Island. She last appeared in 1915 registry.

The schooner *Arawak* joined the San Salvador route in 1912, then North Andros and Inagua up to 1927. She was built of wood in Nassau in 1907 of 33 tons, and owned by Horace Wilson of Duncan Town, Ragged Island. One of her captains was named Wade. *Arawak* substituted in in for *Nellie Leonora* which was wrecked off Rum Cay in 1916. The sailboat *Arawak* sank on a voyage from Jacksonville to Hatchet Bay in 1927, and is not to be confused with a large power yacht of the same name, built over 30 years later, in 1938 by Victor Cleare in Hatchet Bay for Austin Levy; that *Arawak* was 115' long and 201 tons.

The schooner *San Salvador* covered the mail route from Nassau to North Andros in 1912. She was built in 1909 of wood at 19 tons, and owned by Charles W. Brownrigg of Cat Island. In 1912 *San Salvador* substituted in for *Petrel*, which commissioners say had 'lapsed into the most bitter disappointment." This vessel could not be the *San Salvador* built 1934, and owned by Erskine Arnett of San Salvador.

Bertie was a schooner which joined the North Andros route in 1918. She was built in Andros Bahamas in 1901 of wooed and was 19 tons. Owned by Pembroke Charles Smith of George Town, Grand Cayman in the 1902 register, *Bertie* remained in service "throughout 1918." The schooner *Magic* sailed for Nicholl's Town to Kemp's Bay Andros from 1920 to 1929. She was 20 tons, and made of wood in Abaco in 1912. Her owners included Oliver aka Ollie, Forde, and Walter J. C. Moxley of Nassau her final owner in 1929. *Magic* was destroyed by the hurricane of 1929 per Wayne Neely.

Another schooner, the *Repeat*, entered this trade lane in 1923 up until 1927. Built of wood in 1924, the clearly flummoxed commissioner reported that the: "irregularity of trips is excused by her captain and crew under the plea of 'weather conditions;' very often these conditions come from the inside of bottles."

The schooner *Laura Louise* sailed for North Andros between 1927 and 1940, later adding Lignum Vitae Cay, Berry Islands. She was constructed to 31 tons of wood at Man-O-War Cay, Abaco in 1915. Under the ownership of William D. Weech, Jr. of Bimini, *Laura Louise* last appeared in the 1940 registry. The motor vessel *William Charles* served North Andros from 1927 to 1929. Built in the Bahamas in 1911, she was 31 tons, and was previously named the *Wallace* and registered in Nassau in 1922. An American-built vessel named *Gaskill Bros.* entered the North Andros market in 1928. Completed the same year in Sealevel, North Carolina, the 29-ton wooden boat was 55 feet long and owned by Charles A. B. Johnson of Nassau, with her registration last renewed in 1930.

In 1929 a new motor vessel named *Ollie Ford* joined the merchant mail fleet serving North Andros. She was built in Scranton, Mississippi in 1903 of 28 tons and 56 feet length. Owned by Edward J. V. Armsden of Nassau, she left the US registry in 1927. A sloop empowered with an auxiliary motor named *Bimini* sailed the mail route to North Andros from 1931 to 1939. She was built as the *Chloe* in Jacksonville, Florida in 1907 then rebuilt as the *Bimini* in 1927, at 30 tons, wood, and 55 feet, with a 75-horsepower auxiliary engine. Her owner was Henry F. Duncombe of Bimini in 1939; she appears in the 1930 ship's registry, yet not that of 1939.

The *Richard Campbell* began service to Abaco Bimini and the Berry Islands in 1937 and into the 1950's, and North Andros from 1962, adding San Salvador in 1938, Grand Bahama Island from 1937 to beyond 1961. Named for a son of Sir George Robert, the *Richard Campbell* was built in Symonette Shipyards, to a Jenkins Roberts design in Nassau in 1937. Of 89 tons, her wood hull was 86 feet long and she was powered by a motor. Her owners were the Roberts family and organization, d/b/a *Richard Campbell* Limited, a holding company at the City Lumber Yard for over a dozen mailboats. One of her captains was Robby Russell of Hope Town, supported by George Saunders as mate, from Green Turtle Cay, and a crewman named Errold Burrows, who sadly was lost overboard in 1965. *Richard Campbell* was one of the mailboats which has to add an overland route from Green Turtle Cay in 1924 to Norman's Castles and Turtle Cay, and in 1932 another spur to Cooper's Town, Old Place, Great Guana Cay utilizing "*Two Sloops*." At one point her crew put out an engine fire in Cherokee Sound.

Between 1945 and 1961 the motorized mailboat *Caribbean Queen* served various Bahamian routes, including North Andros. She was built at Symonette Shipyards to a design by foreman Jenkins Roberts in Nassau in 1945, and was 335 tons, wooden, and 220 feet long. Her owners were the Eastern Shipping Company, and one captain was

Albert Shippee, with crew said to have been Honduran. In January of 1961 the *Caribbean Queen* sank in Bahamian waters off Cay Sal Bank *en route* from the Florida Keys to the Dominican Republic. The motor vessel *Betty Ann* sallied forth to Fresh Creek, North Andros with the mails between 1947 and 1968. Bahamas-built in 1947, she was wood and over 90 tons. Her owner in 1968 was named Lowe. By 1969 *Betty Ann* was beached at Fresh Creek Andros and, as the story goes, when Her Majesty Queen Elizabeth the II was expected to visit in October, 1984, anxious politicians had the unsightly hulk of the *Betty Ann* burned to the waterline to avoid an eyesore and any awkward questions. Fortunately photos of it exist before it was burnt.

Between 1950 and 1977 the motor mailboat *South Andros Express* served South Andros' mail needs. She was built in the Bahamas around 1950 of wood and in 1977 sank off Andros. Several vessels, including the US Navy boat named *IX* from their nearby base at AUTEC helped to rescue survivors. From 1958 the *Aline* served North Andros, adding Behring Point, Pure Gold, and Drigg's Hill. The government mail tender for those ports required "a vessel of at least 60 tons." It is possible that *Aline* is a new name for the *Coraline*, built in Symonette Shipyards to 60 tons in 1957. The motor vessel *Madam Elizabeth Rolle* contributed to the mailboat services to Andros between 1958 and 1970. She was built of wood to 78 tons in 1954 and owned by John Newton of Lowes Sound, Andros. *Madam Elizabeth Rolle* was attacked by Cuban poachers alongside *Andros Trader* in March of 1964, until fortunately the Royal Navy and US Coast Guard went to their aid. The vessel has been the subject of a painting by Bahamian artist William Johnson, Jr.

The motor vessel *Wissama* joined the North Andros trade from 1959 until 1961. Previously known as the *Zizi* in 1945 and Bermudian owned *Wissama* was built Haiti in 1942 out of wood, and was 114 tons and 240 feet long. Her Bahamian owners were Sir George Roberts, d/b/a *Noel Roberts* Limited and *Richard Campbell* Limited at City Lumber Yard, Nassau. Commissioners in 1960 and 1961 at Nicoll's Town commended the vessel and crew. The *Nassau Guardian*'s shipping news cites her on 4 January, 1961. The ship was wrecked at Long Bay Cays, East of Bluff, Andros, on 8 April, 1961. The smaller wooden mailboat *Andros Trader* carried mail to Andros from 1963 and was also fired on by Cuban poachers near Cay Sal Bank, west of Andros, along with *Madam Elizabeth Rolle* in March, 1964, yet were rescued by US and UK forces.

In 1965 the mail fleet to Andros was supplemented by the sloop *Astonish*, which was built of wood in 1903 and was 13 tons. During 1967 commissioner reports detail how the *Astonish* was substituting in for the *Spanish Sea Queen*. *Astonish* appears in the 1902 ship's register. The motor vessel *Bahama Land* served the northern Bahamas from 1965 to 1973. Built as the *Black Creek* by Walker Marine in Pascagoula, Mississippi in 1955, the *Bahama Land* weighed 184 tons of steel and was 83 feet long. From 1973 the boat is no longer listed. The *Spanish Sea Queen* covered the mail needs of Fresh Creek, Staniard Creek, and Behring Point from 1965, occasionally being covered by the smaller vessel *Astonish* substituting in. The 90-ton motor vessel *Bahama Trader* served northern Bahamas from 1968 to the early-1980s. Constructed of wood, the vessel was 90 feet long and owned by A.C.L. Limited of Nassau. *Bahama Trader* was listed as a mailboat in September, 1975, indicating that was active, yet not listed on registries or schedules after 1985, suggesting it was no longer active in the mailboat trade.

In 1971 the motorized mailboat *Pleasant* provided mailboat service to Drigg's Hill, Mangrove Cay, Long Bay Cays, Bluff, Kemp's Bay, Deep Creek, Pleasant Bay (probably where she got her name), then on to Mars Bay by truck from Drigg's Hill, after 1969. The following year another motorboat, the *Andros Express* carried mail, freight and passengers to Andros. A steel boat named *Cat Island Princess* is revealed in leaked diplomatic cables with United States officials to be on a list of all active mailboats in the Bahamas in 1975. *Andros Express* appears in the *Frommer's Guide* of 1988 to 1989. It is not to be confused with another vessel named the *South Andros Express*, which sank off Andros in 1977 per AUTEC. The 82-ton steel ship *Delmar L.* motored to Androsian ports including Congo Town between 1972 and the 1980. Other spellings of its name include *Captain Delmor*. She was built at St. Augustine Shipbuilding to a design by DeJong, Lebet in Florida in about 1970. The boat was listed active in 1975, however not listed a decade later her service can be considered ended by 1985.

The *Goldfinger* delivered mails to Andros, the Berry Islands, and Bimini, then North Eleuthera between 1972 and 1977. The ship was built in 1935 as *Jant Je Eppiena* by Scheepswerf Gebr. van Niestern & Company of Delfzijl, Netherlands. Her tonnages was 200 of steel and length was 117 feet. Other names for the same ship included *Alja-V* to 1957, and *Brigadoon II* in 1970. In the Bahamas her owners, starting in 1972 were the Northern Eleuthera Shipping Company. Her officers and crew included David Cleare, Ronald Duncombe, Everett Roberts, John Spurgeon Archer, and Samuel Archer. Reflecting the very real tensions which culminated in the sinking of HMBS *Flamingo* by the overpowering Cuban military in Bahamian waters on 10 May, 1980, just under six weeks of the Royal Bahamas Defense Force's official establishment, in 1977 *Goldfinger* was sunk by Cuban-American terrorist bomb in Miami Florida. She was not the only vessel so attacked, with other mailboats fired on at Cay Sal Bank in armed conflict over perceived fishing rights. In August of 1975 *Goldfinger* served the H. M. Imperial Lighthouse Service. Having been salvaged in Miami, the *Goldfinger* ultimately sank in a storm northeast of Andros on 5 April, 1977.

The wooden motor vessel *Miss Andros* was designed and hand-built as the largest vessel so made in Andros to serve Nicholls Town, Morgan's Bluff, and North Andros. She was 140 feet long when completed, yet sadly it took days even to launch her, and even with expert shipbuilder Sir Roland Symonette flown in from Nassau to assist. Because of many design and performance faults which lead to excessive shaft vibrations and water ingress, this lovely but flawed swan of a vessel was ultimately deemed unsuitable, unsafe, and uninsurable and was pulled from service. Fortunately members of the nearby AUTEC community were able to spend time with the kindly builder and document *Miss Andros* while it was being built and launched.

The European passenger ferry *Lisa J.* undertook the North Andros route in 1973 up until 1981. Built in Denmark, she began her career as the *Ellen-Søby* from 1960 to 1973, then reverted to the Danish name *Runden* in 1999 while awaiting a buyer in Freeport, Grand Bahama, and her final, scrapping name was *Lisa J. 3* in 2005, upon sale. *Lisa J.* was fabricated by H. C. Christensen Steelworks in Marstal, Denmark in 1960, and weighed 347 tons and stretched 122 feet. Her Bahamian owners were the Woodsides of Andros, d/b/a North Andros Shipping Company.

In 2010 a Mr. Bowleg purchased her, however he passed before she could be reactivated. Officers and crew included members of the Woodside and Adderley families, George Johnson engineer, and Joseph Moxey, engineer. From 2005 to 2010 the team at Bradford Marine in Freeport, who refit, scrap, sell, and store all manner of vessels, listed her as Lisa J. 3. She was ultimately sold to Honduran interests in 2010 and scrapped; there has long been a maritime connection between the Bahamas and British Honduras and Roatan, with English-speaking mariners and fellow islanders serving as officers in Bahamas and vessels being sold back and forth as well.

The motor mailboat *South Andros Queen* was next to serve southern Andros, from 1973 into the 1990s. Built of wood, she was owned by interests in Driggs Hill Andros per Joseph Moxey, who described it is a sort of cooperative. By 1995 the mailboat was inactive, and may have caught fire. The *Lady Moore* was a primarily a government tender which substituted in on the Andros market and sank there. From 1974 to the 1980s she served both the mail market and the Royal Bahamas *Defense* Force in a cargo and support capacity. Built in 1945, her previous names include *Twenty Grand*, from 1952, and her maiden name, *El Mexicano* when built of 422 tons of steel and of 139 feet length. The only known captain was RBDF Commander Whitford Neilly, after 1977.

Once again illustrating how important mailboats have been to events of national and international importance, on 12 November, 1980 the *Lady Moore* was a central participant in the controversial 1980 Cay Lobos incident This pitted the Bahamian police and RBDF personnel versus 116 shipwrecked Haitian immigrants, ashore for nearly two months and terrified of being sent back to Baby Doc's regime. After attracting the glare of worldwide attention, the conflict resulted in an amphibious landing caught on tape, with *Lady Moore* visible, then male and female Haitians being injured, Bahamians being filmed injuring them, and a helicopter returning that night to Andros full of US journalists being lost with all on board without a trace. *Lady Moore* was laid to rest as a mailboat and supply boat, scuttled off Morgan's Bluff North Andros in the early 1980s. It sits upright in fairly shallow water and is a dive site.

One veteran mailboat captain described her role as a standby rescue boat for the RBDF, and said she went to the aid of many a vessel and crew in the Bahamas over its career. Mailboats have brought relief to hurricane survivors, reported aircraft parts to the RAF in World War II, solved critical shortages of supplies, carried medical patients as well as goods to market, and been the targets of foreign aggression at home and abroad. Indeed the armed feluccas which carried Bahamian mail in the Napoleonic Wars were armed and manned by the military and at least one was captured.

The motor mailboat *Miss Beverly* served Andros with the mail from 1975 to 1983 and beyond. She was built of wood at 114 tons and 100 feet length in 1942. Despite she and *Air Swift* being severely damaged and sunk in the freak winter storm which hit Nassau and the northern Bahamas on January 9, 1977, *Miss Beverly* was salvaged, and is listed in the in 1983 as taking passengers to Andros for $10. That same storm, according to the Abaconian, is the same one which allegedly (hoteliers refute this) brought a few flakes of snow to Grand Bahama. The first motor mailboat *Captain Moxey* arrived on the shores of Andros in 1982 and served southern Andros up until 1998, when a new boat of the same name took up the baton. Made of wood, she was owned by Moxey Shipping, captained by Moxeys (possibly Hezron or Kaya), and her engineer and Joseph Moxey (unrelated) is from Mangrove Cay. This *Captain Moxey* appears on mailboat schedules in 1988, 1989, and 1992. She sank west of Great Exuma during or after 1998.

The bluff-bowed motor mailboat *Lady D.* set out from Nassau to Fresh Creek Staniard Creek, Stafford Creek, Behring Point, Blanket Sound, and Browne Sound, Andros in 1983 and kept at it until unfortunately it sank at Potter's Cay Dock in July of 2014. More unfortunately, the spot it sank was prime mailboat real estate, and there are so many other wrecks there already that it only sank about halfway, and remained there for years until finally stabilized and towed clear in the fall of 2016. Once known as the *Central Andros Express* before 1983, she was 62 tons, steel-hulled, and owned by Prince Munroe, a mariner who was also the ship's captain, Spellman Munroe was one of the crew. *Lady D.* was cited in schedules, articles, and travel guides in 1989, 1994, and 1999, sank Potter's Cay in July of 2014, and was removed in the fall of 2016. Like many mailboats serving central and northern Andros, *Lady D.* often went west from Potter's Cay over the Nassau bar, and thus was often photographed by passengers high above on the cruise ships, resulting in great images of her from there and Fort Charlotte. Depending on weather, boats headed to Drigg's Hill and South Andros tend to head east out of Nassau Harbour and take a route south of New Providence.

The *North Andros Princess I* started the North Andros mail run in 1984, touching at Mastic Point among the other ports. She was built at the Chu-Chu Perez, No. 1 Boat Manufacturing Company on Stock Island, Key West, Florida, and is one of the few mailboats in Bahamas made of fiberglass; *Current Pride* is wooden but sheathed in glass. Measuring 75 tons, *North Andros Princess I* is owned by another owner-mariner, Harley Simms, d/b/a Camp Bay Shipping, in Andros, and is no longer active. The motor mailboat *Big Yard Express* carried mail to Mangrove Cay, Andros from roughly 1986 to the mid-1990s. She is made of steel at 102 tons and owned by Big Yard Shipping of Nassau. According to mariner Joseph Moxey, a veteran of 15 mailboats born in 1937, all of this boat's owners and captains are drawn from Andros. The motor vessel *Lady Gloria* began her mailboat career in 1985 to Andros and carried it beyond 1992. Built of steel, she is owned by Ivan Johnson, who was also her captain, with one of the engineers being Joseph Moxey. Captain Johnson named *Lady Gloria* after his wife. She appears on the schedule in 1992, yet thereafter ran aground in a channel along the long barrier reef along the east coast of Andros.

Lisa J. II followed her predecessor to Andros in 1985 and beyond 1994. Her previous names were the *Schokland* from 1952 to 1965, then the *Netty* to 1981, and *Alphen ad Rijn*, in the Netherlands. She was built in Holland by the De Vooruitgang, D. & Joh. Boat Manufacturing Company, in 1952 and weighed 298 tons. Constructed of steel, she was 144 feet long and owned by Carlton Bowleg and relatives Louise Adderley and Eunice Adderley from 1981, then the North Andros Shipping Company, Limited from 1994. Officers and crew included Ulric Woodside and Joseph Woodside, Louise and Eunice Adderley, cook, crew Kirkwood Bowleg, and Joseph Moxey, engineer. The ship was repowered in 1985 and in June, 2010 was "reported sold to unnamed interests," probably for scrap via Bradford Marine in Freeport. Joseph Moxey who took her to refit in US more than once, said she was much bigger than the first, Danish *Lisa J*.

The motor mailboat *Central Andros Express* in 1987 began the mail service to central Andros until beyond 1993. Manufactured of wood, she appears on official mailboat schedules, 1988, 1992, and up to the late 1990s, thereafter is presumed to be inactive for the mail sector. The motor boat *Mangrove Cay Express* initiated her service to her namesake port in 1988 as well as Lisbon Creek, Andros up to 1995. There was a short-lived first version of the *Mangrove Cay Express* which sank prior to 1988, after the owners hired Joseph Moxey to take delivery of her from the US, convert it to a mailboat, and delivery it to Andros, then assumed command briefly. The name was simply transferred over to the steel boat of 72 tons, which was owned by the Rev. Herbert King, and captained by he and his son, with Joseph Moxey as an engineer. The boat is listed to 2009, yet by 2018 was no longer listed on registries or schedules.

The mailboat *Mal Jack* was a Ro-Ro, landing-craft-type vessel which served South Andros from 1989 to 2001. She was built in 1989 of steel, weighed 172 tons, and was 122 feet long. Her owner was Jack Andrews, d/b/a Mal-Jack Construction. In 2001 the vessel grounded in either Andros or Hatchet Bay, Eleuthera, yet managed to work free and trade again. In April 2001 the Bahamas Development Bank listed it for sale, and by 2005 *Mal Jack* was sold to Connors of Roatan, Honduras as *Capt. Berto II*, utilizing its bow ramp as an open-deck cattle carrier. The *Lady Margo II* entered mail service in 1995 to North Andros up until 2010. Her previous name was *Frankie Lynn,* and she was built by Master Marine of Bayou La Batre, Alabama in 1971. The steel ship's dimensions were 127 tons, steel and some 74 feet long. Although still listed in 2009, the following year it was no longer in service.

The second *Captain Moxey* took over the route of the first in 1998, hauling mail, passengers, freight and crabs among other items, to and from Kemps Bay, Driggs Hill, Bluff, Long Bay Cays in South Andros, and on occasion to Abaco, Berry Islands, Ragged Island (as a substitute for *Captain C.* She was built by Russell Portier Shipyard in Chauvin, Louisiana in 1998, which is the same yard which has built many Bahamaian vessels, including about four for Tom Hanna). *Captain Moxey* is 370 tons, made of steel, and 135 feet long. She is owned by Moxey Shipping, and officers and crew include captains Boycel Moxey Jr. and Kevin Moxey, and crew Joseph Moxey (unrelated). The ship is still operating, utilizing the route south of Nassau to and fro.

The Ro-Ro, landing craft-type ship *Lady Kathreina* sailed for Mangrove Cay, Driggs Hill, and Fresh Creek, South Andros in 2005 and with her cheerful light-blue livery is still on the route in 2020. *Lady Kathreina* was built by Russell Portier Shipyard in Chauvin, Louisiana in 2005. The steel hull is 276 tons and 123 feet long, and her owners are Captain Thomas Hanna d/b/the Ro-Ro Company, Carib-USA. Her officers included Captain King, who is the son of the Rev. King, owner of the first ship. A wooden-hulled *Lady Kathreina* about 60-feet long was delivered from Miami by Joseph Moxey in about 1987. The motor vessel named *K.C.T.* has served Fresh Creek, Andros, as well as Acklins, San Salvador, Rum Cay, and Clarence Town and Seymour, southern Long Island, since 2012. Built of steel in 2012 of 165 tons, she is owned by Captain Tom Hanna, d/b/a Ro-Ro Company, Carib-USA and is also still operating.

Exuma Islands

Over 30 mailboats have served the Exumas (population 7,300), and probably many more that went on to San Salvador, Cat Island, Rum Cay, Long Island, Ragged Islands, and beyond. For the sake of simplicity and perhaps because today Georgetown Exuma and Duncan Town, Ragged Island are along the same route served by *Captain C.* owned by the Maycocks, we address 18 vessels allocated to Exuma and an additional 13 to Ragged Island, with its proud maritime traditions in producing both wooden boats and steel captains over centuries. Together therefore we address the boats, with Exuma and its lovely chain of cays, likened appropriately to an emerald necklace. Ragged Island has been the cradle of many prominent maritime families from Duncan Town, including the Curlings, Hepburns, Joffres, Lockharts, Maycocks, Moxeys, Munroes, Pintards, Wallaces and Wilsons, many of whom by necessity can no longer live there, some considering survival barely tenable.

Hattie Darling was a schooner which in 1894 sailed from Nassau for Rolleville, Georgetown delivering the mail; it was thence carried over land to Steventon, Exuma. From Simms the mail also went over land to Clarence Town, Long Island. *Hattie Darling* was built of wood on Harbour Island in 1878 and weighed 81 tons. Her owner was Thomas H. Pearce of Harbour Island, and once the new route was established, on 7 October. 1895 it was contracted with him by the government for fortnightly service.

The schooner *Pilgrim* initiated service in the same route half a decade later in 1899 into 1900. She was built of wood in the Bahamas and weighed 16 tons. The vessel's owner was David A. Brice of Nassau who won the contract to Clarence Town from Simms on 1 April, 1900. Another Bahamian vessel named *Pilgrim* was a sloop of 5 tons, sloop built in 1885 in Eleuthera and owned by Henry T. Smith of Nassau. Both *Pilgrim*s appear in the 1915 register. The schooner *Renown* covered the same route to Exuma and Long Island from 1902. She was built of wood in 1867, was 22 tons, and owned by Timothy Culmer in 1900, Jason Alexander Sands in 1910, and James R. C. Young in 1940. All owners were based in Nassau, and Renown appears in the 1940 registry.

Estrella was a wooden, 52-foot, 15-ton schooner which in 1905 added Roker's Point, Exuma to the route, then The Ferry, Little Exuma and on Long Island, Deadman's Cay, and finally Inagua, which it served from 1902 to 1909. *Estrella* was built in Nassau in 1899 and owned by William J. Pinder, also I the capital. He won the 1 April, 1908 mailboat contract renewed for fortnightly service, at a per-trip subsidy of £12.12s. The ship was registered in 1915. Another schooner, the *Olivette*, began the Exuma mail run in 1905. She was constructed of wood in the Bahamas in 1891 and was 36 tons. The vessel's owner was Orlando Francis Pritchard of Nassau, who won the 1 April, 1907 contract for the mail route. However by 1919 commissioners, whose input often determined the viability of boats since they spoke for the end-users, called the 20-year-old *Olivette* "a leaky tub for a schooner, that is no good for this route. The crew spend much of their time pumping, and the passengers spend theirs complaining."

In 1908 the schooner *Celeste* entered the Exuma mail route, and the Long Island leg in 1909. She was built in Abaco of wood in 1898 and was 15 tons. Uriah T. Knowles of North End, Long Island was her owner, and she appears in the 1920 register. The schooner *Eclipse* began the same mail route in 1920, adding Cat Island and San Salvador the same year and Rum Cay in 1921. Built in 1892 of wood, *Eclipse* was 29 tons and owned by Jeremiah U. Dupuch of Nassau. She appears in the 1911 registry. At the time there were two post offices in the Simms district, so mail from boats was taken overland to Deadman's Cay and Burnt Ground. In 1924 the schooner *Serene* replaced the *Eclipse*, which was becoming leaky.

The schooner *Invincible* participated in the mail route to the Exumas and Long Island, starting from 1921. She was built of wood on Abaco in 1899 and weighed 23 tons. Owned by Lorenzo G. Brice of Nassau, in 1922 the commissioners deemed *Invincible* "...too small for so long a voyage, the sufferings of passengers during light head winds is better imagined than described." She appears in the 1940 registry, however not thereafter. Another schooner, the *Blanche Eva* took up the route from 1926. The boat was made of wood in Marsh Harbour in 1925 and was 24 tons. Her owners were Reuben A. Gibson of Simms, Long Island. She received the opportunity by substituting for *Columbia*, which "has ground disappointment and delay so thoroughly into our bones, that no one complains." *Columbia* was wrecked that year in the hurricane, and the *Blanche Eva* is featured in the 1940 register.

The large, 138-ton motor vessel *Castlerag* entered the Exuma and Long Island mail route in 1931. The owners were commended by commissioners on October 15, 1931, who observed her to be "a very fine one from appearance, and it is hoped will remain in service. Passengers are well accommodated..." The *Madam Queen* joined this route in 1932 to 1933, adding Farmer's Cay, Exuma. The *Captain Roberts* entered service to Exuma and Long Island, after a tragic early career, from late 1945 or 1946, then Grand Bahama to 1961. The boat was named for Sir George Robert's father, and built by Earl Johnson and Gerald Johnson in Harbour Island in mid-1945. *Captain Roberts* was made of wood, 82 tons and 111 feet long. Her owners was Sir George W. K., Richard d/b/a *Richard Campbell*, Limited of Nassau. Her very first captain, John Morell Carey of Abaco, was tragically killed while seeking the lee of Andros during a hurricane in September of 1945. He is said to have perished assuring the safety of those remaining on board. The boat has to be salvaged thereafter. Then William Roy Lowe of Green Turtle Cay took over, and other officers and crew included Vernon Albury, J. Fox, G. Fox, H. Bethel, J. Pratt, H. Harding, H. Pinder, and A. Bowe in 1961. In 1946 the commissioners observed how "mail service was satisfactorily performed by M/V *Captain Roberts*. Another port, Williams Town, was added, and then Forbes Hill was added in 1949. The boat had a shallow draft, Fairbanks Morse engine, and during a long career served Grand Bahama.

The motor vessel *Gary Roberts* covered the route including Black Point, Forbes Hill, and Moss Town, Exuma, Long Island in 1960, and Harbour Island, then Spanish Wells, North Eleuthera from 1944. Built in 1941 and first owned by Edgar L. Rolle of Lowes Sound, Andros, which she served in the 1940s, before covering Spanish Wells and Harbour Island. She was sold to Sir George Roberts d/b/a *Richard Campbell*, Limited of Nassau. In 1960 and 1961 both *Captain Roberts* and *Gary Roberts* together made weekly trips per commissioner reports. By 1971 *New Day* and *Eastern Isle* replaced them. *Gary Roberts* appeared in the *Nassau Guardian* in 1960, and the Manitoba *Selkirk Enterprise* in 1975, and was lost, sold or scrapped by October 5, 1978.

The *Staniel Cay Express* was designed as a fishing boat, and carried mails for Staniel Cay, the Exumas Cays, and Abacos from 1968 to 1975, then Alice Town and Cat Cay, Bimini in 1972 when he *Bimini Gal* sank suddenly. Built in the US before 1968, the wooden boat was 76 tons and captained and owned by frequent regatta winner Rolly Gray of Exuma. Captains and crew included Rolly Gray, his son Frederick Gray, and Joseph Moxey, engineer. On September 3, 1975 Manitoba's *Selkirk Enterprise*, carried a story on her. She sank off Elbow Cay, Hope Town Abaco on 11 June, 1975, when her seams opened up, however all were rescued. In 1973 the 97-ton, 75-foot wooden mailboat *Lady Blanche* sailed to Georgetown and the Exuma Cays and continued doing so over 20 years, beyond 1994. She is named for Rhonda Miller, who worked at Staniel Cay, Exuma, prior to 1973. Her owners were the Maycocks of Ragged Island. *Lady Blanche* is listed to 1995 and active to at least 1994. Her namesake's son Craig Miller is captain of the multi-hull *Flying Cloud* in Nassau.

The *Exuma Pride* began in the Bahamas in 1978, having started as a British naval vessel, and ended grounded on a cay in a former British colony. She served Georgetown and the Exuma Cays from 1978 to 1987. Built during 1945 in World War II by the Royal Navy as HMS *LCG(M)-192* by Tees-Side Bridge & Engine Works in Tees-Side, England, the 299-ton steel ship was 150 feet. Then she became *Hjelmeland Fjord* in Norway doing coastal trading in 1949. Previous names include *Old Joe* and *Enrus*. A Yorkshireman named John Gynell overseeing Sir Robert McAlpine and Sons in Exuma found himself exiled to Miami after independence but managed to purchase and return to Exuma with this fine British and Norwegian freighter. For conversion from international freighter to Bahamian mailboat, she was entrusted to Ray Ward in Providenciales.

According to his daughter, "He bought this boat with all his life savings and put it in service, as you stated as a mailboat. Once known as "the tyrant of Exuma," some unknown person(s) with a grudge, set it adrift from the dock one night and since my father was not on the island at the time, there was nothing he could do to stop anyone from salvaging it after it was adrift for the number of hours stated by law, it was stripped. It drifted and ended up here." Mr. Gynell's heart was broken, as "He thought he was doing something good for the island, upgrading the old wooden boat for this ship." He named it the *Enrus* for the god of the east wind, then *Exuma Pride*. It is now known locally as the *Exuma Shame*.

The first *Grand Master* became the hometown boat to serve Georgetown, Great Exuma and the Exuma Cays in 1993, and up to the present. She was built by San Sebastian Marine in St. Augustine, Florida in 1983. The steel hull weighs 214 tons and is 116 feet long. The owners are Gray Marine d/b/a *Grand Master* Shipping, believed to represent the Rolly and Frederick Gray and Lenny H. Bozozog and Lance Bozozog. Skippers have included Rolly Gray, his half-brother Lance Bozozog, and Lenny H. Bozozog, and Joseph Moxey, engineer. *Grand Master* was very popular as it affords a comfortable ride far enough away to be adventurous, weaving amongst lovely cays and almost always in shallow waters, and close enough for one to arrive within a day. She appears in schedules, magazines and the news in 1988, 1992, 2019, and 2020 and is still operating with a white hull and green trim.

The *Sealink* initiated service in 2000 and has carried government mails to Mayaguana, Inagua, San Salvador, and Cat Island, from 2017. Sometimes called the *Sea Link*, she was built out of aluminum in 2000, is 273 tons and 137 feet. Her owners and operators are Bahamas Ferries, she can carry an impressive 250 passengers, 33 vehicles, and has both a catamaran hull and Ro-Ro capabilities. The second *Grand Master II* entered the fleet in 2018 for Georgetown, Exuma. She was constructed of steel by St. John's Shipbuilding of Palatka, Florida in 2017 and is 496 tons and 198 feet long. Her owners are *Grand Master II*, LLC, of Panama. Launched on 28 July, 2017, Bahamas Ferries of Nassau took delivery. She boasts 6,400 feet of cargo space, twin 700-hp Cummins diesels, and is designed along the lines of a Ro-Ro passenger ship with landing craft capabilities.

Ragged Island

This sparsely-populated island group centered around Duncan Town Ragged Island boasts a long and distinguished boat building heritage and has produced notable captains, Moxeys and Lockharts among them. By way of illustration, in 1956 there were 22 sail cargo vessels built or owned in Ragged Island, out of a total of just over twice that number in the Bahamas. With a population post-hurricane of just 72, Ragged Island has been served by more than these vessels and captains, but for a small community they can rightfully proud of supporting this many. Captains on the Ragged Island route have included John Samuel Pintard, Kaya Moxey, Hezron Moxey, Etienne Maycock, Sr., Emmett Munroe, Alfonso Johnson, and many captains Lockharts, however several of them, like Hezron Moxey, sailed deeper waters, on global international routes as officers in the merchant marine.

In 1895 a schooner named *Experience* arrived in Duncan Town, Ragged Island, known as the basket of boating aristocracy – captains, owners, and builders - in the Bahamas. She was built in 1889 of wood and weighed 9 tons. Owned by John Samuel Pintard of Ragged Island, he was also one of her skippers. The boat last appeared in the 1915 registry. Eight years later, in 1903, the wooden schooner *Maria Ellen* arrived at Ragged Island, followed the next year by the schooner *Herman*. The *Julius* was also a schooner and served Duncan Town with the mail in 1905 up until 1911. *Julius* was built in Ragged Island in 1900 of wood and was 11 tons. In 1911, her owner was Walter S. Wilson of Duncan Town. She appears in the registries in 1903 and 1910. Another schooner, this one named *H. J. C.* arrived at Ragged Island in 1909. She was built in Green Turtle Cay, Abaco in 1902 and was 15 tons and made of wood. Her owners were Horace A. Wilson of Ragged Island. The commissioners reported in 1912 how the "*H.J.C.,* belonging to this place." In 1924 it was reported "sunk, raised, and repaired in Nassau," and remained up to 1940 in the register.

The schooner *Pearline* sailed for Ragged Island in 1916, and in 1910 added Black Point, Great Guano Cay, Farmer's Cay, Staniel Cay, Exuma. The wooden vessel was built in Cat Island of 23 tons and owned by William Munnings of Cat Island in 1930. Her officers and crew were from Ragged Island. In 1916 her ownership was in Nassau, and she appeared in the ship's registry up to 1930. A wooden 25-ton schooner named *Saale* entered the Ragged Island trade in 1927, serving Exuma along the way, as have many mailboats before and since. Her owner was James R. C. Young in 1940. Constructed on Ragged Island in 1927 by Alonzo F. Hepburn, the commissioners reported in 1949 that *Saale* was a "slow type sailing vessel on a three-weekly schedule. Quite spacious in her cabin. With a motor added, it could do bi-weekly service." In 1933 the schooner *Rescue* contributed mail service to Ragged Island, as well as Exuma Cays. She was built on Grand Bahama in 1881 of wood and was 20 tons, owned by James W. Culmer of Nassau.

The *Lady Baillou* went to Ragged Island from 1950, serving there and Exuma up to 1961. She was named for Baillou aka Blue Hill Road, a main thoroughfare in Nassau. She was built of wood in Andros in 1947, weighed 64 tons and was 75 feet long. Owners included Kaya Moxey of Andros, and she was commanded by Kaya Moxey and mate Hezron Moxey, was well as Joseph Moxey of Mangrove Cay, as engineer from 1960. In 1961 commissioners noted that: "*Lady Baillou* was thrown ashore by Hurricane Donna in 1960. Her hull was twisted. Refloated, but broken propeller shafts. Mechanical troubles. Replaced by local power boat." On 30 November, 1961 she repatriated Haitians for the Bahamian government. From 1966 the 21-ton wooden motor boat *Daily Gleaner* served Duncan Town and Exuma, up to 1971. The vessel was owned and operated by a father-son team, with Leland, aka Blue Boy, Curling, serving as captain. The vessel appears on the ship registries of 1955; one possible derivation of the name is the Kingston Jamaica newspaper named *The Gleaner*.

The motor mailboat *Gleaner Express* joined the Ragged Island service for roughly a decade from 1972 into the 1980s. She was built of steel in 1970 and owned by the same Ragged Island father-son team which has owned the *Daily Gleaner* up to 1971. Leland aka Blue Boy Curling was her captain, and from 1985 the boats was de-listed. The more modern, purpose-built *Captain C.* arrived on the Exuma and Ragged Island run in 1990, and remained a stabilizing fixture since. She was constructed in 1990 and weighs an impressive 500 tons, spread over 125 feet of length. The owners are the Munroe and Maycock families, including Etienne Maycock, Sr. and Jed Munroe. She is still in operation and has been featured in numerous articles, blogs and innumerable photographs with its dark blue hull and smart lines. A painting of the vessel and officers is prominently in the main café at Duncan Town, which suffered severely from depopulation arising from devastation caused by Hurricane Irma in 2017.

The motor mailboat *Emmett & Cephas* served Ragged Island from 1988 to 2001. Other names include *Etlene C.*, and *Lady 9*. She was built by St. Augustine Marine in Florida in 1988 and was 142 tons burthen. Munson Shipping Company, believed to be a joint ventures between the Maycocks and Munroes of Ragged Island, were the owners. Captains and crew have included Emmett Munroe, Maycocks as mates and other roles, and Alfonso Johnson in 2001. *Emmett & Cephas* is on the 1992 schedule, and was part of a test given to students nationally. She sank in 2001, per Bahamian government open-file listings.

Long Island

Long Island has 3,100 persons living in its 230 square miles, which, true to its name is long and shallow. Situated between the Exumas and southern and eastern islands, it is large enough to merit its own fleet of mailboats. Over the years these have included at least a dozen seagoing boats and ships, from the *Columbia* in 1901 which B. W. Malone and James R. C. Young invested in, to *Madam* in 1929, a boat named *Albury's* in 1938, and the *Gary Roberts* of 1944 owned by Edgar L. Rolle of Lowes Sound, Andros and Sir George Roberts of Harbour Island and Nassau.

In 1901 the government schooner *Columbia* took the mails from Nassau to Spencer's Point (Little Harbour), Cherokee Sound, Hope Town, and Green Turtle Cay, Abaco. She followed that route up with service to Eleuthera in 1919, Rum Cay, Cat Island, San Salvador, Fortune Cay, Acklins, and Inagua in 1913, and Simms and Clarence Town, Long Island, for a total of a quarter century, up to 1926. *Columbia* Abaco was built of wood in 1901 and weighed 50 tons. Her owners were B. W. Malone from 1901 to 1920, then James R. C. Young, of Nassau, from 1920. Although her owners won the mail contracts tendered on 17 October, 1908 and in August, 1909, by 1925 commissioners complained that *Columbia* had "outlived her usefulness; the zinc pail which is called a privy is very untidy, and nauseous." The vessel was wrecked in the hurricane of 17 September, 1926 at Simms, Long Island, and beached there, though it also may have salvaged, it was no longer a government mailboat.

The motor vessel named *Madam* began its service to Rolleville, Roker's Point, Georgetown (thence overland to Steventon, The Ferry, Little Exuma), Exuma, and Simms (land to Clarence Town), Deadman's Cay, Long Island, from 1929. There were two post offices in the Long Island district served by boats, so the mail had to be taken overland north and south from the main post office from Simms to Burnt Ground and Clarence Town. In 1938 the *Albury's* served the same route. Also known as *Albury*, or *The Alburys*, this 32-ton wooden boat was owned by an Albury and registered in Nassau in 1937, not thereafter.

The motor mailboat *Gary Roberts* serviced the mail needs of Lowes Sound, Andros, and Simms, Long Island from 1957 to 1978. She was built in 1941 by Earl Johnson and Gerald Johnson in Harbour Island, and was 59 tons, wooden, and 66 feet. Her owner was Edgar L. Rolle of Lowes Sound, and later Sir George W. K. Roberts, d/b/a *Richard Campbell* Company of Nassau up to 1978. Other sources say there was a different ship named *Gray* (or *Gary*) *Roberts*, and this one was built in 1956. This vessel appears in the *Nassau Guardian* in 1960, and the Manitoba, Canada *Selkirk Enterprise* in 1975. Whether lost, sold, or scrapped, the date of *Gary Robert's* demise is given as October 5, 1978.

The motor ship *New Day* hauled the mails, freight and passengers to Clarence Town and southern Long Island starting in 1971, and Acklins and Crooked Island from 1966 to 1972. Built in Boston in 1947 and changed from naval ship to salvage vessel by Symonette Shipyard in 1947, *New Day* was 388 tons of steel and 164 feet long. Freedom Shipping Co. took her over in 1972, assuring that the Clarence Town district post office sent mail from the capital three times a week. Deadman's Cay was at that time only able to receive its mail by air. The service did not last long, as the *New Day*, former *Sea Salvor*, was destroyed by fire in 1972 and a new *New Day II* was cued up to take her place. In 1971 the *Eastern Isle* brought mail for the residents of Salt Pond and northern Long Island.

In 1978 the large Dutch steel ship *Miranda* covered Long Island, Georgetown, and the Exuma Cays up to 1996. Previous names included the *Geulborg* up to 1977, and after her service in the Bahamas the *Paradise Express*, *El Compa*, and finally the *Gilbert Sea*. *Miranda* was built as the *Geulborg* by Sander Gebroeders [brothers] of Delfzijl, The Netherlands in 1966, and weighed 399 tons, her steel hull being 176 feet long. Her owners were the Taylors of Pirate's Well Investments, d/b/a The Taylor Corporation. Captains included Bob Garroway and Eddins Taylor. In January, 1986 the *Miranda* ran aground off Miami. Soon she was sold to Hondurans, became *Paradise Express* and *El Compa*, and in 1996 she was arrested in Miami. In an effort to rid the Miami River of derelicts, she was towed out to create an artificial reef with and in 2002 sunk east of Palm Beach, Florida, thenceforth known as the *Gilbert Sea* wreck, or reef.

The 431-ton steel ship *Abilin* covered some of the mail needs of Long Island from 1984 to 1998. As with most mailboats, this vessel has a colorful history: she was built in Germany by MAN GHH Dock & Schiffbau, in Duisburg in 1962, her steel hull measuring 179 feet. First, from 1962 to 1977 she was the *Dinslaken*, and from 1977 to 1984 the *Emsstrom*. Then in 1987 she was purchased by Homeboy Shipping Limited, and by Androsian captain Harley Simms in 1991. One of *Abilin*'s captains was Jason Cartwright of Deadman's Cay. The ship was detained by authorities in 1998 and sank, or was intentionally sunk, on a reef in 2007 on reef per shipping consultant Captain Calum Legett. Another version has it that she was sold out of Bahamas in 2010; in any event, *Abilin*'s mailboat career in Bahamas was over before 2000. Harley Simms also owned *Harley & Charley*.

The *Nay Dean* added the resort at Long Island's north tip, Stella Maris, in 1985 to the North Long Island run. At times known as *Nadine* (phonetically), she was built in Florida in 1980 of 91 tons and wood manufacture. Dean Shipping is the owner, and John Dean, his father Ernest A. Dean, and Willie Knowles, have been captains, with Joseph Moxey as engineer. The *Nay Dean* is still operating with her cheerful bright red and blue color scheme; she is featured at length in an *Island Expedition* book by the Popov brothers, from circa 1989.

The *Mia Dean* began serving Clarence Town, then Cat Island and the Abacos in 1990, the year she was built of wood in Abaco to 146 tons. Her owners are the Dean

Shipping Company, Limited, and does not appear to be steadily active in 2020. Per the *Abaconian* her said schedule was 'erratic' in 1997, on government lists in 1992. Listed as still operating in 2020, it is also not unusual to find as many as three Dean-named vessels stacked along the dock face at Potter's Cay beneath the first Paradise Island Bridge. *East Wind* headed for Simms and Clarence Town, Long Island in 2007, then Governors Harbour and Rock Sound Eleuthera. She was built of steel by Rodriguez Coden in Coden, Alabama, in 2007, is 177 feet long and 498 tons burthen. Owned by Bahamas Ferries, and/or Inter-Island Shipping, the Ro-Ro, landing-craft-type vessel is still operating.

The steel catamaran *Island Link* embarked in 2014 for Salt Pond and Deadman's Cay, Long Island, having served Georgetown, Exuma, since 2004. Her makers were South Pacific Marine Construction of Caboolture, Australia in 2004, and it tipped the scales at tons and over 120 feet of length. Her owners are the Munroes of Munson Shipping; other iterations being SeaRoad and Intamico Shipping. Captains include Jed Munroe and Emmett Munroe. In 2007 the first mailboat (pre-2019) named *Captain Emmett* shared same registration number in 2007 government list, indicating that the two boats may at one point have shared the name *Captain Emmett*; however reporting and recording errors are not unknown. *Island Link* is still operating, and is particularly in demand during regatta time in Georgetown.

Cargo on the dock face awaiting the mailboat, Georgetown, Exuma, 2017, by Dave Blake Photography.

San Salvador and Rum Cay

The first recorded mailboat calls at San Salvador, aka Watling's Island, which has a population of 930 persons and is 63 square miles in area, was by the *Linnet*. The schooner *Linnet* began serving Cockburn Town, Sandy Point, and Grahams Harbour, San Salvador in 1916, then later added Andros. The 25-ton wooden boat was built in Nassau in 1906 and owned by Mrs. Lilian A. Bone of Mangrove Cay, Andros in 1920. Initially *Linnet* substituted for one trip in October, 1916 for the *Arawak*, a smaller sponge fishing vessel, according to district commissioners, and she was off the register by 1920. The schooner *Resolve* joined the mailboat fleet in 1920, serving San Salvador and Cat Island. The 23-ton wooden boat was constructed in Man-O-War Cay, Abaco in 1912 and owned by Harrison L. Russell of that island in 1920 and appears in the ship registries up to 1940.

The tragic schooner *Brontes* served San Salvador, Rum Cay, Ca Island, and the Exumas from 1921 to 1926. Weighing 43 tons and made of wood, *Brontes* was owned by W. P. Styles and possibly a Mr. Burrows, who drowned in 1925. A vicious hurricane swept the Bahamas in July of 1926, catching the *Brontes* on the night of 25-26 July with 30 souls on board, many of the residents of the communities they left. The schooner wrecked near Highbourne Cay, northern Exumas, and sank, with the loss of all persons on board. The effect on the communities it had served was devastating. Wayne Neely, in *The Great Bahamian Hurricanes of 1926*, describe the mail boat *The Brontes* leaving for San Salvador at the outset of the 1926 hurricane:

> Including the crew, there were 30 persons on board, among them Rum Cay's Commissioner Mr. T. A. Greenslade's wife, four other members of his family, and the wife and children of H. A. Varence, the schoolmaster at Roker's Point, Exuma. At the time of *The Brontes* departure, the hurricane was …approaching Hispaniola. The captain of *The Brontes*, W. P. Styles, was a much-admired figure in the maritime life of the colony. Renowned for his reliability as a mailboat captain and exceptional skill as a sailor, he was in the words of Sir Etienne Dupuch, a *"very, very valuable mariner."*

The Brontes, then, was a ship that had many lives because a year before the hurricane, it had sunk between Graham's Harbor and Riding Rocks (Cockburn Town), San Salvador, taking its then captain, a man named Burrows, to his grave….

The schooner *Serene* began San Salvador and Cat Island in 1924. She was built in Hope Town, Abaco in 1909 of wood and weighed 22 tons. Her owner was W. Richard Sweeting of Man-O-War Cay, Abaco. Commissioners described her in 1924 as an "inferior boat in size and speed," adding that "Service is lamentable, and there are no accommodations; a great defect." Usually such scathing reviews are reserved for the ending rather than the beginning of vessel's careers, so it would appear that the boat was not carefully vetted prior to entering service that year. The schooner *William H. Albury* joined the San Salvador and Cat Island service in 1925. She was built in Man-O-War Cay in 1890 at 70 tons of wood and owned by Miss Maude E. A. Morris of Nassau as a namesake of William H. Albury, aka Uncle Will, who was a boat-building legend at Man-O-War Cay in the 1940s, per *Out Island Portraits* by Ruth Rodriguez.

The schooner *Graceful* served Sandy Point Creek and other ports in San Salvador and Devil's Point, Port Howe, and others on Cat Island (formerly Watling's Island) from 1926. She was built of wood in the Bahamas in 1898 and weighed 18 tons. Her owners included Thaddeus George Johnson of Nassau and David Poitier of Arthur's Town; possibly David Franklin Poitier, born on San Salvador in 1876, died in Arthur's Town, or David Poitier, born 1878. On the first year of service the commissioner complained that she was "too small, and management is unsatisfactory in every respect." Furthermore each leg took six to ten days, the vessel could not accommodate livestock and if she could, the passage would be too long for that critical cargo to retain their weight and health for market. She last appeared on the registry list in 1940.

The fast motor mailboat *Air Pheasant* entered service to San Salvador, Long Cay, Crooked, Acklins, Inagua, and Ragged islands from 1948 to 1982. Other ports served include Clarence Town, Long Island and Inagua, from 1966, and Georgetown, Exuma starting in 1972. The ship was constructed of wood in 1942 at Luder's Marine Construction, on Cook Point (now occupied by the Ponus Yacht Club) in Stamford, Connecticut. The 148-ton boat was 111 feet long, launched in August, commissioned in October as the US Navy patrol chaser USS *PC-1015* and submarine chaser *USS SC-1015* from April, 1943 until struck from the Naval Register in November, 1945. From October, 1945 to January, 1948 she became the US coast guard cutter USCGC *Air Pheasant* (*WAVR-449*).

The Morton Salt Company of Matthew Town Inagua (owned by the Bill Erickson and family), purchased her as the *Air Pheasant* on January 14, 1948. In July, 1949 she was registered in Nassau at 162 tons, which is 14 more than when built seven years previously. The Ericksons then sold her to Sir George Roberts, doing business as *Richard Campbell* Ltd. at City Lumber Co. in Nassau. A 1964 article my Michael Mardon in the *Bahamas Handbook* informs readers that *Air Pheasant had* both first and second class accommodation. Since Mr. Erickson was Haitian Consul in Inagua, he loaned *Air Pheasant* to the Haitian Government, however they mistreated and overcharged the captain and crew, who returned to the Bahamas. The ship's master at the time was Anton Lockhart of Ragged Island. He was 58 years old and had been going to sea since age 16 in 1922. He lost his sister, brother-in-law and wife in a collision between the *Robert Luckenbach*, an American Liner, off Castle Island Light on 7 June, 1931. They had been married only six months. Her captains also included

John Spurgeon Archer of Abaco in the 1970s, and Willie Knowles of Long Island, in the early 1980s. Commissioners reported in 1967 that *Air Pheasant* was "not large enough to handle all freight" on her demanding run, and she was replaced by *Monarch of Nassau* on some routes in the 1950s and scrapped in 1982.

Another former US Navy vessel was the motor vessel *Drake*, which began the run to San Salvador in 1957, Tea Bay, Cat Island, and Rum Cay, between 1956 and 1968. Built by Robinson Marine Construction in Benton Harbor, Michigan in April, 1942, *Drake* was 143 tons of steel and 111 long. Commissioned a month later into the US Navy as patrol craft USS *PC-541*, a year later she was renamed a submarine chaser as USS *SC-541*, and in October, 1945 as the coast guard cutter USCGC *Air Drake* (WAVR-418), and struct from the Naval Register the following month. She was sold in 1948 to Thorton & William Lawson of New York as the 123-ton fishing vessel *Drake*. In 1954 they sold her to the Crosland Fish Company, aka Frozen-at-Sea Corporation, of Marathon, Florida and based it at Key West. In 1956 the vessel was sold to Bahamian ship owner Sir George W. K. Roberts, who had brought the two sister ships *Air Pheasant* and *Air Swift*. The *Drake*, sometimes known as the *Bahama Drake*, was then flagged to Nassau, Bahamas.

Drake's new owners, *Richard Campbell* Ltd., employed captains including Claudius Storr in 1961, Erroll Burrows crew, and Fred Sawyer, port engineer in 1968. In early January, 1957 the *Drake* replaced *Alice Mabel*, with much anticipated improvement. She appeared in the *Nassau Guardian* shipping list of 1960. Bahamas *Drake* sank off Cave Cay, Musha Cays and Farmers Cay, in the Exumas, on December 29, 1968. The *Drake* appears in a maritime column by well-known Miami shipping journalist Benedict Thielen, in an article entitled *The Bahamas – Golden Archipelago*:

"Among the sloops are the mail boats, high-sided, clumsy and fancifully colored as a child's drawing. They carry cargoes of rum and beer, oil drums and tractors, crayfish pots, cows and sometimes grand pianos. The *Air Swift* has come from Eleuthera, the *Lady Dundas* from Cat Island. The *Church Bay* is bound north for Grand Bahama, the *Drake* far south to Rum Cay and San Salvador. Coming and going, they and others like them call at little settlements like Palmetto Point and Eight Mile Rock, Savannah Sound and Castle Island, Pleasant By and Pure Gold." (*Holiday*, December, 1964, pp. 62-73, 135-140, "Bahamian Fragments," World War II U.S. Navy Vessels in Private Hands, 2014, Williams). It is fair to say that the adaption of the three World War II-era "Air-class" vessels; *Air Pheasant*, *Air Swift*, and *Air Drake* in the 1950s added considerably to the speed, safety, comfort, and culture of the Bahamian mailboat system and have made a lasting impact. Interviewees from the 1950s to 1980s almost always lead with a reference to an "Air" boat and a big smile and ready story.

The *Wissagua* headed for San Salvador, Rum Cay, and Cat Island in 1964. She was built of wood in 1921 at 96 tons and 75 feet in length, and in 1944 her name was *Ruth*. During the 1960s the *Wissagua* was advertised in Nassau papers as serving the "eastern islands." The *Plymouth Queen* served The Cave, Knowles, McQueen's, Cockburn Town, Sandy Point Creek, and Grahams Town, San Salvador from 1969, then Cat Island also. That year the commissioner wrote that her "route was Nassau, Rum Cay, San Salvador, and *Plymouth Queen* was often called to substitute for disabled boats." The second *San Salvador Express*, served San Salvador between 1972 to 1974, then became the mailboat *Johnette Walker* in 1975 following an accident. She was built by F. B. Walker & Sons at the *Innocent Express* in Pascagoula, Mississippi in 1953, being 112 feet long and 136 tons of steel. In May, 1974 the second *San Salvador Express* sank at Ship Channel Cay, Exuma, was salvaged, and renamed *Johnette Walker* in 1975. Under different ownership as the *Superfly II* flagged to Panama, she was rumored to have been carrying drugs in 1979, and finally became the *Pack One* in 2017. One captain was Roy Oral Lockhart of Ragged Island.

The large steel European mailboat *Willaurie* entered service in 1980 to San Salvador, southern Cat Island, and Rum Cay between 1980 and 1988. Formerly named *Willmary*, the 199-ton, 138-foot ship was built Hoogezand Shipworks, Netherlands in 1966 as the *W. B. Hart* for the British coastal trade. The ship had a tortuous end, with *Frommer's* travel guides saying in 1989 that she sank three times. To simplify it, that would be on initial impact, then on being towed to the Clifton Pier area where she (not uncommonly) broke her tow during the Christmas holidays of 1988, and finally she was literally wrenched off the rocks on Christmas Eve by diving entrepreneur Stuart Cove and colleagues, who then towed the hulk to a location southeast of Goulding Cay, of Clifton Bay, and sank her as a dive attraction, where it continues to draw visitors.

The industrial-built offshore supply boat or OSV, *Treasure Lady* joined the Taylor family fleet to serve San Salvador and Rum Cay between 1997 and 2012. She was built in the US Gulf as hull 77, *Tar Heel V* by Scully Brothers Boat Builders in Morgan City, Louisiana in 1981, and weighed 320 tons of steel, being roughly 180 feet long. Her owners were Pirate's Well Investments, as crew moved from *Lady Rosalind* in 2012. In 2001 the communities of Rum Cay and San Salvador eagerly awaited family and friends aboard *Treasure Trader* for homecomings. Believed to have been sold in 2012 out of the Bahamas market, though with this vessel specific dates proved difficult to verify. The supply vessel *Maxine* carried mail to United Estates, San Salvador, and Cat Island and Rum Cay from 1988 to 1999. Of 90 tons, she was built of steel in 1972 and owned by Louis Williamson, Eddins Taylor's uncle. Referenced in various schedules and publications from 1989, she is believed to have sunk in 1999.

The *Lady Frances* began serving San Salvador, the Exuma Cays including "private cays" starting in 1989. She was built of steel in Houma, Louisiana in 1989 of 154 tons and over 90 feet in length. Her captain was Reverend Gladstone Patton, Sr., and owners Mrs. G. M. (Maureen) Patton, who are related to the Taylors of Pirate's Well Investments. Other officers included Eddins Taylor and engineer Joseph Moxey. The ship is still operating, based out of Black Point, Exuma. Due to the need for periodic surveys and overhauls in the US, and a different layer of licensing requirements, captain and engineer Joseph Moxey of Mangrove Cay, Andros, brought her on three trips to the Jones Boatyard in Miami for refit, and overhaul, each lasting some two weeks.

The *Lady Emerald* joined the route to San Salvador, Rum Cay, and Cat Island between 2003 and 2014. The ship had more than one iteration in the mailboat fleet when it was sold to Tom Hanna in 2017 and became *Tolyn*, until Hanna sold her on to the Sawyers and she became the latest in *The Daybreak* series in North Eleuthera, from 2018. Built in Chauvin, Louisiana in 2003, the steel ship is 464 tons and 151 tons. As the *Lady Emerald* for over a decade, her owners were the Pattons of Black Point Exuma, possibly in partnership with the Taylors of Mayaguana. Bill Williams was a captain. In 2014 she was laid up at Potter's Cay and briefly out of service before becoming the *Tolyn*. She is operating in 2020 under Quincy Sawyer as *The Daybreak*.

Cat Island

Cat Island is an historic island 48 miles in length, with a population base of 1,500 persons spread along the lee, or western shore and mostly in the middle. Fewer than 10 mailboats have made Cat Island their focus, as many were on their way to and from other islands, but nevertheless an island cooperative has funded the *North Cat Island Special*, and with one of the main airports knocked out, as well as an airline that served them, the mailboat is as important a link to the commercial world beyond as ever. Confusingly in historic documents Cat Island is sometimes referred to San Salvador or Guanahani, and some philatelists mistakenly named it Watling's Island).

The wooden sloop *Mountain King* served Cat Island as a mailboat from 1915 until its tragic demise in 1926. She owned by Rev. James Smith of Port Howe, Cat Island, and was under the command of Elliston Bain and Napoleon Rolle when lost off Little San Salvador and Bird Cay. After the two men could not agree on the best course of action during the 1926 hurricane 25 lives were lost. The *Monarch of Nassau* began its Cat Island service in 1947 and also covered Eleuthera and San Salvador up to 1951. The ship arrived in the Bahamas directly from builders in just 19 days from J. Crighton & Co. Ltd. of Cheshire, England as the *Sir Charles Orr* and sailed under that name from 1930 to 1947. She was built by, weighed 215 tons, had a steel hull and was 116 feet long. Her owners were Sir George Roberts, the Monarch Line, and the Carl Sawyer Steamship Agency after 1947. One captain was Roland Roberts in 1952. After her sale by Sawyer in the US she was renamed *Carl Shmedeman* 1952 and was reported by the *Kingston Gleaner* of Jamaica as trading in those waters.

The *Cat Island Princess*, or *Cat Island Express* began service to Cat Island and Andros in about 1967 and continued into the 1970s. Built of wood, she is said by Joseph Moxey of Andros to have been owned by the North Cat Island Cooperative Society. In 1969 veteran Rd Fruendt of the AUTEC US Navy base there reports their sending TRBs, AVRs to the aid of the *Cat Island Princess*, which experienced a radio room fire *en route* from Exuma to Andros. She was fitted with a single screw, Cummings engine, little passengers space, narrow. Because it was not well suited for passenger and breakbulk cargo work, she became *Diamond Express* around 1978 and sank off the Berry Islands *en route* from Grand Bahama with cement on 13 March, 2018 per *The Tribune*. While the RBDF, OPBAT, BASRA, and others managed to rescue four men who were found clinging to the overturned hull, two other crew remained missing and are presumed dead.

The *Johnette Walker* called on Cat Island from 1975 to 1979. She was known as *San Salvador Express* from 1972 to 1974, when it sank and was salvaged, sold and renamed. The vessel was built of steel by F. B. Walker of Sons of Pascagoula, Mississippi in 1953, was 136 tons, and 112' overall. She was owned by Lockharts of Ragged Island and commanded by Roy Oral Lockhart in 1979. As the *San Salvador*

Express she sank in Ship Channel Cay, Exuma, during May of 1974, was salvaged, and became the mailboat *Johnette Walker* in 1975, *Superfly II* in 1979 and *Pack One* in 2017.

The *Lady Eula* began service to North Cat Island from 1978 to 1981, later serving Freeport and Andros. She was built by Jerry Thompson of St. Augustine Trawler Company in Florida in 1978. With a wooden hull, the vessel was 149 tons and 90 feet long. John Dean, son of patriarch Ernest Alexander Dean, commanded her. In 1981 she ran aground and sank off San Salvador due to a navigational error. The first *North Cat Island Special* began service to Cat Island in 1986 to Bennett's Harbour, Orange Creek, Dumfries, North Bight and South Bight, Bluff, Zion Hill, and Arthur's Town, from 1986 and 2003, occasionally serving the Berry Islands as well. Built in 1986 of steel, she weighed 98 tons and was 80 feet long. The owners were the North Cat Island Cooperative Society, and one captain was Roy Oral Lockhart. She was listed in service on schedules and registers in 1988, 1989, 1992, and replaced by *North Cat Island Special II* in 2003. When the author rode aboard her in 1986 she was so new that the engines were still being broken in with low RPM.

The *Lady Eddina* served Cat Island for the Taylors of Mayaguana from 1989 to 2000. She was built at VT Halter Marine in Moss Point, Mississippi 1989 as the *Stonewall Jackson*. The ship's tonnage was 270, the hull was steel and length overall 156 feet. Pirate's Well Investments and the Taylor Corporation, managed by Eddins Bruce Taylor owned her. In 2005 the Bahamas Development Bank listed her as an asset on their books and it was sold on to Roatan Honduras. According to Bradford Marine in Freeport, she subsequently sank at either Utila or Guanaha in Honduras. The *Sea Hauler* motored to and from Cat Island for owners from there in 1989, up until 2011. Built of steel and 98 feet long, her owner was Allan Russell, Sr. who was also captain. The ship was involved in a fatal collision with another mailboat, the Tom Hanna-owned *United Star* in 2003 and was wrecked by 2011.

The *North Cat Island Special II* was financed by the North Cat Island Cooperative Society and entered service to Cat Island in 2003 until the present. Originally named the *Cahaya Agung* when built in January, 2001 the vessel is made of 289 tons of steel and it 153 feet long. She replaced *North Cat Island Special*, and one of the captains is said to have been Roy Oral Lockhart. The Ro-Ro vessel *New G.* began serving Cat Island, Acklins, Crooked, and Long Cay, then Central Andros from 2015. She is built of steel in 2015, weighs 486 tons, and is 178 feet long. Her owner is Captain Thomas Hanna of Consolidated Marine Group, who designed and engineered her in a "private yard," suggested to be SF Sea. Since the agents, Harvey Jones, are in Slidell, Louisiana, and since *Sea Spirit II, United Spirit, United Star*, and *VI Nais* are all Tom Hanna-owned and built at Russel Portier Shipyard in Chauvin, Louisiana, this author posits that *New G.* was more likely than not built there as well. In 2020 she is still operating.

Mayaguana

There are 277 persons on the 110 square miles of Mayaguana, although that population spiked with the siting of a large US air base there and the recent major resort development which was begun but soon fizzled. Of the 23 boats to serve Mayaguana since the early 1900's, the following 15 have been or are owned by the Taylor family and affiliated companies and families, primarily from Pirate's Well and then Nassau, who have travelled the world from China to Europe to build and buy the right vessels for the market.

The sloop *Wisdom M.* began serving Abraham's Bay and Pirate's Well, Mayaguana in 1925; these were the only two options on the island. The vessel was built of wood in 1918 at 12 tons for Frederick Black of Pirate's Well; starting a dynasty. In 1927 *Wisdom M.* won a tender for one year, for not less than 20 tons (odd, given the boat was 12 tons) and was still registered in 1930. Captain Fred and mary jane black are parents to Nathaniel Bruce Taylor, grandparents to captains Eddins Bruce Taylor, Limas Taylor, and Elvin Taylor. The sloop *Dove* joined the route in 1930, having been built in Bambarra, Middle Caicos, Turks & Caicos in 1928. Made of wood and 6 tons, her owner was Arnold L. McCormack of Cockburn Harbour, Caicos.

Dove of 1930 was owned by Arnold L. McCormack, of Cockburn Harbour, Caicos, followed by Ruthie Melrose, which arrived in 1931 was owned by Wilbert B. Griffin of Governor's Harbour, Eleuthera. Then in 1932 the schooner *S. C. Louise,* sailed in, followed by the schooner *Go On,* which arrived from Acklins in 1933. Owned by Rev. William M. Maycock, and by 1942 by Rev. Alfred Samuel Collie, Captain Collie used the *Go On* to rescue 47 American sailors beached at Hard Hill, Acklins. *Sea Wonder* sailed to Mayaguana with the mail in 1937; she was owned by John Burrows of Mayaguana. Then, in 1938 by a boat named *Child* and another called *High Purchase* joined the route. *Miss BJ* in 1990 was owned by George McKinney through Trans-Bahama Shipping Ltd., Mail & Ferry Services, MVBS. *United Star* in 1999 arrived from the fleet of Thomas Hanna, d/b/a Ro-Ro Co., Carib-USA.

The schooner *Ruthie Melrose* carried mail to Mayaguana from 1931; she was built of wood in 1898 and was 25 tons. Her owner was Wilbert B. Griffin of Governor's Harbour, Eleuthera, and was on the ship's register into 1940. The wooden sloop *S. C. Louise* sailed for Mayaguana with mail in 1932, probably as a substitute boat. The Ragged Island-built schooner *Go On* served Mayaguana from 1933, having been built in Duncan Town in 1927 of 25 tons, wooden hull, for Reverend William M. Maycock, who then sold her to Reverend Collie. In July, 1942, Captain Collie rescued 47, and buried 1, survivors of the American steamship *Potlatch* who washed ashore at Anderson's Settlement, Acklins after 29 days, adrift, with a couple days in the Inaguas. Speedboat racer Marion Carstairs of Whale Cay, Berry Island, took her Bahamian power yacht *Vergemere IV* to off Bird Rock, Crooked Island, intercepted the *Go On*, and carried the survivors to Nassau, arriving 1 August.

The sailboat *Nonesuch* also took the mails to Mayagauna from 1933 at the behest of the Black and Taylor family of Pirate's Well, all the way up to 1940. She was built either by Matthew Gates of Green Turtle Cay, or Joseph Curry on Abaco. Built of wood in 1880, *Nonesuch* was 21 tons, and she had several owners, including Mary *Jane* and Frederick Black, Benjamin W. Roberts from 1880 to 1900, and William H. Edgecombe, from 1910 to 1915, and James R. C. Young from Nassau from 1920. Her masters included Eddins Bruce Taylor and his father Fred Black from 1933 and 1940, possibly with Daniel Gibson. In 1940 she was believed destroyed at Mayaguana, having already been damaged in the 1926 hurricane, then been repaired. From 1940 *Nonesuch* was de-listed from 1940, and gradually sunk at Pirate's Well, and is inactive.

The sloop *Sea Wonder* sailed to Mayaguana in 1937, having been built in 1933 of wood at 14 for John Burrows of Mayaguana. Another sloop, the *Child* became a mailboat in 1938, with the sloop *High Purchase* of wood serving Mayaguana the same year. Based on interviews on the island, with Higgins and Williamsons, this is not to be confused with the *I Purchase*, active from 1913 to 1927; she was a 6-ton sloop of Turks & Caicos owned by Edward S. Walkins. The motor vessel *ML 371* joined the Mayaguana service in 1946, also calling at Crooked, Acklins, Inagua, and Ragged islands up to 1951. The boat began as HMS *ML-371* in the Royal Navy, having been built in Belmont Dock, Kingston, Jamaica in 1940 for service in World War II. Weighing 129 tons with a wooden hull of 112', she was bought by Louis Williamson in 1946, and Henry L. Roberts of Nassau in 1951, who still owned her in 1956. Captains included Daniel Gibson in 1956.

The former Royal Navy torpedo boat turned-getaway yacht *Frecil* is said by Higgins and Taylors to have served Mayaguana from about 1953 into the early 1960s, but only on an intermittent, probably substitute or chartered-in basis. Few boats have had such exotic careers: built for World War II in 1942, she was 58 tons and her wooden deck was 112 feet long. When the middle-aged owner of an engineering firm named Cecil Edward Heath of St. Leonard's and Hastings, England purchased the vessel to follow his doctor's advice and head for the tropics, he planned for he and wife Freda and their 7-year-old son Bryan to motor for the British West Indies from Rye in 1952. The name *Frecil* is a portmanteau of *Freda* and *Cecil*; their first names.

Well, the voyage ending in the Bahamas took a different turn, to say the least. A French newspaper noted that *Frecil* was on the way to Africa then the Caribbean. Soon thereafter the wire news services reported how eight men and a woman were crossing the Atlantic to escape post-war Europe; and the woman was a 27-year old doing all the cooking. On January 22, 1953 the boat was reported aground in the East River, in the Bronx, New York – a far cry from the tropics. Finally, by 1960 the *Palm Beach Post* reported her loading freight there for Marsh Harbour. It does not appear that she was owned by Mayaguanans, however if so then it was by Louis Williamson: with this boat, one never can tell.

The sailing vessel *Silver King* sailed for Mayaguana starting in 1955, and added Inagua, Crooked, and Acklins up to 1968. Cornelius Collie of Acklins, then Mayaguana owned the wooden vessel, then Louis Williamson. Daniel Gibson was one of her captains in 1968. The boat substituted for *River Queen* from 1962 to 1968 and then been beached at Pirate's Well, submerged, and rotted. Another fate proffered is that she was destroyed by fire in Bimini. The motor vessel *Mayaguana Queen* joined this mail run in 1960, also serving Acklins, Crooked Island, Long Cay, and Inagua for several years. Built of wood in 1931, the 31-ton, 56-foot long boat was owned by Louis Williamson (uncle to Eddins Bruce Taylor), and captained by Daniel Gibson. She appears in the *Nassau Guardian* shipping columns in 1960 and 1961, until wrecked on the samana or French Cays.

Cape Hatteras was a wooden motor boat of 56 tons built in the US in the 1950s which started serving Mayaguana in 1962 and up until 1968. Her owners were Nathaniel Bruce Taylor and Pirate's Well Investments, who sold her to craw fishermen in Spanish Wells, Eleuthera in 1968. The sailing vessel *River Queen* served Mayaguana, Crooked Island, Acklins, and Inagua from 1962 to 1968. A wooden vessel of 68 tons, she was constructed in the Turks & Caicos in 1941 and purchased by Louis Williamson, with one captain being Daniel Gibson. According to Mr. Higgins, in 1968 *River Queen* was beached in Pirate's Well. Earlier on, in 1945, she was reportedly wrecked in the September hurricane at Landrail Point, Crooked Island, and salvaged.

The first motor vessel *Marcella* (also *Marcella I* or *Marcella 1st*) was named after the Taylor's grandmother. She was built of wood by P. K. Trawlers of St. Augustine, Florida in 1968. Weighing 90 tons, *Marcella* was 148 feet long, and captained by Nathaniel Bruce, Eddins B. Taylor, Daniel Gibson, and Joseph Moxey, and she hauled mail, passengers and freights to Mastic Point Andros and Freeport Grand Bahama as well as Mayaguana for 18 years. A 1968 report states "she unloaded the entire cargo for the District. Freight and passengers... transported by trucks." Other data has her completed in 1969. Her owners were the Taylor family and Pirate's Well Investments. The vessel caught fire, burned and sank at Salt Pond, Long Island in 1986, per interviews with Mr. Higgins and others on Mayaguana." The *Lady Rosalind 1st* entered the mail service in 1986 to Mayaguana, Acklins, Crooked Island, Inagua, and even North Andros, up to 1997. The large steel, 233-ton, 156-foot ship was built as the *Misty Briley* in 1967 by Bollinger Shipyards in Lockport, Louisiana. Around 1984 she was sold to Pirate's Well Investments, Taylor Corporation, and operated by Limas Taylor, supported by a mate named Jake. In 1997 *Lady Rosalind* struck a rock, and was damaged and towed to Potter's Cay, where she sank. Her hull was donated to DB Bahamas, with fate uncertain.

Miss BJ was a European boat whose service in Bahamas began in 1990 to Mayaguana, Crooked Island, Acklins, Inagua, and Ragged Island up to 1999. She was built as the *Sambre* by Apol A., Scheepswerf C.V. in Wirdum, Netherlands, in 1965, weighing 330 ton, of steel and 152 feet long. Her owners included Trans-Bahama Shipping Ltd., and Mail and Ferry Services, MVBS, under George McKinney. In 1999 the ship was scuttled off Atoll Cay, east of Nassau (or 1994), split in half, and lays on its side as a dive attraction. In 1988 the Popov brothers and their Island Expedition team featured the boat in their books. The McKinney brothers are said to also have owned the motor mailboat *Jeleta*, also of Europe, in 1988. From Lovely Bay Acklins own a liquor retail establishment on Wulff Road, Nassau

The *Lady Mathilda* (believed to have been the second *Lady Mathilda*) began service in 1998 to Acklins, Crooked, Mayaguana, and Inagua. She Was named after Eddins Taylor's mother, also known as Tilly. The steel, 135-foot ship was built by Russell Portier Shipyard in Chauvin, Louisiana, and purchased by Nathaniel Bruce Taylors' Pirate's Well Investments. One captain was Nigel Davis; in December of 2010 the vessel sustained a minor fire at Potter's Cay, and in October, 2012 her crew managed to fish a car out of Nassau Harbour. *Lady Mathilda* is still operating in 2020.

United Star served the southern islands from 1999 to 2009. At 178 feet long and 498 tons, the Ro-Ro ship was built by Russell Portier Shipyard in Chauvin, Louisiana in 1999. Her Bahamas buyer was Captain Tom Hanna, d/b/a Ro-Ro Co., and Carib-USA. One captain was Rodney Miller, in 2010. This ship was in a fatal collision with *Sea Hauler* in 2003. She is listed serving Acklins and southern islands to 2009. The *Lady Rosalind I* began in 2002, going to North Andros, San Salvador, Mayaguana, and Inagua. Her previous names included *John F. Walker, Jr., G. W. Pierce, Fugro I,* and *Offshore Venture*. She was built *OMS Maverick* by Halter Marine Chickasaw, Alabama in 1967. Weighing 391 tons of steel and measuring 158 feet, *Lady Rosalind I* is owned by the Pirate's Well Investments, Taylor Corporation. Captains included Willie Wilson, V. H. Black, and crew Jairo Osorno Camacho. The ship is still operating in 2020.

Lady Rosalind II began hauling the mail in 2006 to North Andros. She is 498 tons of steel, 198 feet long, and constructed by Portier Shipyard in Chauvin, Louisiana in 2006. Named for Eddins Bruce Taylor's wife, the ship's owners are Pirate's Well Investments, and Taylor Corporation. Captains included Eddins Taylor, Gifford Johnson, V. H. Black, and she is still operating in 2020. The motor ship *Trans Cargo II* sailed to Mayaguana with the mails in 2014, replacing the *Lady Rosalind*, 1987-1997, and *Marcella III*, 1997-2014. She was built by Mickon Shipbuilders in Singapore in 1986, and is 1,015 tons of steel and 191 feet long. *Trans Cargo II*'s owners are Pirate's Well Investments, and Taylors Corporation, and her recent captain is David Hyde, originally of Roatan. If one looks carefully on the transom, you will see Arabic script where the ship names are. That is because they Taylors and Captain Hyde delivered her from Egypt, anticipating fulfilling a government contract, which ultimately a competitor from Acklins won instead. Nevertheless, *Trans Cargo II* is still operating, mainly as a substitute vessel along various routes as the Potter's Cay dockmaster, the government, and other operators' needs dictate.

The offshore supply vessel (OSV) *President Taylor* joined the mailboat fleet in 2017 to perform the Mayaguana, Inagua, San Salvador, and Cat Island runs for the Taylor Corporation. Her prior name was *Seabulk Carmen* from 2013, and before that *C/Centurion* from 2005. Candies Shipbuilders of Houma, Louisiana built her in 1998, of steel, weighing 824 tons, and being 174 feet in length. Pirate's Well Investments are another Taylor family ownership vehicle, and she is commanded by David Hyde, originally of Roatan. In Betsy Bay, near Pirate's Well, the flat-bottom boat has to put the bow into a shallow inlet cut from the rock at high tide, and rests on the bottom while discharging.

Crooked Island, Acklins Island, Long Cay (Fortune Island)

MICAL stands for Mayaguana, Inagua, Crooked Island and Long Cay. Of those, only Crooked Island and Acklins, perhaps occasionally small Albert Town on Long Cay or Fortune Island, are treated. Acklins has 150 square miles and roughly 555 persons, with Crooked Island, connected by short ferry ride, having 330 persons in 57 square miles. Long Cay or Fortune Island is barely a shadow of the former self, which had a cathedral, major international post office, for thousands of Bahamian stevedores all throughout the Caribbean with major German, British, and other European shipping lines, and two communities with a police force. Now the eight square miles host less than 30 persons. So, taken as a whole, from Castle Island and Salinas Point to Landrail and Bird Rock and from Colonel Hill to Albert Towns' Batelco station, there are roughly 215 square miles utilized by around 900 inhabitants.

Because the communities basically surround a large bowl or multi-mile, flamingo-filled cauldron of shallow water which makes the bow-ramp Ro-Ro model of mailboat very useful in Spring Point and on Crooked Island as well. It is fascinating to watch a mailboat struggle across the shallows in low tide, throwing up a churn of yellowish sand visible from the air as the ship's propellers send particles into the water column in what Bahamian mariners call a "rub." Also, the places where the struggled up the shallows in the past can be seen in streaks across the banks, leaving markers of sorts, similar to the turtle grass between Spanish Wells, mainland Eleuthera, and Gun Point.

Captain Hannah has gone from the *United* and *Sea* series (i.e. *United Spirit* or *Sea Spirit*) naming conventions to more obtuse hat-tips to members of his family, which are almost encoded, like *Tolyn, K.C.T.*, and *VI Nais*. Captains on this run have mysteriously often included the same man, Captain Hanna, on multiple boats on the same days on the same weekly schedule; in fact, he has an experienced and reliable team of master mariners in his employ. Captain Fisher was followed in the 1800s on the government contract by William G. Fulford, Daniel Gibson, Leroy Ferguson, Arlington E. Farquharson in the 1960s, and his brother Nevis Farquharson, Nigel Davis, and of course the indefatigable Captain Thomas Hanna of Acklins himself.

Long Cay, also known as Fortune Island, to the south of Crooked Island, has perhaps the longest history of handling mail from Europe and North America, as it was a trans-shipment point for mail and stevedores for vessels entering and leaving the Caribbean via the *Windward Passage* in the days of sail as well as steam. Particularly British mail vessels and German liners would call there until the First World War and beyond.

The armed schooner *Mary & Susan* connected the mails between Crooked Island and Long Cay aka Fortune Island, starting September, 1804 up until 1812. She was built of wood and chartered by the government, who appointed Captain Fisher to command her. In January of 1805 the first mailboat named *Nassau*, set out for

Crooked Island, Long Cay aka Fortune Island, and served the route until 1812. The wooden schooner was chartered by H.M. Government from James Edgecombe Gibson. This schooner is not to be confused with either the larger government steamship *Nassau*, which was a tender of the 1960s, nor former *Spey Royal*, 1931 to 1940. Then in February, 1812 the wooden felucca named *John Bull* set off for Crooked and Fortune Islands, up until 1820. Also chartered by H.M. Government, the captain was William G. Fulford.

In January, 1821 the wooden schooner named *Dash* joined the route to Fortune and Crooked islands, even going as far as the Turks & Caicos up to the 1830s. She was government-chartered, and met her fate in 1858 when it beached off Clarence Town, Long Island. Although salvaged, *Dash* was delisted, her commercial career over. The wooden sailing schooner *Paragon* substituted in for the *Dash* from 1821 on the Crooked and Fortune islands run, and was also on government charter and de-listed after 1858. The wooden schooner named *Rising Sun* served Crooked Island and Fortune Island from April, 1835 up until the late-1840s. On government charter, she too is not listed after 1858. One of the few steel steam ships in the Bahamian mail service, the SS *Corsica* entered the market in 1865, mostly calling in Nassau with carried mail from overseas to Bahamas dispersal points. Although she was not on the dedicated inter-island mailboat service, philatelists include her in the 1800's fleet as an exception worth citing.

The schooner *Pelican* served only Long Cay, aka Fortune Island, starting in 1894. Built in the Bahamas of wood at 14 tons and owned by Daniel D. Sargent of Inagua, the vessel was registered in 1895 registry, yet not the following year, in 1896. The sloop *Return* called at Fortune Island only, starting in 1894. She is not to be confused with the 12-tonner built in Cherokee Sound, in 1929 owned by James E. Seymour of Nassau. In 1906 owner W. J. Pinder chartered out his vessel for the vessel *Raven* for the San Salvador route, then in 1908 it was transferred to the *Hazel Dell*.

The two-masted schooner *Hazel Dell* served Crooked Island District from 1920 to 1960, however her earlier career covered High Rock, Golden Grove, Smith's Point, Eight Mile Rock, Settlement Point, and Sweeting's Cay in Grand Bahama, as well as southwest Abaco and San Salvador. She was built in Bimini in 1901 out of wood and weighed 28 tons with 50 feet on deck, had an 18-foot beam, and six feet of depth. She was owned by W. J. Pinder in 1908, Ellis O. Burnside in 1920, and F. G. Deleveaux of Crooked Island as the *Hazel* which caught fire and sank in 1960. Among books and articles featuring this boat which covered the breadth of the Bahamas was Amelia Dorothy Defries, *In A Forgotten Colony,* published by the *Nassau Guardian*, in 1916. Upon her loss in 1960, the owner petitioned the government for recompense.

The motor vessel *Lillian* began serving Crooked Island from 1963, then Inagua, Mayaguana, Fortune Island and Acklins into the 1970s. She was built in 1944, was 347 tons of steel, and owned by the Windward Shipping Company. Her captains included Arlington E. Farquharson and his brother Nevis Farquharson, in the 1960s. The vessel was sold in 1972 and became the *Sealane V*. The motor mailboat *Lady Tasha* entered service in 1971 to Crooked, Mayaguana, and Acklins islands, up to the 1990s. Also known as *Abastash* before 1973, her steel weighed over 45 tons. One of her captains was Daniel Gibson. Sometime after 2010, she was partially sunk at busy Potter's Cay, taking up valuable space, and so around 2017 she was raised and towed to the southwestern end of Arawak Cay. She lay there for several months until towed to deep water and sunk off New Providence, possibly by the government as part of wreck-removal efforts.

The *Sea Salvor* sailed for Crooked and Acklins islands from 1972, though under different ownership she served the Bahamas from 1947, for example calling at Long Island and Inagua starting in 1966. *Sea Salvor* began in Neponset, outside Boston, in 1943 when built by George Lawley & Son, out of steel, with a length of 164 feet and 388 gross tons weight. Up until 1947 she was in the US Navy as patrol craft USS *PC-464*. In January, 1947 the A. G. Schoonake Company in New York purchased her and sent her to Nassau where Symonette Shipyards converted her to a salvage vessel renamed *Sea Salvor* from 1947 to 1972. She was then acquired in 1972 by the Freedom Shipping Company in the Bahamas, converted to a mailboat, and renamed *New Day* until 1985. Although her license was renewed in 1973 it was inactive by the mid-1980s. The *San Salvador Express* was later renamed *New Day II*.

The motor vessel *Commonwealth* sailed to Crooked and Acklins islands from 1975 to 1990. She was built in 1956 of steel and weighed 134 tons and was once named *State Star* and owned by Windward Shipping Company. Her captains Arlington E. Farquharson and Nevis Farquharson; the ship traded to about 1993. The motor mailboat *Windward Express* sailed for Acklins, Crooked, Long Cay, Mayaguana and Inagua between 1988 and 2007. The steel ship was 95 tons and owned by the Windward Shipping Company. Her captains included Leroy Ferguson, Arlington and Nevis Farquharson. *Windward Express* is cited in government lists in 1988, *Frommer's* in 1989, 1999, 2005, and 2006 going to the southern islands, after which it became inactive.

The *Lady Mathilda* began serving Crooked Island in 1989, as well as Mayaguana, Acklins, and Inagua up to 1998. This is the first *Lady Mathilda*, named for Eddins Taylor's mother Tilly. Pirate's Well Investments owned this wooden vessel, and Nigel Davis was a captain, as were Taylors. She is listed in the press serving Crooked Island in 1992, and begin fitted with twin diesel engines. The motor vessel *Jeleta* started serving Acklins and Inagua, then southern Long Island from around 1990. She was built by Apol A., Scheepswerf C.V. of Wirdum, the Netherlands in 1965, being 330 tons of steel and 152 feet long. *Jeleta* was owned by Trans-Bahama Shipping Ltd., Mail & Ferry Services, MVBS, under George McKinney and his brothers, from Lovely Bay, Acklins, who owned a liquor store on Wulff Road. In 1999 she was scuttled off Atoll

Cay, east of Nassau, split in half, on its side. She is owned by the same owner as *Miss BJ*, and featured in *Island Expedition* books of 1988.

The *Sea Spirit II* entered service for Tom Hanna's fleet in 1999, serving Acklins, Long Cay, and southern Long Island, up to 2011, when she was renamed *United Spirit*. The Ro-Ro vessel was built by Russell Portier Shipyard, Chauvin, Louisiana, in 1999 and is 498 tons of steel and 167 feet long. Captain Thomas Hanna is the owner, d/b/a Ro-Ro Co., Carib-USA. In 2011 she grounded and was abandoned off Long Island, however a vessel named *Sea Spirit* was still on the mailboat schedule in September, 2018. The same physical ship under the new name *United Spirit* then served Acklins, Crooked Island, Mayaguana, Matthew Town, Inagua from 2011. One of her captains was Tom Hanna, another was Capt. Rodney Miller for RoRo Co., Carib-USA. Since sold, the ship is now *Princess Samiah II*, flag of Togo, West Africa, trading in the Virgin Islands and Caribbean.

The *VI Nais* began its service to Cat Island in 2007, adding Acklins and Crooked Island. She was built that year by Russell Portier Shipyard in Chauvin, Louisiana, as were at least five of the Tom Hanna fleet. A modern landing-craft ship of the Ro-Ro type, she docks in the northwest corner of Potter's Cay, weights 487 tons, and is 190 feet long. The owners, headquartered on Soldier Road, Nassau, are the Ro-Ro Company and Carib-USA, and she is still operating in 2020, with good air conditioning, many long benches for sleep, and direct access to the galley and heads on the same level, though squeezing through rolling stock to get to accommodations can be a challenge.

The steel Ro-Ro landing craft *Sea Spirit* initiated its mail service to Acklins, Long Cay, and southern Long Island in 2011. Her owner is Thomas Hanna, Ro-Ro Company, and Carib-USA. Though the ship is still in service, because *Sea Spirit II* wrecked in 2011, it can be confusing. *Tolyn* began hauling mail to Rum Cay, San Salvador, Long Island from 2017 to 2018, after it was sold from the Taylors, who operated her as *Lady Emerald* from 2003 to 2017. Finally (perhaps), in 2018 the ship became *The Daybreak* under the ownership of Eleutheran Quincy Sawyer, from 2018 to present. A steel ship of 150 feet length, her owners as *Tolyn* were Captain Tom Hanna, d/b/a Ro-Ro Company, and Carib-USA of Nassau.

Inagua

Great Inagua is 375 miles from Nassau, the population there, even with an impressive saltworks and a light house with a hand-wound Fresnel lens, is just over 900, on an island of 648 square miles with many fascinating fauna, including nesting flamingos to admire. Serving this community which is closer to Haiti and Cuba than most Bahamian ports, have been over 20 mailboats in the past 150 years, starting with government vessels including in 1849 the *Palestine*, which began its mail route to Inagua, San Salvador, Little Exuma, Long Island, Rum Cay, Crooked Island, Long Cay, Acklins, and Mayaguana, up to 1866. The wooden vessel was 35 tons and registered to Turks Island, Turks and Caicos. In 1861 her owners were His Majesty's Government, in 1850 Cunningham and Bain, and in 1851 she was owned by a Mr. Williams. In the hurricane of September, 1866 the *Palestine* was wrecked with all hands in Sapodilla Bay, Providenciales, Turks. The government-chartered schooner *Experiment* provided mail service to Inagua and the "southern, windward islands" (Mayaguana, Acklins, Crooked islands, Long Cay) from April of 1852 to July of 1853, and then later from 1858 to 1862. She was built of wood in 1898 and weighed 29 tons. In 1862 *Experiment* replaced *Palestine* on some routes, and was in turn, replaced by *Electric* on others the same year.

From July, 1853 the schooner *Union* replaced the *Experiment* for a year on the route to Inagua and the southern, windwards. She was built with a wooden hull in 1853 and weighed 17 tons. She was chartered by H.M. Government and in July of 1854 was replaced by the *President*, and broken up in 1869. The 42-ton schooner *President* entered the Inagua and southern windwards route from July to August of 1854. She was built on Grand Turk, Turks and Caicos in 1853 of wood and weighed 42 tons. Her owner was J. H. Symonette of Nassau, who chartered her to the government, and the schooner was still listed in government service to 1870. The *Electric* served Inagua and southern, windwards from 1865 to 1866. Built in Abaco in 1855, she was 50 tons and built of wood. Her owners include John Smith and Mott Johnson of Nassau, who chartered her to the government. In 1862 the schooner replaced the *Experiment*, and in 1866 was replaced by the *Amelia Ann*. Sold to interests in Jamaica in 1890, she was still listed to 1900.

The schooner *Eugene* covered Inagua and southern windwards from July to August, 1865, as a substitute for the *Electric* on charter to the government. *Eugene* was built of wood in 1864 and weighed 54 tons. The schooner *Amelia Ann* was really an Imperial Lighthouse Service tender which replaced the *Electric* from 1867 to 1868 served Inagua and the southern windwards with mail. Also known as *Amelia, Alelia Ann Findlay*, the boat was constructed of wood in 1863 and was 10 tons. She is listed as "captured," in 1868.

The schooner *Jane* entered mail service to Inagua and southern windwards from 1875 to June, 1876, then again from 1877 to 1878). Although replaced by the *Arabella* in 1876, the *Jane* resumed mailboat duties between 1877 and 1878. She was built in 1895 of wood and was 44 tons. Her owners were John Saunders of Nassau.

In June of 1876 the schooner *Arabella* covered the Inagua and southern windwards mail route, but only until December of the same year. She was built of 15 tons, of wood, and chartered by H.M. Government. From June to December of 1877 the *Arabella* was a substitute for *Jane*. In 1883 the schooner *Argosy* began its service to Inagua, Cat Island, Long Island, Rum Cay, and Acklins, for two years up to 1885. She was built of wood in 1883 of 78 tons, and owned by Robert H. Sawyer of Nassau. She replaced, or supplemented, the *Carleton* in 1883, and was pushed out by the *Eastern Queen* in 1895 when that vessel entered the route to Rum Cay, Long Cay Fortune Island, and Inagua. The schooner *Carleton* sailed for Inagua and the windwards with the mail from 1883. She was built of wood in Abaco in 1848 and weighed 69 tons. Her owner was Robert H. Sawyer of Nassau. *Carleton* was replaced by the *Osborne* in December of 1883, and the *Argosy* shared the same route for some time.

The schooner *Osborne* sailed for Inagua and the southern, windwards starting in December of 1883. She was built to 24 tons burthen of wood in 1877 and owned by Francis Bullard of Nassau. At first she substituted for *Carleton* before the *Argosy* displaced her in 1883. The schooner *Eastern Queen* became the Inagua mailboat, also calling at Cat Island, Long Island, Rum Cay, and Acklins, beginning in 1895. Constructed of wood in 1882, she was 38 tons and owned by Samuel O. Pinder of Nassau. *Eastern Queen* is featured in the influential study of the Bahamas, *Land of the Pink Pearl*, Powles, in 1888. In 1896 the steel steam ship SS *Antila* called on Inagua, Cat Island, Long Island, Rum Cay, Long Cay, and Acklins. The same year, 1896, the schooner *Tropic* set off from Nassau for Inagua, Cat Island, Long Island, Rum Cay, Long Cay, and Acklins, all the way to 1917, 21 years later. She was built in Nassau of wood in 1884 and 23 tons. Her owners were Hilton C. Albury of Nassau. Although featured in the 1915 vessel registry, *Tropic* was not registered in 1917.

The schooner *Siren* first sailed for Inagua in 1898, then Cat Island, Long Island, Rum Cay, Long Cay, and Acklins Island. She was built of wood in Nassau in 1887 and weighed 32 tons. Her owner was Lewis Taylor of Nassau. She made just two trips, and only appears on the ship registry in 1890. The schooner *Sarah E. Douglass* sailed for Inagua, Cat Island, Long Island, San Salvador, Crooked Island, and Long Cay in 1906 then until 1909. Built of wood in 1859, she was 90 tons and owned by W. J. Pinder in 1907, and Jason W. Culmer of Nassau in 1890. In 1908 the owners and commissioners thanked the German Hamburg American Steamship Line for bringing mails to Long Cay free of charge from New York, Haiti, and Jamaica.

The motor vessel *Nonesuch* served Inagua from 1926, then Cat Island, Long Island, Rum Cay, Long Cay, and Acklins, up to 1928. She served Mayaguana beyond 1933. She was built in 1880 of 21 tons and owned by Frederick Black, grandfather to the modern Taylors, in Mayaguana in 1930, James R. C. Young of Nassau in 1920. The commissioner reports that 1928: "gave good service, and was damaged, recent hurricane." From September to October she was substituted by a "small craft belonging to Acklins," possibly Rev. Collie of Hard Hill's schooner *Go On*. In 1920 a vessel of the same name is listed at 47 tons; a sloop built in 1889. Another *Nonesuch* of 10 tons was owned by Robert Woodside of Staniard Creek, Andros. The sloop *Evangeline* served Inagua and Rum Cay, Long Island, Long Acklins, Long Island and Cat Island starting in 1947. She was constructed of wood in 1947 and subsidized for mailboat service under the Out Islands Department.

The second motor tug *Nassau* served as a mailboat in 1947 to Inagua, Cat Island, Long Island, Rum Cay, Long Cay, and Acklins up until 1948. She was built in New York of wood in 1878, was 100 tons and 91 feet long. Her Bahamian owner was John S. Darling, of Nassau in 1947. Nassau only substituted in for three months, ending on 31 March, 1948, when the *Alice Mabel* owned by Sir George Roberts took its place. The motor vessel *Eastern Prince* joined the Inagua route in 1960, then Mayaguana, Long Cay, Acklins, and Crooked Island up to 1974. She was built of wood and owned by Windward Shipping Company, with brothers Arlington E. Farquharson and Nevis Farquharson serving as captains in the 1960s. Her schedule was listed in the 1975 Bahama Out Islands Association leaflet, per *Selkirk Enterprise*, in Manitoba, Canada on 3 September, 1975. The *Bahama Land* got off to a rocky start in 1972 when it sailed for Inagua and Long Island. She suffered engine failures at the height of a shortage and holidays, so that the Member of Parliament, J. R. Ford sequestered the Government tender M/V *Eastore* for an urgent Christmas voyage. She was built in 1966 and was not long in service.

The *New Day II* served Long Island from 1972 and Inagua from 1973 to 1985. Her other names included USS *LCS(L) 120-130*, and *San Salvador Express*. George P. Lawley and Sons of Neponset, outside Boston built her in 1943 at 388 tons and 164 feet. Owners were Freedom Shipping Company, said to be from Acklins, per Joseph Moxey. In 1972 *New Day* was destroyed by fire, and replaced by *Sea Salvor*. Then, the vessel which has been named *San Salvador Express* was renamed *New Day II*, and its license renewed 1973, inactive after 1985. The first *San Salvador Express* served Long Island and Inagua from 1971.

Family-Owned Mailboat Dynasties

Owners with multiple vessels: Albury: 5, Archer: 5, Bahamas Ferries: 4, Bethels: 4, Bozozog: 2, Brice: 2, Farrington: 3, Griffin: 3, H. M. Government: 16, Hanna (for Windward Shipping): 5, Johnson: 3, Kelly: 3, Knowles: 2, Levy: 2, McKinney: 2, Moxey: 3, Munroe: 5, Musgrove: 5, North Cat Island Cooperative Society: 3, Pinders: 13, Roberts (not Sir George): 2, Russell: 3, Saunders: 4, Sawyer: 7, Simms: 3, Smith: 6, Sweeting: 5, Symonette: 9, Weech: 3, Wilkinson: 2, Wilson: 3, Young: 2.

Family names: 32, vessels owned: *139*

Owners with one vessel: ACL Ltd., Andrews, Armsden, Arteaga, Big Yard Shipping, *Bimini Mack* Association, Bone, Bowleg, Bowles, Brown, Brownrigg, Bullard, Burnside, Burrows, Carstairs, Cleare, Cox, Culmer, Curry, Darling, Duncombe, Dupuch, Elden, *Eleuthera Express*, Exuma Shipping & Trading Co., Forde, Fox, George, Gibson, Gray, Hart, Hepburn, Higgs, Hodgkins, Isaacs, King, Levarity, Macarthy, Malone, Maura, Maycock, McCormack, Menendry, Morris, Munnings, Newton, Northern Eleuthera Shipping Co., Ogilvie, Pearce, Pintard, Poitier, Pritchard, Sargent, South Eleuthera Shipping Co., Thompson, Wells, Wilchombe, and Woodside:

Total: *58*

Four Largest Fleets:

    Dean: *14*
    Hanna: *10*
    Roberts: *18*
    Taylor: *29* –
    Totals: 71
    No known owners: *69*

    Total: *340*

Roberts Family Dynasty

Sir George William Kelly Roberts, KT, CBE, lived between 19 July, 1906 and 24 June, 1964. During that time – particularly in the late 1920s – he transformed and standardized the subsidization of mailboats as well as financed the construction and operation of at least eight vessels. In order of year built they were the *Alice Mabel* (purchased in 1923, when he was 17), *Richard Campbell* (1937), *Gary Roberts* (1940), *Air Pheasant* (1942), *Drake* (1942), *Noel Roberts* (194), *Air Swift* (1943), and the *Captain Roberts* (1945). According to Anne and Jim Lawlor in their book, *The Harbour Island Story*, they were owned under the holding company *Richard Campbell* Limited, located at the City Lumber Yard in Nassau. This is their story.

Sir George was born on Harbour Island, Eleuthera the son of Captain George Campbell and Nellie Maud Roberts, whose ancestors arrived from Bermuda with *the Eleutheran* adventurers in 1647. According to the Lawlors, as a young man George "sailed before the mast on the three-masted schooner *Bentley*, under his father before moving to Nassau at the age of 12. As a self-made man, he grew to own the City Lumber Yard…" He married Freda Genevieve Sawyer at Trinity Wesleyan Church in Nassau on 7 January, 1929, when he was 23. Together they had three sons: Richard Campbell (in 1929), Gary William Kelly (born 1934), and Noel Sawyer Roberts (in 1938). From the late 1950s the family residence was "Lucky Hill" on Eastern Road, near Dick's Point Road in eastern New Providence.

Sir George was active in politics and served in the House of Assembly from 1935 (aged 29) to 1955 and was a member of the Executive Council between 1946 and 1954. He led the Government between 1949 and 1954 and was president of the Legislative Council (LegCo) in 1954. He served briefly as the President of the Senate of the Bahamas, from January, 1964 until his death on 24 June of that year. On New Years' Day, 1958, he was awarded the Commander of the Most Excellent Order of the British Empire (C.B.E.) and knighted. He is buried on the grounds of the library named after him in his hometown of Dunmore Town, Harbour Island.

The sailing vessel *Alice Mabel* was a 47-ton schooner with more than one mast and an auxiliary motor. She was built in Marsh Harbour, Abaco in 1923. It is not known which islands the vessel served, though it is safe to assume that Eleuthera was among its ports of call. Richard and Susan Roberts say that one of her skippers was Captain John Carey. By 1940 the small ship was no longer listed in mercantile navy lists.

The *Richard Campbell* was built in Nassau in 1937 of wood. At 89 gross tons, she was 85.6 feet long, 16.3 feet wide and 8 feet deep. The vessel is described as a single-masted sailing sloop with an auxiliary motor. For ten years, until roughly 1947, she plied between Abaco, Miami, and Nassau. In *Islanders in the Stream*, Volume II, Craton and Saunders quote an account of the vessel in 1947 as a "rickety, cockroach-infested boat (nicknamed *Wretched Campbell*), with its Conchy Joe captain [Russell] and mate and all-black crew." According to author Kevin Griffin, the *Richard Campbell* was employed in "12-day voyages through the Out Islands."

The motor vessel *Gary Roberts* had two masts but was primarily propelled by a 100 horsepower Cooper-Bessemer diesel motor. She was 66 feet long, 16.5 feet wide and 7.2 feet deep. Weighing 59 gross tons, she was built in 1942 of wood by Earl and Gerald Johnson, family friends of Sir George's, in Harbour Island. She was named after the Roberts' son, Gary William Kelly. The Lawlors, in their history of Harbour Island, have collected a photo of the vessel.

The *Air Pheasant*, built of wood in 1942, was a sister ship to the *Drake* in as much as her dimensions were 110.8' long, 17' wide, and 6.5' deep. Constructed by Lauder's Marine Construction Co. in Stamford Connecticut in 1942 she had two General Motor's 1,540-horsepower engines, could make 21 knots, and weighed 148 tons. She was known as *USS PC 1015* (patrol craft) until 1942, then *USS SC-1015* (sub-chaser), and USCG *Air Pheasant* (WAVR-449) from 1945 to 1948. Presumably sold to the Bahamas in 1948, she replaced the *Monarch of Nassau* on the San Salvador mailboat run. Then it appears that Roberts chartered her to the Erickson brothers for their Morton Salt Company to serve Inagua. One of her captains, at least in 1964, was Anton Lockhart of Ragged Island, who was born in 1906. Tragically he lost his young wife, sister, and brother-in-law in a collision with the American freighter *Robert Luckenbach* off Castle Island on the 7 June, 1931. According to published reports, the *Air Pheasant* also served Fortune Island/Long Cay, Crooked Island, and Acklins in the 1950s and San Salvador in the 1970s. The ship was scrapped in 1982, signifying the end of a 44-year career in the islands.

The motor vessel *Drake* was built by Robinson Marine Construction in Benton Harbour Michigan in 1942 for the US Navy as USS *PC 541*, a patrol craft. Weighing 136 tons, she was 110.9' long, 17' wide, and 6.5' deep. Her twin 1,540 horsepower engines propelled the boat at an impressive 21 knots. After serving in the navy, the vessel went to the US Coast Guard between 1945 and 1948 when it went to a New York fishing company until 1954 then onto the Crosland Fish Company, based in Key West as the *Drake*. George Roberts purchased her in 1956 and put the vessel to use between Nassau, Rum Cay, and San Salvador in the south-eastern Bahamas. She traded through 1964 when she was mentioned in a *Holiday* magazine article. A vessel of similar dimensions but named *Bahamas Drake* is listed as having wrecked and sunk off the Exuma chain on the 29 December, 1968. Probably this was the *Drake*.

Earl and Gerald Johnson in Harbour Island built the *Noel Roberts* of wood in 1943. She was named after George and Freda Roberts' son, Noel, who went on to represent Harbour Island in parliament between 1972 and 1977, and then from 1987 to 1997. Immediately upon being launched with considerable fanfare alongside the Government Dock in Dunmore Town, the Symonette-owned former minesweeper HMS *BA 2*, built for the Royal Navy in WWII, towed her to Nassau to be fitted with an engine. In 1948, she is recorded by the *Kingston Gleaner* as having carried a load of lumber as far as Kingston Jamaica. In 1957, she was on the British mercantile marine lists, and was recorded as still trading in 1961. The vessel's final disposition is not known.

Thomas Knutson Shipbuilding of Halesite, New York, on the north shore of Long Island, built the *Air Swift* of wood in 1943. Her dimensions were the same as *Air Pheasant* and *Drake* (111' X 17' X 6.5'). Her original name until 1945 was USS *SC 1340*, then USCGC *WAVR 471 Air Swift* until 1948. A member of the shipbuilding Knutson family of Long Island, New York told this author an extraordinary anecdote. The Knutson family were enjoying a family vacation in either Eleuthera or Abaco in the 1970s when the patriarch's attention was immediately drawn to a run-down freighter in the harbour. He scrambled over to the *Air Swift*, hurried aboard, took out his penknife, and scraped away at an old metal placard buried up forward. It was the boat's nameplate (kind of a dog-tag for boats), and it confirmed that his family and he had indeed built her in distant Halesite during WWII, over 30 years before!

George Roberts purchased her in 1948, as she became an institution in the Bahamas, serving right up until the *Bahamas Daybreak* replaced her on the Harbour Island run in the 1970's. During the 1960s the vessel served Harbour Island and North Eleuthera. Kimberly King-Burns determined that after Sir George her owners were Carlyle Albury, David Curry, aka Old Socks, and a Doctor Maloney. Her final owner was Humphrey Percentie Sr. of Harbour Island. His son, Dr. Leatendore Percentie, writes that she was irreparably damaged in Nassau Harbour when "the boat broke off and got damaged during a freak storm in 1977." Once free of Potter's Cay it ended up elsewhere in Nassau Harbour. Another source places the loss during Hurricane David in 1979, and yet another report has her bones lying in Six Shilling Channel, east of Nassau, where many boats have wrecked.

Anne and Jim Lawlor chronicle the short life of Sir George's 111-foot motor vessel, *Captain Roberts*, named after his father, best. The boat was commissioned by Roberts and built of wood by Earl and Gerald Johnson in 1945. She was fitted with a Fairbanks Morse diesel motor. According to the Lawlors, "This was the third boat built for him in four years by Earl and Gerald Johnson. Unfortunately, in October, 1945, freakish winds destroyed a number of small boats on Harbour Island and the *Captain Roberts* was wrecked on its maiden voyage." According to the website wrecksite.eu, the location of the Captain Roberts' final resting place is near Great Isaac Light north of the Bimini Islands, suggesting she may have been on her way to or from Florida when wrecked.

Sir George Roberts is believed to have been a driving force behind An Act to Establish an Improved Inter-Insular Mail Service passed in August, 1948. It establishes that the "Governor may establish mail service between Nassau and the Out Islands." Roberts was a member of the Executive Council at that time. The influential Inter-Insular Mail Shipping Act of 1966, based on the 1948 act and the basis of legislation since, is largely credited to Roberts' efforts in the legislature. It standardized aspects of the carriage of mail, passengers and cargo within the Bahamas, as well as government subsidization of the fleet of mailboats, which carried them. According to the entrepreneur and ship-owner Craig Symonette, son of Sir Roland Symonette, "It was Sir George that designed the first MailBoat Subsidy Act...still in place to this day."

Roberts Fleet List:

Alice Mabel, to Abaco from 1923, *Monarch of Nassau*, to Cat Island from 1930 and Abaco from 1936, *Sir Charles Orr*, Eleuthera, 1930, *Richard Campbell*, Andros, 1937, *Midinette* and *Gary & William*, to Bimini starting 1938, Three Bays, Eleuthera, 1940, *Noel Roberts*, Harbour Island, 1943, *Captain Roberts*, Exumas, 1945, the *Rock Sound* and *Joyce Roberts*, Eleuthera, 1947, *Air Swift*, Harbour Island from 1948, *Air Pheasant*, to San Salvador from 1948, *Drake* to San Salvador, 1956, *Gary Roberts*, Long Island in 1957 and Exuma in 1960, and the *Wissama* to Andros in 1959.

Taylor Family Dynasty

The Taylor family's mailboat dynasty began in 1933 with Captain Fed and Mrs. mary jane black, of Pirate's Well, Mayaguana, which is a small community nestled in an expansive and beautiful bay on the northwest coast. Women in the Taylor family have been the inspiration of most of the Taylor vessels: *Marcella* for Eddins' late grandmother, *Lady Rosalind* for his late wife, and *Lady Mathilda* for the Taylor's mother, Mathilda "Tilly" Taylor. *Lady Emerald* is owned in the name of Maureen Patton, in honor of the late Rev. Gladstone Patton, Sr. An early family schooner, built in 1891 of 21 tons and registered to Mayaguana in 1936, was named *M. B.*, for Mary Black, Captain Fed's wife; another matriarch of the family was Stephanie Miller.

Captain Nathaniel Bruce Taylor, a nephew of Captain Fed Black, continued the family tradition of providing mail and passenger service to Mayaguana and beyond. He formed a company called Pirate's Well Investments and in 1962 purchased a 56-foot-long wooden mailboat named the *Cape Hatteras*. The boat, which was propelled by a 671 General Motors diesel engine, was built in the US in the 1950s. Under Captain Taylor's command she served Mayaguana from 1962 to 1968, when it was sold to fishermen in Spanish Wells, Eleuthera. She was Bahamian flag from 1962 until her unknown demise.

The next vessel that the patrician Taylor purchased he named the *Marcella*, or *Marcella I*. She was a 90-foot wooden cargo boat built in 1969 by shipwrights in Saint Augustine, Florida. Most of her superstructure was to accommodate passengers, though the vessel had a derrick located on the fore deck for cargo. She served both Mayaguana and nearby Andros from Nassau during a career lasting nearly 20 years. The captains were Nathaniel Bruce Taylor and his son Eddins. Late in 1987 she burned to the waterline in Salt Pond, Long Island and was a constructive total loss.

Nowadays ownership is split amicably between the Mailboat Company Ltd., with Elvin, Limas, and other family in control, and Pirate's Well Investments, with Eddins Bruce as head. Each have their own fleets and websites, however for the sake of this study are being treated as Taylor-derived entities and ownerships stemming from Fred Black. Captain Eddins is proud of the many "firsts" achieved by the family, including the first steel-built modern mailboat owned by a black-Bahamian family; the 170-foot *Marcella II* in 1972. The *Lady Mathilda* was another example of innovation, with 20 feet added, and the *Fiesta Mail* has offered live bands and movies for the Nassau – to Freeport overnight run. Of you stroll Potter's Cay and catch up with Eddins in person, he will show family portraits in the company office, and speak of Taylor family and affiliates having some hundred-plus years of ownership and operational experience with mailboats in the Bahamas. "Taylor Corporation are the biggest mail boat firm in the Bahamas, period," he states, and with two dozen vessels, this is accurate.

The family owned many vessels which were not categorized as mailboats, from the small trading schooner named *Cairo* built in the Turks and Caicos Islands around 1905. At 5 tons, the schooner was listed in 1935 as the property of Abraham Michael, of Matthew Town, Inagua. Another which Eddins calls his first boat was named *U. G. Dice* in the early 1960's, though it never plied the mail, and some vessels like *Trans Cargo II* is more of a bulk than a mail carrier and is often on charter, substituting in for mail when needed. *President Taylor* for example, has enough tanks to fill the gas stations on most Bahamian islands in one go. Captains who have made careers with the Taylors – on top of all the brothers, who are captains themselves – have been Bob Garroway of St. Vincent, Nigel Davis, Gifford Johnson, and David Hyde of Roatan, who helped delivery *Trans Cargo II* from Egypt and now runs the new arrival *President Taylor* to name a few.

Set in the far south-eastern Bahamas, Mayaguana has a population about 250 persons. Other families involved in mailboats and Taylor enterprises over the years have included the Williamsons and Higgins. The vessel which they purchased was named *Nonesuch*, and was 21 tons, and had two masts, making her a schooner. Built of wood in 1880, presumably in Abaco, her first owner was Benjamin W. Roberts of that island. Between 1900 and 1910 he sold her to William Henry Edgecombe of Andros, who then sold her to James R. C. Young of Nassau in about 1920.

According to Captain Fed Black's grandson, Captain Eddins Bruce Taylor, Black used the *Nonesuch* to carry freight and passengers between Nassau and Abrahams Bay and Pirate's Well, Mayaguana. This lasted less than a decade, and from 1940 the vessel no longer appears in the Mercantile Navy register. Another vessel they owned then was named *G. J. Wisdom*, built or owned by Jonathan J. Lockhart, of Ragged Island and registered up to at least 1935. Since then the Taylor family have commissioned or bought vessels made in Alabama, Louisiana, Florida, Singapore, China, Netherlands, and Germany. They have never stopped their entrepreneurial investments in the country's trade.

The *Marcella II* was built in Germany in 1956 of steel and was purchased by the Taylor family in about 1987. Less than a year later, in 1988, the vessel was severely damaged in a storm and became an artificial reef off Long Island, which still draws divers. According to Captain Eddins Taylor, this vessel was the first steel-hulled mailboat to be owned by black Bahamians. She began her career as the Wilhelmshaven, Germany-built *Jade* in 1959. The yard itself was named Jadewerft, or *Jade* works, and her hull was kept *Jade* green by the Taylors. In the Bahamas, the vessel served Freeport as well as Mayaguana and other island groups as the need arose. She was 364 tons and could carry 480 tons of cargo. Less than 10 feet deep she could steam at 8.5 knots. Her captain was Captain Limas Taylor, who presently commands the *Fiesta Mail*, also to Freeport.

Marcella III, ex-*Jade* but with the same green colour scheme, at Prince George's Dock, Nassau. Completed in Germany in 1959, she sailed from Europe to the Bahamas in 1981 and replaced the *Marcella II*, also owned and commanded by the Taylor family. Captain Limas Taylor skippered her to and from Freeport. She could carry 480 tons of cargo at 8.5 knots and was 9.2 feet deep.

This photo shows Captain Eddins Taylor purchasing the *Jade* in Germany in 1981, with the Bahamas flag showing proudly off her fantail in the right distance. She would go on to serve many years as a Bahamian mailboat as the *Marcella III*.

The Taylors purchased *Jade* in 1981 and traded it under the Bahamas flag under that name before naming her *Marcella III*. The Taylors sold her to Haiti early in the 21st century, and she became *Miss Eva I*, then *Michelda*, and is presently trading under the Bolivian flag in South America, some 55 years after her launch. With her low freeboard and extensive length, she was a familiar site to many along the Bahamian waterfront in the 1980s and 1990s. The Taylors sold her for further trading to Haitian interests, who then sold it to owners in the South American country of Bolivia, where she is still trading as the *Michelda*.

Next the Taylors purchased the *Miranda*, which was built in Delfzijl, Netherlands in 1966 as the *Geulborg*. The Taylor Corporation purchased her from the well-known ship-owning firm Wagenborg Shipping in 1977 and put the ship to work trading between Miami and the Turks & Caicos, serving Long Island, Exumas, and Mayaguana with mail services between 1977 and 1993. Her captain was Bob Garroway. Then the 176-foot-long, 399-ton ship was sold to Haitian buyers around 1993 and renamed the *Paradise Express*. Under new ownership, Honduran flag, and the name *Gilbert Sea*, the vessel was impounded, by US authorities, on the Miami River. Ultimately, in 2002, the ship was towed to sea 1.5 miles from Palm Beach Inlet and sunk as an artificial reef.

In 1998, the Russell Portier Shipyard in Chauvin, Louisiana, built the steel freighter, *Lady Mathilda*, and the Taylors purchased her. She is 135 feet long, having been extended from 110 feet some years ago. Her captain on the mailboat run to Acklins, Crooked Island, Inagua, and Mayaguana is Nigel Davis. She has twin engines and can carry as many as 70 passengers. In December, 2010, the ship had a minor fire while at Potter's Cay Dock, Nassau, and on 16 October, 2012 her crew fished an errant car from the harbour – its occupant was not found. Apparently, the hapless victim was manoeuvring his car on the unfamiliar dock in the dark and the vehicle plunged into the harbour. A good Samaritan made it into the car, but by that time it was empty of people. The roll-on, roll-off (Ro/Ro) landing craft *Trans Cargo II* was built at Mickon Shipbuilders in Singapore in 1986. In 1998 the Taylors purchased her from Egyptian owners, and with one of their nephews on board for the passage, had it delivered from the Mediterranean Sea to the Bahamas. The ship is 191 feet long, 46 feet wide, and 1,015 gross registered tons, with cargo capacity of 1,400 tons. She can also carry passengers. Her captain is David Hyde of Honduras. Like the *Lady Mathilda*, the ship had twin engines and twin propellers for redundant reliability.

Initially the ship had contracts for the Bahamas *Electric*ity Corporation (BEC) but after they failed, it was put to use carrying aggregate and sand from Freeport to Bimini, among other jobs. The *Lady Rosalind* was 156' long and built by Bollinger shipyards in Lockport, Louisiana. She was 233 gross tons and made of steel. The Taylors bought her in 1987 and she traded under Captain Limas Taylor to the southern Bahamas. Then in 1997 the vessel struck a rock and was damaged beyond repair. Halter Marine in Chickasaw, Alabama in 1987, built *Lady Rosalind I* as the *OMS Maverick*. The Taylors purchased her from sellers in Texas in 2002 and she serves North Andros from Nassau. At 391 gross tons, she is painted grey and has a large cargo deck astern of the wheelhouse. Her captains over the years have included Captain Willie Wilson and Captain V. H. Black. *Lady Rosalind II* was built by the Portier Shipyard in Louisiana in 2006 and presently serves North Andros from Nassau. She is 198 feet long, 43 feet wide and is 498 gross tons. Her captains have included Captain Eddins Taylor and Captain Gifford Johnson.

The largest of the Taylor Corporation and Pirate's Well Investments' fleet is the *Fiesta Mail*, which can carry up to 450 passengers between Nassau and the country's second largest city, Freeport. The ship is 228 feet long, 50 feet wide, and draws 11.5 feet. It is 2,485 gross tons, can speed at 12.5 knots, and carry 710 tons of cargo. With a cargo ramp at the stern it can carry rolling stock. Xinhe Shipbuilding of Tianjin built it in China in 2002. The owning entity is the Mailboat Company Ltd. of Nassau, which is run by Captain Elvin Taylor and an able team of family and staff. Not only does the *Fiesta Mail* carry freight and passengers to and from Freeport, but it calls at Port Everglades Florida as well. Overall the Taylor family – Captain Fed Black, Captain Nathaniel Bruce Taylor, Captain Limas Taylor, Captain Eddins Bruce Taylor, Captain Elvin Taylor, and other family members who help run their companies – have contribute a great deal to inter-island trade amongst particularly the southern Bahamas over the past 80 or so years. They certainly have already achieved – and continue to contribute a great deal to interisland trade in the Bahamas.

Taylor Fleet List:

Siren began the Taylor dynasty's cooperative fleet ownership with the Williamsons and Blacks at Pirate's Well, Mayaguana in 1989, followed by the *Nonesuch*, which also served Inagua, but starting in 1926. These fifteen Taylor-controlled vessels served their home island of Mayaguana: *Wisdom M.,* 1925, *Nonesuch*, 1933, *ML 371*, 1946, *Frecil,* 1951, *Silver King*, 1955, *Mayaguana Queen*, 1960, *River Queen*, 1962, *Cape Hatteras*, 1962, *Marcella* 2nd, 1968, *Lady Rosalind 1st*, 1986, *Lady Mathilda*, 1998, *Lady Rosalind I*, 2002, *Lady Rosalind II*, 2006, *Trans Cargo II*, 2014, and the *President Taylor*, starting in 2017.

Their three boats serving Grand Bahama have been *Marcella II* in 1972, *Marcella III*, 1981, *Fiesta Mail* from 2002, and *Cape Mail*, from 2017. *Lady Mathilda* served Crooked and Acklins since 1989, *Marcella 1st* carried mail to Andros from 1968, and *Lady Eddina* Cat Island since 1969, with the *Miranda* going to Long Island since 1978. San Salvador has had the mail carried to it by Taylor-owned or controlled vessels since 1981, when *Treasure Lady* began, followed by *Maxine* in 1988, *Lady Frances* (with the Patton family), since 1989, and *Lady Emerald* in 2003.

Dean Family Dynasty

Captain Ernest Alexander Dean was born the son of a fishing boat captain in 1915 in Sandy Point, Abaco. His parents were James Alexander Dean (1889-1966) and Leah Hunt Dean (1886-1923) who died when Ernest was a boy of eight years. His father's fishing smack was a two-master named *Champion* and he had a part ownership interest in the vessel. At the time, Sandy Point was not connected with other communities in Abaco except by the sea and the people of the small settlement eked out their existence by fishing and sustenance farming. A year after his mother's death, at age nine, Ernest was sent to assist the lighthouse keeper of Cay Sal Light in far southern Bahamas, bordering Cuba. In exchange, the boy would learn to read and write, as the keeper, Chatham Albury, had educated Ernest's uncle the same way.

At the age of 14 Ernest served about his father's schooner, the *Champion*, and by 17 the young man was in command. He would remain a captain – and very much a community leader – since, and until his death in the early 2000s. Much of the material of this article is drawn from his autobiography entitled *Island Captain*, co-written by Gary W. Woodcock and published by White Sound Press in 1997. Ernest first met Eula Clarke of Cherokee Sound when he was 18, in about 1933. She was the daughter of Wilfred and *Lillian* Clarke. They were married on 19 November, 1936, a union that would last until her death almost 60 years later. The wedding had to wait until Ernest had built them a house next to his father's on West Bay Street, Sandy Point. Together they kept a shop – or rather she kept a shop, as he was mostly at sea – called E. and E. Grocery and Dry Goods, the motto of which was – and is – "all under one roof."

A home wasn't the only thing that Captain Ernest built with his hands – in order to enter the mail freighting business, he spent three years hand crafting, mostly alone, a 35-foot sailing vessel named *Captain Dean* after his father, himself, and his infant sons. Begun in 1949 and not launched until February, 1951, the boat was made from hand-hewn pine from the pine fields as far afield as Hole-in-the-Wall Light and madeira and dogwood roots from Gorda Cay. The roots of these hardwoods had to be dug out by hand, and when found unsuitable for the joinery required, were rejected. He hand-cut the keel in the forest then towed it with a small dingy back to Sandy Point from Cross Harbour, sometimes drifting windless for hours, other times tacking against the wind. It was backbreaking work and only someone gifted with true determination would have completed it. With as much help from local craftsmen as they could afford, their income supplemented by Ernest's fishing, the couple achieved it.

Ernest cut and bent the sails and headed to Nassau to convince the Colonial Secretary in charge of mailboats – a Bahamian – that he deserved a mail contract to serve Sandy Point, Moore's Island, and the Berry Islands. At the time, there was no mail service to those small communities, which were cut off on the landward side by a lack of reliable roads. The one mariner, who had tried, Charles Sawyer from Marsh Harbour, in his quaintly named vessel *AutoGo*, had failed to make a go of it. But Dean persisted; pointing out that the fishermen who carried the mails provided unreliable and intermittent service and young families like his could go weeks without fresh milk from the capital for their children. Eventually the Commissioner relented, and the *Captain Dean* was put to work with the first mail service to southern Abaco and the Berry Islands. The craft was sloop-rigged, 30 feet at the keel, 40 feet on deck, with a 15-foot beam, and a five-foot draft. At first, she had no engines but relied instead on the Trade Winds to propel her.

The *Captain Dean* plied her trade, eventually adding Sweeting's Cay, Grand Bahama to a busy route. Her owner said, "She was built strong because my life and the lives of my crew depended on her." Carrying people rather than just cargo changed Captain Dean's perspective: "I couldn't think just about the money anymore. I was providing a service at reasonable fees and fares that these people hadn't had before. They were depending on me to keep going . . . Passengers ate what the crew ate, basically fishing boat food." He made room for six to eight passengers as well as four crewmembers to work the cargo and manage the vessel. As he wrote, "The government paid me only to carry the mail and set all the rates for freight and passage. Any passenger fares and freight charges were paid to me." Eventually an engine was added to the vessel. In 1953, Ernest Dean released the *Captain Dean* to his son James to go crawfishing with and purchased the larger, wooden-built *Margaret Rose*. She was five feet longer on deck (45 feet). The vessel was also sloop-rigged and had a Perkins diesel engine.

Dean only ran the *Margaret Rose* for "a few years," before trading up again, this time for the 112-foot motor ship *Clermont*, which had twin General Motors engines, but was "big, old, wooden, and leaky." By this point Dean was supplementing his income by hauling live crawfish from the various out-ports to Nassau. He also tried carrying live conch, but it didn't pay due to unscrupulous receivers who would take the conch on credit then refuse to pay, claiming the mollusks had died in his absence. The crawfish purchased at Butler's in Nassau was packed on ice. Dean rationalized that if the ice melted the crawfish were in cold water, but if refrigeration – which was more expensive – failed, then the creatures died and rotted. After less than a decade, in 1962, the *Clermont* sank off Abaco. Fortunately, there were no passengers and the two boats – with mailbags – managed to make it to shore. The *Captain Dean* then filled in as the mailboat again.

Right away Dean ordered the *Captain Dean II*, which was built by Johnny Albury and Walter Hatcher in Marsh Harbour. She was wooden with a 60-foot keel, a 14-foot beam, and five feet of draft. As well as the main deck where cargo was handled and stored, the passengers and crew quarters fitted out, etc. there was a top deck and pilothouse for the officers to steer the ship from. The boat was built entirely of native woods, 4 X 4 inch with two-inch planking. Rather than sails propulsion it came solely from two Perkins diesel engines. To have the hull fitted out with housing, Captain (later Senator) Sherwin Archer towed the hull behind his vessel the *Anita Queen*. Six years later, in 1968, the *Captain Dean II* caught fire and sank between the Berry Islands and Abaco. Two boats with seven people each, including a four-year-old and a two-year-old, survived a blustery night and were blown to Whale Cay, Berry Islands using the flat oar blades as sails. To Captain Dean's immense relief everyone survived to be flown to Nassau from Chub Cay.

Meanwhile Dean chartered the mailboat *Captain Moxey* to fulfil the mail run to Abaco and the Berry Islands – a common but exhausting practice of substituting boats that continues today. True to form Dean commissioned the *Captain Dean III* from St. Augustine, Florida. The lumber mills were closing and more men were returning to their communities, becoming fishermen or farmers, settling down and providing a growing market for building materials, fuel for their small boats, and obviously groceries. But the boatyards in Abaco were no longer building large vessels, hence the look westwards to the States for new-builds. The *Captain Dean III* was 90 feet on the keel, 18 feet wide, and had a five-foot draft. She could carry 16 passengers and had a large cargo capacity. She was wooden and had a large Caterpillar engine. Launched in 1969, she barely made it to Freeport because the seams had not properly soaked and sealed, but they made it. Plus, sawdust and wood chips from the construction clogged the bilges in the Gulf Stream, with a northern wind. Eventually, in 1973, the vessel was sold to interests in Bimini to provide mail service there and was sunk on the Mackey Shoal Buoy between Bimini and the Berry Islands.

The *Captain Dean IV* was in the works soon enough, and Dean's son, James, filled the mail run with his boat, the *Miss Dean*, in the interim. This ship was also made of wood and very similar to her predecessor, only stronger. Ernest Dean handed command of the *Captain Dean IV* over to his son John and in about 1977 the vessel was lost off Abaco in a storm. Fortunately, a mayday was sent and received by the US Coast Guard, who managed to hoist all 15 men and women aboard their helicopter. The ship was salvaged and towed to Miami where it was learned that several planks had been stove in. After that Captain Dean decided to build his next vessel, the *Captain Dean V*, of steel, and so he did. It would be "the first steel boat in all of the Bahamas designed and built just for the mail service." At that time, there were steel boats operating in the Bahamas, but most of them originated in Europe or the US Gulf. The *Captain Dean V* ran from 1979 to 1985, first under Ernest Dean then under John Dean. It sank at the Frederick Street dock in Nassau in a fire that claimed the life of Captain Stanford Curry. Her hulk was sold to Haitian interests.

Captain Ernest supplemented his runs to Abaco and the Berry Islands with calls at Freeport, Andros, and Cat Island when time permitted. On assurances that he would be given the mail contract he constructed the *Lady Eula*, named after his wife.

She was 90 feet on keel and had a single Caterpillar engine: "a very spacious and modern boat." Ernest's son John took over running her to Andros, Freeport, and Cat Island. At this time, there were political moves by individual island groups to have their "own" mailboat and skipper, as in from that island. Some resented being served by an Abaco skipper and entrepreneur. So, as he had done in Bimini, Captain Dean sold *Lady Eula* to interests in Cat Island. Due to a navigational error, the boat was run aground on San Salvador and pummeled on the coast. Finally, in 1986, Captain Dean modified the scope of his ambition and built a smaller vessel, the *Champion II* (after his father's fishing smack on which he had experienced his first command. She was 75 feet long – that way she could trade to the US without having to obtain a load line certificate required of longer vessels.

Decades after having built her by the sweat of his brow, Captain Dean and his daughter came upon her amongst a crowd of fishing craft at Potter's Cay Dock. It was 1993, 44 years after her keel was hewn in the Abaco pine fields. A main on board protested that the boat wasn't the *Captain Dean*, to which Ernest retorted, "This was the *Captain Dean*. I should know; I built her. Captain Dean's beloved wife Eula died in 1995. By then Ernest was a revered patriarch in the community of Sandy Point, and his opinion on matters such as the new high-speed ferry's terminus in his community was highly valued.

Dean's family continue to operate their store – providing for fishing and passenger vessels such as the *Nay Dean* and the *Mia Dean* throughout the Bahamas as well as to the US. In June of 1988 Governor-General Taylor presented Captain Dean with the Queen's Medal along with a Certificate of Honour. In 1995, he was invested with the British Empire Medal, again at Government House in Nassau, this time by Governor General Turnquest. Captain Dean learned of these awards via mailboat. When his wife's body was returned to Sandy Point from Nassau she was carried home – to the strains of the song *Amazing Grace* – across the bar to the community by their son's mailboat, the *Mia Dean*, which is still plying today.

Dean Fleet List:

The first five Dean Family vessels were on the Berry Islands and southwest Abaco run carved out by Ernest A. Dean: the *Captain Dean*, 1951, *Margaret Rose*, 1953, *Clermont*, 1962, *Captain Dean II*, 1963, *Captain Dean III*, 1969, *Captain Dean IV*, 1973, and *Captain Dean V*, in 1977. The *Lady Eula* went to Cat Island from 1978, *Nay Dean* to Long Island from 1985, *Champion II*, back to Berry Island and Abaco, 1986, *Mia Dean*, 1990, *Captain Gurth Dean*, also Berry Islands to Abaco, 1999, *Legacy*, 2002, Abaco, and their Ro-Ro *Legend II* has served Bimini since 2006 as well as other ports in Andros and Abaco.

Hanna Family Dynasty

From the early 1800s to 1911 members of the Hanna family owned ten vessels of various sizes in the Bahamas. The patriarch of the Hanna clan in the Bahamas appears to be John Hanna, who was born in Aberdeen Scotland and set sail for the Bahamas with three children, John, George, and James, with Edward Tobias being born on the voyage to the colony (his nickname was "Salt Water"). John senior went on to become a Member of the Houses of Parliament in the Bahamas. However, most of his descendants appear to have settled in the southern island of Acklins. J. Hanna was listed in the *Bahamas Gazette* as a slave owner on Crooked Island in 1799. One of his grandsons was named Thomas.

In 1868, William H. Hanna of Long Bay, Crooked Island owned a 19-ton schooner named *Augusta Justina*. In 1935, Castell Rivas Hanna of Pompey Bay, Acklins owned the sloop, *Delightful*. By 1911 five other Hannas from Acklins owned the locally built schooners *Barbara Ellen*, *Charm*, *Excite*, *Mary*, and *Sea Bird*. Their owners were John James, Philip Hannah, Conrad C., William H., and Thomas Benjamin Hanna. J. E. Hanna owned the schooner *Molly* registered to Grand Bahama. So, 100 years ago the family were already a vessel-owning dynasty, however modest some of the craft may have been (all were from 4 to 18 tons). Additionally, Alexander Hanna owned the 9-ton schooner *Venus* in Crooked Island. He was born in 1840 and passed away in Pompey Bay in 1923. Five years before Arthur Dion Hanna, later Governor General of the Bahamas, was born there.

While little is known about his exact connection to the Hannas of Acklins 200 years ago, Captain Thomas (Tom) Hanna has been a substantial ship owner in his own right, contributing significantly to inter-island as well as international seaborne trade between the Bahamas as well as Florida in the last quarter century. Capt. Hanna has owned at least five large vessels, most of them with bow-ramps called roll-on, roll-off, or Ro-Ro type which are shallow draft and well suited to cargo work to remote islands with limited infrastructure like Spring Point Acklins.

Over his career some of Hanna's trading firms have gone under but Hanna has managed to rebuild under new names, sometimes with the same vessel. His business has also survived one of the deadliest accidents in recent Bahamian history – the collision of *Sea Hauler* with the *United Star* on 3 August, 2003, resulting in four deaths, an amputation, and 25 injuries.

On a more positive note, following Hurricane Irene in August, 2011, his vessel, the *K.C.T.*, was one of the first on-scene to bring relief to Cat Island, and last year the *New G.*, which he designed, commissioned and had built, was introduced as the newest mailboat into the Bahamian fleet. Past vessels have included the *United Star* (served 1996-2007), *Sea Spirit II* (ex-*United Spirit*), *VI Nais*, *K.C.T.*, and *New G.* – all still operating today for Carib-USA Ship Lines Bahamas, Limited, of Nassau, with Hanna as president. Though not all are always strictly mailboats, they fill in for each other and provide essential services to the Bahamas and are Bahamian owned and operated.

The motor vessel *United Star* was built in 1996 by either Chauvin Shipbuilding or Portier Shipyard in Chauvin, Louisiana. She is 178' long, 36.5' wide, 417 gross tons, and 500 deadweight or cargo carrying tons. It is a Ro-Ro cargo vessel with accommodation and bridge aft made of steel. She was owned and operated in the Bahamas by Hanna from launch to 2007. The ship served the Bahamas on long-haul voyages to Mayaguana, Acklins, Crooked Island, Long Cay (Fortune Island), and Inagua. In 2003 her master was Capt. Rodney Miller. On the 3 August, 2003, she was in a severe collision with the *Sea Hauler* 14 miles south of Eleuthera. The Prime Minister termed the event a tragedy of national importance.

A committee was formed to investigate the incident. That report, through a government-appointed Wreck Commission, was presented to the Minister of Transport and Aviation on 4 January, 2005, however efforts by this author to unearth it have so far been unsuccessful. The incident led to a number of lawsuits, including at least nine civil actions filed in the Supreme Court against the government. In 2007, the *United Star* was sold the Compania Internacional Maritima (Coimar Transport) of Roatan, Honduras.

The *Sea Spirit II* was built as Russell Portier in 1999. In September, 2007, she was renamed the *United Spirit* for one year, or until August, 2008, when she became *Sea Spirit II*. She is 498 gross tons, 750 cargo-carrying tons, and was built of steel at Russell Portier Shipyard, Chauvin Louisiana. Hanna has been her owner since 2007, under different companies. She serves Acklins, Long Cay and southern Long Island, leaving Nassau on Tuesday afternoons. According to a *Tribune* article dated 7 February, 2011, Hanna was chased by a number of creditors and removed his vessel from the Bahamas Maritime Authority Registry in December, 2007, changing ownership from Carib-USA to Ro-Ro Company Ltd. Despite all this the vessel's trading seems to have been uninterrupted.

The boat *VI Nais* is 487 gross tons, 587 cargo-carrying tons; 190 feet long, powered by two Mitsubishi engines rated 927-horsepower at 1,400 rpm. The engine manufacturer stated that "provide owners with much better fuel consumption than the older engines that [Hanna] had been operating." They related that the engines are rated Tier 3 with the US Environmental Protection Agency. Portier Shipyard built her in 2007. The vessel serves North and South Cat Island, taking about 24 hours, and costing $60 each way. Over her career it appears she was also chartered to GG Shipping to ply from Florida to the Bahamas. For a time, her owners were MMS Ship Management of Palm Beach. Another owner was the Ro-Ro Company of Nassau. She is flagged to Panama.

Hanna's fourth vessel, the *K.C.T.*, is 165 feet long, powered by Mitsubishi engines rated 630-horsepower at 1,600 rpm. She serves Fresh Creek and Central Andros, spending Wednesday to Saturday there and Sunday to Tuesday in Nassau. She has also served Acklins at $90 each way for a 26-hour voyage every ten days. Since she was built in 2012, Hanna has owned it, under either the Ro-Ro or Carib-USA brands.

In August, 2011, the *K.C.T.* was one of the first ships to arrive in Cat Island with relief supplies from the Bank of the Bahamas following Hurricane Irene. *K.C.T.* brought "a container packed with love and crammed with proof that people cared. It bore furniture, paper goods, cleaning supplies, food, toiletries, clothing and more. The owners of the M/V *K.C.T.*, refusing to accept pay for shipping relief supplies." Furniture donated from homes in Lyford Cay was re-purposed for those in need on Cat Island.

The ship *New G.* is indeed new: it is 178' long, 40' wide, 10' (aft) to 6.6' deep forward. Her speed is 10.5 knots, and holds crew, 486 gross tons, 145 net tons, and 587 cargo tons. *New G.* is a landing craft type Ro-Ro vessel, flagged to Panama. She was built of steel in 2015 delivered in February. According to a Carib-USA spokesperson, *New G.* was "designed and engineered by Tom Hanna at a private shipyard." Officially her owners are the Consolidated Marine Group located in the United Building, Soldier Road, Nassau. As well as being a relief ship on other routes, the *New G.* serves North and South Cat Island, arriving in Nassau Monday, taking freight Tuesday, and leaving Wednesday evenings. We hope this vessel has an illustrious and successful career in the Bahamas.

Overall, Captain Thomas Hanna is an exemplar of those owners who adapt to changing market conditions, take immense risks by expending considerable funds for new-built ships in foreign yards (the US is a cabotage shipping market, protected from foreign competition, and thus an expensive place to build vessels), and providing innovative design solutions custom-fit for the Bahamas, as well as forward-looking propulsion technologies which are better for the environment and also more fuel-efficient.

Though Hanna's maritime roots can be traced to remote Pompey Bay Acklins (also the site of the largest Lucayan settlements in the country), and go back hundreds of years, including a dozen or so vessels, this entrepreneur's outlook is thoroughly modern, and practical. He has shown that even in legal and financial adversity he and his colleagues can re-invent themselves and survive, rising from the ashes. Hanna is one of the most private owners that this author has contacted, as in, not even a website. When we finally met the captain, he was busy cleaning up his company's small working area on western Potter's Cay with a forklift and by hand – in person, working alongside the officers and men from his ships.

Hanna Fleet List:

The ownership of mailboats by a Thomas B. Hanna of Acklins began in 1910 with the *Ghost,* which served Grand Bahama. Jumping ahead, the *United Star* covered Spring Point Acklins and Crooked from at least 1998, followed by *Sea Spirit II* in 1999, and the *United Spirit* the same year, the *VI Nais* in 2007 and the *Sea Spirit* from 2011, and the *Tolyn* for just a year in 2017 before she became the *Daybreak* under different owners. Beginning in 2005 the Ro-Ro ship *Lady Kathreina* served Andros, followed by *K.C.T.* in 2012, and the *New G.* carrying mail, passengers and freights to Cat Island from 2015.

Lisa J. II, formerly *Schokland*, in dry dock showing what a European mailboat looks like underneath the waterline. Courtesy of E. Schumacher, Shipspotters, and Bradford Marine, Freeport, Grand Bahama

Mailboat Photographs

The Captain of the *Lady Frances* leaving Black Point, Exuma. Built of steel in 1989 in the US Gulf, this 154-ton mailboat served the Exumas including Black Point, Port Nelson on Rum Cay, and Cockburn Town, San Salvador. She carried emergency supplies to Rum Cay and Cat Island in August, 2011 following a hurricane. From riding this vessel for a week or so, it is believed that the Captain is also a religious minister and brought spiritual inspiration as well as cargo for his shippers..

The captain of the *Legend* working in the wheelhouse with guest. The bow-ramp roll-on type ship was built in Alabama in 2006 and has traded within the Bahamas and back and forth to Florida since. Owned by Dean Shipping of Nassau. Listed for sale in 2015. Serves Green Turtle Cay, Abaco, Spanish Wells, and Great Harbour Cay, Berry Islands. Whether it has carried the government mail contract is unconfirmed, but *Legend* is well known in the Bahamas.

The Captain of the *Champion II* driving rolling cargo off his ship at Sandy Point, Abaco. This diminutive, 75-foot-long was intentionally built short in length so as to duck under US Coast Guard regulations requiring load lines, or Plimsoll marks, for ships calling at Florida. Finished in 1987 at St. Augustine Marine, she plied the route serving Bullocks Harbour in the Berry Islands, Hard Bargain on Moore's Island, Abaco and Sandy Point, its homeport and that of the Dean family. Note how very close the rear wheels are to slipping off!.

Captain Dean of *Legend* in his wheelhouse.

Captain Miller of the *United Star*, from Roatan Honduras, overseeing discharge near Spring Point, Acklins. This 170-foot ramp-type roll-on ship was built in Louisiana in 1996. She plied the long-haul routes for Mayaguana, Acklins, Crooked Island, Long Cay, and Inagua. Her owner has been Captain Tom Hanna under various iterations (Carib-USA), and both he and Rodney Miller have skippered her. In 2007, she was sold to Coimar Transport of Roatan, Honduras.

A captain casually chatting from the bridge with those ashore during cargo operations. On small vessels over short distances, starchy formality would not be the most effective long-term strategy for crew and customer retention. So captain and customer alike learn to roll with the punches and adapt to delays due to weather, propulsion overhaul, refrigeration maintenance, crew change, waiting for that last passenger or cargo delivery to arrive, whatever the case may be.

Captain Eddins Taylor, centre, and a trusted Taylor Corporation shipmaster, right, with the author. This was the day before Hurricane Matthew struck in late fall, 2016.

Captain Eddins Taylor, brother of Elvin and Limas Taylor, sons of Captain Nathaniel Bruce Taylor, who was son of Captain Fed Black, patriarch of the three-generation mailboat dynasty founded in remote Pirate's Well, on the northwest coast of Mayaguana, where the population of 90 persons is shrinking.

Sir George William Kelly Roberts, KT, CBE, 1906-1964, founder of the Roberts mailboat dynasty as a young man. Starting in the late 1920s after he established himself as a rising merchant in Nassau (where he arrived with seagoing experience at age 12), this Harbour Islander transformed and standardized the subsidization of mailboats. Starting at age 17, he financed the construction and operation of at least eight vessels. Though several of his children, notably his son Noel, a representative of North Eleuthera, continued to run his investments, the family is believed to be divested of their interest in mailboats. There is a library and a park named after Roberts in Dunmore Town, Harbour Island, where the featured bust rests. Prominent in national politics, Roberts is credited with crafting and guiding the posthumous passage of the *Inter-Insular Mail Shipping Act* of 1966

Richard Campbell Roberts, whose father founded the Roberts mailboat dynasty in Nassau and Harbour Island, and who named a mailboat the *Richard Campbell*. The Nassau Corporation, under which most of the eight Roberts vessels were held was also named after him. His eponymous mailboat was 85.6 feet long and was built of wood in 1937 at Nassau. Though a sailing craft, she was fitted with an auxiliary motor as well. She is believed to have plied to Abaco and Miami from Nassau for at least a decade. One of her captains was named Russell.

A man and woman from the nearby AUTEC US Navy base on Andros, talking with the owner and builder of the ambitious mailboat *Miss Andros* of 140 feet, around 1972. The sailing ship's propeller shafts didn't align, meaning the vibrations could loosen the wooden seams, and she was quickly pulled from service and into ignominy in the mid-1980s. Sir Roland Symonette was photographed on-site trying to help get her launched from the beach. Ultimately the ambitious vessel was towed like Icarus after failing to reach the sun, into a creek at Mastic Point, Andros, where its ribs lie today.

The elusive Captain Tom Hanna, at the right, talking to an associate aboard one of his vessels. Although entirely friendly and a hands-on boss, he has proved difficult to photograph. He named thelatest of his many vessels after a daughter who had worked for the shipping firm, but recently passed. The Hanna family of Pompey Bay, Acklins have owned nearly a dozen boats over 200 years, and Capt. Tom Hanna recently added his sixth to the mailboat fleet. Most of his are the ro-ro type with landing-craft bows, accommodation and wheel-house aft, and open deck configuration, capable of accessing shore-side locations even bereft of any infrastructure. Hanna's career has not been without financial and legal complications, yet he perseveres and can be found operating a forklift and overseeing cargo operations on Potter's Cay.

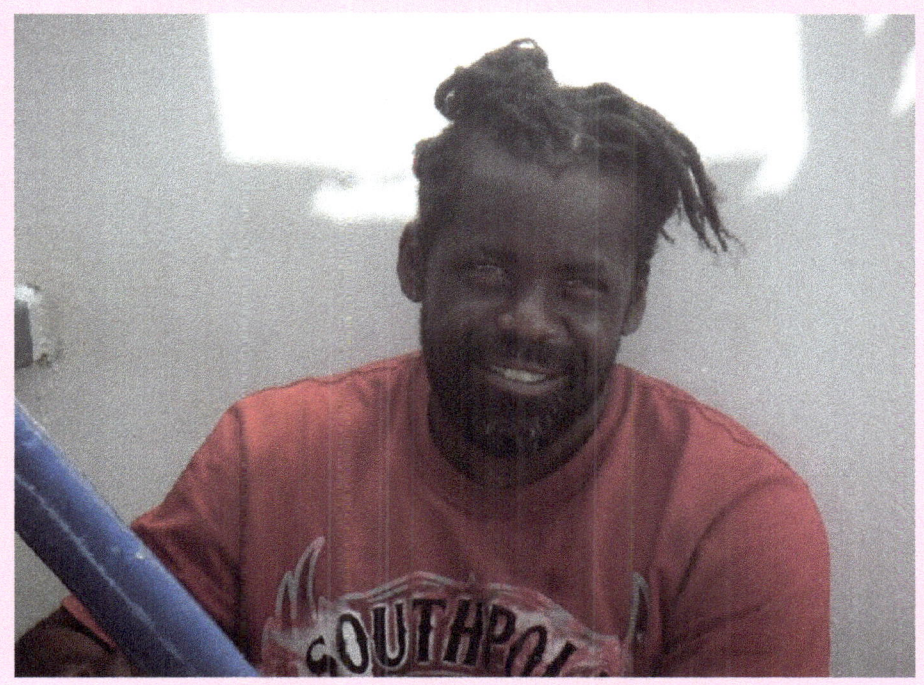

Crewmember of *Bahamas Daybreak*.

A crewmember aboard the *Captain C.* grabbing a quick meal in the galley. The *Captain C.* was built of steel around 2000 and serves Staniel Cay and Black Point, Exumas as well as Duncan Town, Ragged Island. Other vessels owned by Capt. Etienne Maycock Sr. and his family have included the *Etlene C., Emet & Cephas*, and *Lady 9*. Maycocks also own a restaurant, bar, and five-room motel in Duncan town, where the matriarch still lives there. The mailboat dock is about a mile and half from the settlement. The dock is on one end and the airport is at the other end of the island with the settlement in the middle.

A crewmember from the *Lady Rosalind* gives a cheerful thumbs-up during hectic cargo operations. This vessel, itself replacing a ship of the same name which grounded and sank in 1998, has had many names: *John F. Walker, Jr., G. W. Pierce, Fugro I, Offshore Venture*, and *OMS Maverick*. She was built in Mississippi in 1967 and serves North Andros for the Taylor Corporation and family. In the past, she has called in Cat Island. Her captains have included Willie Wilson, V. H. Black, and Gifford Johnson. The Taylors bought her in Texas, and she has also served as a substitute boat for the rest of the mailboat fleet, on call to fill in holes in itineraries created by breakdowns, servicing etc.

Whether this gentleman is affiliated with the mailboats or not, he was working beside the *Captain Moxey* and *Captain C.* on Potter's Cay. Note his unique use of ship containers to spread and repair his fishing nets.

Sailors aboard the *Bahamas Daybreak* waiting for the word to push off to either North or Central Eleuthera.

Finding shade as the *Island Link* prepares to sail, most likely to Georgetown, Exuma. This large catamaran-hulled vessel was built in Caboolture, Australia in 2004 and is 443 gross tons. Her trade route takes her to Salt Pond and Deadman's Cay in Long Island, plus George Town, Great Exuma. One of her Captains is Jed Munroe. Ownership is a bit obtuse, variously named as Munson Shipping, Intamico Shipping Ltd. and Sterling Group, all of Bank Lane, Nassau.

This crewman at the stern of the *North Cat Island Special II* (at left, in yellow shirt) is checking out a work job, or perhaps a barely visible location for a quick nap?

These creative crewmen are using a large boulder in place of a bollard to hold their mailboat in place in George Town, Great Exuma.

This passenger was very happy to be heading home to the southern islands aboard the *Lady Emerald*, and came up to wish these visiting American yachtsmen well. *Lady Emerald* was built of 464 tons of steel in Louisiana in 2003 and has been serving the Bahamas – specifically Rum Cay, San Salvador and Smith's Bay, Old Bight, and New Bight Cat Island – since. In March, 2014, she was laid up for repairs but is now back in service. Her owner is G. M. Patton of Nassau. The cost to sail for the far southern islands is $60 each way. Past Captains have included Bill Williams, and it is believed that Mr. Patton has skippered her as well.

Cephas Maycock, First Mate of the *Captain C.*, leaving the Exumas for Ragged Island.

Drudge work – chipping paint on the ramp of *Trans Cargo II*. This is another cargo ship owned by the industrious Taylor family, for Pirate's Well Investments. It has the unusual distinction of having been built in Singapore in 1986 and is 191 feet long and 46 feet wide. Its captain is David Hyde, from Roatan, Honduras. Capt. Eddins Taylor, a co-owner, said that she was purchased in Egypt and delivered from there to Bahamas with a mix of Egyptians and the relative of one of the Bahamian owners. Originally bid out to carry fuel for the Bahamas Electricity Corporation, it instead hauled sand and aggregate to and from Freeport when the owners lost the bid.

High drama, of the kind that captains and owners dislike. In the last minutes before departure from Potter's Cay on a Friday afternoon, after all the cargo, vehicles, and passengers had been boarded, it was discovered that due to equipment breakage, the loading ramp cargo door would not close. A team of welders, led by the man in the red shirt, was summoned immediately and went to work with a torch in the hot sun. While they frantically try to work their magic on the *Lady Kathreine*, a clearly displeased passenger, in red hat, looks on impatiently while another passenger to the left in hat, seems more circumspect. This illustrates how much teamwork and coordination is involved in getting mailboats to and from their destinations safely, repeatedly.

Mariners always have to work rain or shine, day and night, and be on call around the clock, whether an engine wiper or captain. Anacharsis, a Scythian philosopher observed that there are three kinds of people: the living, the dead, and those who are at sea. There are reasons why every major port around the world still maintains a hostel for seamen who have been away so long that their own family hardly know them anymore. When the author commercially operated a fleet of tankers in southeast Asia, he was taught two maxims from the industry that applied on shore as well as afloat: The ships don't stop, so why should you? And "time off" is a Russian prince ("Timoff") – so shut up and get back to work! Would that these sayings were mere levity. Those ashore, whether out of empathy or personal experience as mariners, work almost as hard as those at sea.

Lady Francis discharging general cargo by crane in Cockburn Town, San Salvador. The same boat has her name spelled different ways (as in *Lady Frances*) on different years.

The mailboat *Eleuthera Express* working cargo in Harbour Island. The vessel was built in Louisiana in 1997 and is 250 gross tons of steel and machinery. Since that time, she has served Harbour Island, Spanish Wells, Rock Sound, and Governor's Harbour, Eleuthera. The owners go by the same name as their ship and are based in Nassau. Confusingly, there was a prior *Eleuthera Express*, which began its working life as the *Spiekeroog* in the Netherlands in 1962. Then Finnish Captain Jan Rautawaara, who had owned the *Spiekeroog*, spotted the discrepancy between the two ships, one older and European, the other American and modern, and called Captain Junior Pinder in Nassau to clarify. The original *Eleuthera Express* was sold in Miami in 1980 and sank between Haiti and Cuba about a decade later.

Lady Rosalind II discharging stern-to in the tight quarters of Matthew Town, Inagua, with numerous boats, including a Royal Bahamas Defence Force speedboat, and rocks nearby.

Crew from the *United Star* trying to discharge dry-board for construction without breaking it, using a forklift. Spring Point, Acklins. Note the absence of sheltered dockfront. Note the letters "T" and "H" in the cross bars above the ramp. Presumably they stand for the owner's name – Tom Hanna; this is his home port.

The wooden mailboat *Current Pride* docked at Hatchet Bay, Eleuthera, and apparently loading and discharging cargo by hand, as there does not appear to be a crane or derrick. This old-school vessel from the Current, North Eleuthera, continues to ply its routes today. She is 88 tons and is the last known wooden-hulled mailboat plying the Bahamas, having since been overtaken by steam ships, steel boats, motor boats, European ships, and modern American mailboats. Her trades take her to Upper and Lower Bogue, the Bluff, Current, Gregory Town, James Cistern, and Hatchet Bay, all in Eleuthera. The one-way fares are $30 and there are pleasant sheltered benches situated aft.

Captain Gurth Dean discharging and loading cargo to and from Abaco at Potter's Cay. This mailboat carries on a long tradition of working boats owned and operated by the illustrious Dean family of Sandy Point, Abaco. She weighs in at 500 gross tons and was built in Alabama in 1999. Her route traces the same as her predecessors, five of them called *Captain Dean*. She sails to Bullock's Harbour, Berry Islands, then Hard Bargain, Moore's Island, and Sandy Point, occasionally calling at Sweetings Cay on the eastern tip of Grand Bahama. It appears that the ship also calls at Marsh Harbour and Green Turtle Cay, but it is always best to check with the Dock Master at Potter's Cay before packing your bags.

An informative few from the deck of *BoHengy II* showing cargo being discharged by the *Bahamas Daybreak* at the Government Dock, Dunmore Town, Harbour Island. Note the coordination and teamwork required by the crane operator, fork lift operator, and stevedores – connecting and disconnecting the crane hook from the various units of cargo. And the boy in foreground is watching the proceeds. An array of cargoes, from petroleum products in barrels to construction equipment to edibles and the pallets used to transport them are all in evidence.

Also at Government Dock in Harbour Island, this special cargo vehicle works bulk material off of the *Caribbean Express I.* It is believed that the multi-wheel equipment travels with the ship. It is fair to say that this level of preparedness is the exception rather than the rule.

The originally Danish mailboat *Lisa J.* discharges a cargo of cement in Andros. It starts in pallets then is shifted by hand into the back of a pickup truck. Part-cargo of cinder blocks at right. Built in 1960 in Marstal, Denmark, this vessel certainly has an interesting history. For over a dozen years it served as the ferry *Ellen Soby*, serving the communities of Soby and Faaborg, Denmark, then Sejero and Havnsoe, as the *Runden* (*Round*), then from 1999 intended for the route from Napoli Italy to Procida, an island in the mouth of the bay. However, she was sold to the Bahamas instead and presumably sailed across the Atlantic on her own hull. This photograph was taken by maritime consultant, Captain Calum Legett, in the early 1990s. *Lisa J.* plied the route from Nassau to Nicholl's Town, Mastic Point and Morgan's Bluff. Bought by Bahamians in July, 1999 and sold on to Honduran owners by after 2005. The author was at a shipyard in Freeport and discovered the *Runden* laid up there. A visiting Danish yachtsman could not believe his eyes when he saw her. He said the vessel had taken him to and from school for his entire childhood!

Sea Wind approaching Simms, Long Island, by Dave Blake Photography.

The *Sea Spirit II* discharging on an unknown (and under developed) site. Note the ruins of a previous dock at right. This ship began as the *Russell Portier* in the shipyard of that name in Louisiana, in 1999. Then from 2007 she was named the *United Spirit* for a year. Her Bahamian owner has consistently been Captain Tom Hanna under the Ro-Ro Company Ltd. as well as Carib-USA. Due to some apparent financial issues the ship was flagged to Panama and though it fills in for other Hanna vessels like *IV Nais, K.C.T.*, and the Dean's *Mia Dean*, her trading pattern in the Bahamas seems unpredictable.

It looks like this mailboat is making a private delivery of construction materials to Exuma. Though the name is illegible in this image, the vessel is almost certainly the *Lady Frances*.

The mailboat reaches! The *Lady Mathilda* arrives in Matthew Town, Inagua – the furthest outpost (relative to the capital of Nassau) in the Bahamas. As a result, this port is the most likely to be cut from mailboat itineraries due to weather, breakdowns, fuel shortage, or a myriad of other reasons.

Lady Mathilda in Nassau. She is 135 feet long, having been lengthened 25 feet, and can carry an impressive 70 passengers. Built in 1998 in Louisiana, the vessel serves Abraham's Bay, Mayaguana, Crooked and Acklins Island, and Great Inagua. One of her Captains is Nigel Davis, and her owners are the indefatigable Taylor clan of Pirate's Well Investments. Note the double radar units and various radio and GPS antennae above the wheelhouse. The ship travels further distances than about any other mailboat in the Bahamas, and must remain in contact and have reliable weather information around the clock. It would appear that the port anchor socket is empty. From other photos taken at the same time, it appears neither anchor is hanging in the customary place, meaning the anchor must be hosted over the rail – a cumbersome task, particularly during emergencies.

Trans Cargo II

The *Current Pride* prepares to jauntily overtake the *Marcella III* in the approaches to Nassau, though in fact both types of mailboat – wooden and European – have been eclipsed.

Legacy loading at the western tip of Potter's Cay, with Atlantis in background.

This mailboat is coming in to dock, churning sand behind it (called "rubbing" in the Bahamas) with a load of regatta sloops as its cargo, ready to discharge. The destination may be George Town Exuma, as a large regatta is held there annually. Because of the highly distinctive letters "T H" (for its owner, Captain Tom Hanna) welded to the frame above the lading ramp, this is the *United Star*.

Mia Dean working her cargo with red crane at Potter's Cay.

The old European work-horse *Marcella III* seems to be utilizing the service of a truck-mounted crane to load or discharge cargo from its forward hold, given the absence of its own cranes and the evidence of a large white crane forward, with at least four men working on the deck.

Grand Master discharging at Highbourne Cay, Exuma, a yachting destination.

Hustle, bustle, deadlines, and anticipation of loading or discharging cargo and sailing.

Lady Frances preparing to load Red Cross emergency supplies to a family island following a hurricane. Note that the same ship spells its name *Francis* and *Frances* at different times.

The all-important mail, upon which fuel and other subsidies depend. Note the ubiquitous but out-of-place US Post Office carton, which is used on several Bahamian mailboats.

Regatta racing boat ready to be shipped to the starting line – note the gleaming shine to the upper and lower hull – fully smoothed for action! A number of mailboat-owning families, like the Moxeys of Andros, compete actively in regattas in the archipelago.

The *North Cat Island Special* with an old Ford pick-up truck on its main hatch. A tragic story tells of two young men bringing a truck back from Nassau to Exuma after Christmas on year about 2000. It was rough. One of them went to get a coffee at the galley after, the other continued resting in the cab of the truck. When the man returned with coffee, the truck was no longer aboard, and his friend had perished.

Loading tyres aboard the *Grand Master*. There will be someone at the other end expecting them. The author "posted" a 2 X 3" sign via crewman named Archie of the *Captain Gurth Dean*. He promised to deliver it to our mutual friend Marcus in Sandy Point, Abaco, which he subsequently did. The cost? $5 cash. Another time the captain of the *Grand Master*, Lenny Bozogrog, had to inform a distressed shipper that it didn't make economical sense for him to run the refrigeration units all night just for the ham which she was sending to family in Exuma (she was quite upset with him!). In San Salvador and Rum Cay there have been urgent scuffles to locate a tiny carburator for a motorbike or a spare to fix a truck before the boat sailed.

Going somewhere precious? Note that while awaiting transport, this custom golf cart is being charged for the customer, who in turn will be charged.

Onions – to make conch salad, peas-rice, minced crawfish? During a recent commodity crunch Eleutherans complained that an imported tomato cost $1, and they were concerned about the pass-through cost to customers (Eleuthera was a successful farming island until nationalization).

Cargo shipped by Bahamas Ferries transits through this Potter's Cay facility but the dock face behind it is blocked by a sunken mailboat on which salvage has been attempted many times over decades without success.

It would appear that the *Captain Moxey* is transferring the most delicate, demanding and important cargo of all – passengers – off Little Farmer's Cay, Exuma, without having to enter port, thanks to the launch alongside and opening in the railing to allow passengers on and off.

Painting the topsides of a vessel, this unseaworthy dinghy is more air and water than boat, but is shared communally for such housekeeping tasks feet from shore.

A mobile gas station. Fuelling, or bunkering as it is called in the marine industry, is an important and expensive part of the cost structure; determining not just subsidies but profits. Here a truck delivers Marine Diesel Oil (MDO) to the *Lady Emerald* via hose at Potter's Cay

Why the dazzle colouring on the bow of the *Grand Master*, you might ask? She is being fumigated. Roaches and other critters come aboard as larvae in boxes, livestock, perishable food, or simply up the docking lines. They need to be kept in check to renew passenger certificates.

What a well-kept foredeck should look like when cargo work ceases and no one is looking. This is aboard the *Bahamas Daybreak*.

171

Detail of a well-maintained deck crane looming over the forward and main cargo hatch. This "North Pacific Crane" is on the *Captain Moxey*.

As can be seen, not all equipment is maintained to the same high standard. Behind some containers, western Potter's Cay.

This truck, utilized by the Dean Shipping Corp., is so fresh off the boat from Asia that it still has Japanese writing on the truck bed above the rear wheel.

General maintenance work. The gentleman painting above the draft-mark numbers appears to be repairing – or at least covering up – some recent damage to the hull plating. The fact the cargo hook to the right above the bow is secured shows that they are not working cargo, and the grey compressor in the foreground suggests more serious repair work may be in the offing.

Sometimes the unexpected gets in the way of schedules and routine. In this case a fishing vessel is repairing or re-installing one of its outriggers, and in doing so has caused the roadway around Potter's Cay to be closed for a section and for a while, during the operations. Car drivers quickly assessed the situation and, without any police presence or direction, found an alternate route which was at least partly against slow-moving traffic. Others – like the author – just stopped what they were doing and watched the unusual activity for the heart of a capital city.

A rare photograph from the Roberts family archives showing the festively festooned little tugboat *BA 2* towing the freshly launched mailboat *Noel Roberts* from Harbour Island to Nassau, on its maiden voyage, to have its engines installed. The boat was launched from the beach immediately to the west of the Government Dock in Dunmore Town, one of many, then fewer and fewer of such baptisms in that harbour, as steel, steam, and motors supplanted wood and sail.

Mailboats in Art

This painting by British-Canadian David Hamilton-Jones in 2002 shows a Bahamian mailboat working cargo. It is difficult to name the vessel, but two possible candidates might be the *Duchess of Topsail* or the *K.C.T.* (Hamilton-Jones' son Felix is a hereditary – and actual – Fijian prince), from the collection of Mrs. Jane Wiberg.

Bahamian artist Chan Pratt painting the humorously named *AutoGo* in Abaco.

A model of the *Almeta Queen* at the Lowe Museum of Art in Abaco.

Author, historian, and sailor, Steve Dodge, and artist Laurie Jones chose to depict the *Albertine Adoue* for several covers of their book *Abaco – The History of an Out Island and its Cays* in 1995. This is the first edition – the others are in colour, but the same subject matter.

This fictional mailboat, the *Lady Marguerite* (possibly named for the Governor General), adorns the passenger exit from Nassau International Airport and is one of the first things visitors see.

A watercolour of the *Noel Roberts* given to Noel Roberts, its namesake, whose widow Mrs. Susan Roberts, shared it with the author. The vessel was 115 feet long, 23.3 feet wide, 11.3 feet deep, and 180 gross tons, with a 180-horsepower engine embedded. Earl and Gerald Johnson of Harbour Island built her in 1943 built the hull, then she had to be towed "light" from Eleuthera to Nassau by the tug *BA 2*, commissioned for the purpose by Symonette Shipyards of Hog Island, where the motors were installed. Noel Roberts, later MP and LLB, was four years old when his namesake was launched. He became a prominent businessman and MP for Harbour Island, which he represented between 1972 and 1977, then from 1987 to 1997. In 1948, a Jamaican newspaper (the *Kingston Gleaner*) reported her carrying lumber to Kingston, and in 1961 she was carrying plate glass from Florida. She is thought to have served the communities of North Eleuthera for at least 15 years, until 1957, which is the final year the boat appears in the definitive catalogue of British and colonial vessels, the *Mercantile Navy List and Maritime Directory*.

A watercolour of the *Gary Roberts* given to Noel Roberts, son of Sir George Roberts.

Painting of Potter's Cay Dock in 1997 by David Hamilton-Jones showing Potter's Cay Dock, main terminal of all Bahamas mailboats, from the collection of Mrs. Jane Wiberg.

A watercolour of the *Lady Dundas,* given to Noel Roberts, son of Sir George Roberts. This vessel, like most mailboats, had a colourful history. Built of wood by Thomas Berlin and Harry Albury in Harbour Island, to designs made by noted American yachtsman, naval architect, and seasonal Harbour Island resident Lawrence Huntington of New York, she was launched in the spring of 1939. At 92 feet long, 19.5 feet wide, 9.3 feet deep and 115 gross tons, she was a sizeable craft for inter-island trade at the time. Her Fairbanks Morse Diesel of 150-horsepower pushed her at 10 knots with up to 80 tons of freight.

Shipwrecks

Lady Gloria run aground and abandoned in Andros. Little is known about this vessel except that either *Lady Gloria* or simply *Gloria* was recorded in secret government exchanges released by Wikileaks, as trading Nassau to Mangrove Cay, Andros and was 94 tons.

Lady Mathilda in trouble, aground on a reef, small boat to its aid, probably helping to set anchors. This photo hangs in the Taylor Corporation dock office, as a reminder of what can happen – often quickly – in hostile waterways and weather.

The infamous, tragic and preventable collision of two mailboats, the *Sea Hauler* with the *United Star,* on a clear and calm night in August, 2003. The accident killed several Bahamians on their way to a festive holiday on their home island and severely injured others, including amputees. Parts of the legal claims for compensation have gone unresolved 18 years later. Both vessels – though not their passengers – survived. The government report on the accident has yet to be publicized.

Untangling wreckage of the fatal *Sea Hauler* crane collapse, which killed passengers, in Nassau.

A mailboat aground, semi-submerged, and rusting away off Long Island. The hull and mast appear to be too large for this to be the *Sea Hauler*. It could be the *Marcella, Marcella II,* or *Sea Spirit II* (ex-*United Spirit*), all of which met their end off Long Island. The fact that a single wreck could be four or more mailboats serves to illustrate the persistent danger of the trade across generations.

Lady Tasha, possibly the ex-*Atabasha* of Andros, sunk at Potter's Cay. This wreck of a boat, believed to have served Andros, was removed in 2016 by Bahamas Ferries. She was built before 1973 and at one point serviced Mayaguana, Crooked, and Acklins Island, and was on the mailboat subsidy list of 1975. She sank at Potter's Cay in the early 2000's. Ironically, once she was raised and salvaged, the vessel was towed from Potter's Cay to nearby Arawak Cay where once again she languished, this time afloat. Ultimately, she is believed (or planned) to have been sunk.

So this is where they bury old mailboats? The *Lady Tasha* at Arawak Cay, the other end of Nassau Harbour, October, 2016. It seemed at the time that someone was merely kicking the can further down the street, however she has, ultimately, been towed away and sunk.

Lady D. of Andros sprung a leak in spring 2014 and remained taking up a berth at Potter's Cay for over two years, until late 2016, after press and public agitation. This is the second *Lady D.* on the Andros run – her predecessor was built around 1979 and sold as (or to) *Coletra* of La Paz, Bolivia after 1992. She was built in 1992, of steel, and served Fresh Creek, Staniard Creek, Stafford Creek, Behring, Blanket Sound, and Browne Sound, Central Andros from Nassau. Her last known captain was Prince Munroe.

Sea Hauler, which had collided with *United Star*, wrecked on the reefs off Long Island. *United Star*'s sister ship, *Sea Spirit II* (ex-*United Spirit*) was also wrecked off Long Island.

The *Legacy* aground in the North Bar Channel, Abaco, 2011. She was floated free safely.

Grand Master aground off George Town, Great Exuma. She survived.

Exuma Pride, once a Norwegian coastal freighter, aground off Crab Cay, Exuma. Built in the UK during WWII, her first name in 1944 was simply HMS*LCG(M)192*, then the *Hjelmeland Fjord* after 1949. She was 155 feet long, 22.5 feet wide and 8 feet deep loaded. After a distinguished career connecting remote communities along the coast and fjords of Norway, in 1978 she was sold to the Exuma Shipping and Transportation Co. of Nassau. On the way from Norway she suffered engine trouble off Bermuda and ultimately had to be towed to the Bahamas, arriving in August, 1979. Soon, the *Exuma Pride* it took over a night passage to George Town, Exuma. By 1987 the benchmark shipping list *Lloyd's Register* declared the ship's existence "in doubt," a final step before de-listing her. Sometime around 1998 the vessel was wrecked off Crab Cay, not far from George Town, half above water. According to a visiting yachtsman in Exuma, *Exuma Pride* was never "officially" commissioned to carry the mails, and she "mysteriously slipped her mooring" and ran aground. Note the plants and rocks in the immediate foreground, right corner – and proximity to land.

Church Bay on fire at Potter's Cay, January, 1973. She was then towed off the jetty and sunk. Note fireman jumping overboard in photo at lower-left. The history of this ship is uniquely Bahamian and forged by the exigencies of war. The Royal Navy ordered Symonette Shipyards on Hog (now Paradise) Island to build two minesweepers, intended to shore up the defences of Singapore, where overflying Japanese planes could drop mines in the harbours and channels. However, since Singapore fell to the Japanese in early 1942, the colony was allowed to keep them, and they essentially got lost in the shuffle. Apparently, the Duke of Windsor (erstwhile Kind Edward VII) launched herand the sister ship, HMS *MMS 195*, which became the *Stede Bonnet* and had a long career serving Abaco. It would appear she was actually commissioned by Royal Navy officers in Nassau, as there is a note that she was decommissioned in March, 1946. The survivors of a British tanker sunk by an Italian submarine off Abaco in March, 1942 insist that they smuggled a machine gun aboard their lifeboat and that it was subsequently, for the balance of the war, mounted on either of the Bahamian-built minesweepers. Built of wood to avoid triggering mines, the boat was 119 feet long and 225 gross tons, capable of going 12 knots.

Mailboat Interiors

Sunlit cabin with bunks aboard the *Captain C.*

The galley, or communal kitchen, aboard the *Captain C.*

Dining and public space on *Bahamas Daybreak*.
Note the US Postal Service tub on table.

A well-varnished hallway between the aft deck and cabins;
aboard the *Bahamas Daybreak*.

Bunk beds aboard the *Captain C*.

Sample Galley on *Lady Rosalind*.

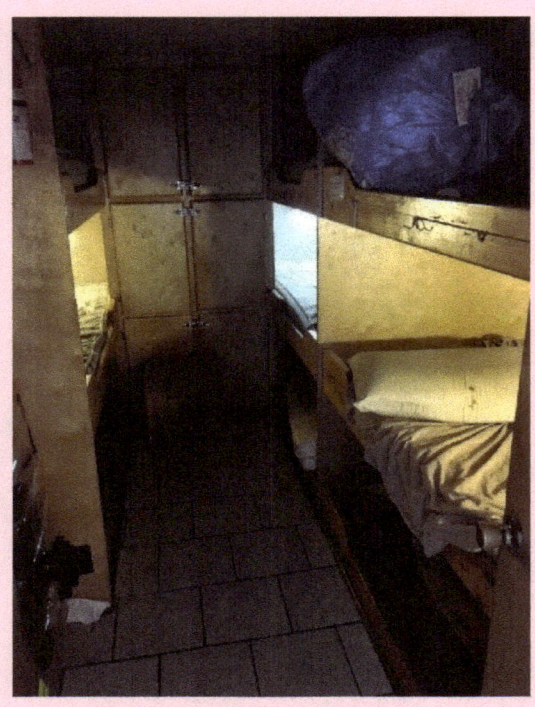

Cabin with bunks on *Lady Rosalind*.

Extra cabin with more bunks, on *Lady Rosalind*.

Communal head on the *Lady Rosalind*.

The galley of a different vessel, believed to be that of the *Bahamas Daybreak*.

Cousins cutting up fish caught in the Ragged Islands, James Wiberg.

Captain C. transiting a narrow, current-scoured cut through the Exumas, James Wiberg.

Boys behind the *Captain C.* in the Exumas *en route* to Ragged Island, James Wiberg.

Patiently fishing, Potter's Cay.

Loading cargo in Nassau for Andros.

More cargo being loaded.

Children ready to set sail from Potter's Cay.

A rush to undock late at night.

A happy child in his bunk.

Passengers settling in.

A box of fruit from the cook in the mid level hallway.

Legend II arriving in Drigg's Hill, Andros: note bow ramp is down

The community converges at dawn on the dock at Drigg's Hill.

Discharging cars at Drigg's Hill.

Crane operator, Captain Moxey.

Wheelhouse or bridge.

Island constable and a young admirer.

Captain Moxey shifted to the spot occupied by *Legend II* after a call at Lisbon Creek.

Disembarking on a shifting gangway.

Fathers keeping vigil at the Dockmaster's Office.

Another mailboat? Note sea hawk's nest atop wheelhouse

A clever if risky way to carry liquids to a nearby eco-resort. Note the absence of a life vest and the proximity of the deck to the water (called low freeboard).

Mailboat at rest. Child not at rest!

Heading out of Drigg's Hill and back to Nassau.

Cargo of conchs and cars. Roll-on, Roll-off, or RoRo, vessels are clearly not required.

Canine companion in the cabin.

Wild land crabs, fresh caught specifically to make the market via the *Captain Moxey*.

The *President Taylor*, newest mailboat in the fleet, greeting the *Captain Moxey* on arrival in Nassau.

Bridge of *Lady Frances* on the southeast side of Potter's Cay Dock.

This is an unusual photo from the community of Hard Bargain on Moore's Island, off Abaco. Previously the island was so isolated that an anthropologist recorded a song with words from the Yoruba language in West Africa being sung there in the 1970s. Now it lies beside a new Disney Cruises island named Castaway Cay. This 1991 image shows the *Queen Dean II* in red and blue, with the *Champion II* in the background, its predecessor, the *Champion*, half-sunk ahead of it, and a small Boston Whaler named *Jesus Saviour Pilot Me* in the foreground! The only men on the island were fishermen and an educator or pastor – those over the youth-age having gone to the capital.

Endion at Government Dock, Dunmore Town, Harbour Island. The vessel had a fascinating history, having been built in Boston in 1898 as a private yacht of the same name. During World War I she was effectively requisitioned into the service of the US Navy, who used her to patrol the coast until the end of the war in late 1918. When her career as USS *SP 707* ended in 1919, she was advertised for sale by the US government for $7,000 as "a motor boat built in Boston, length 100 feet, beam 14 feet 2 inches, draft 8 feet, 61-ton gross, speed 10 knots; has a semi-Diesel engine, 4-cycleindicated horsepower 60." She was converted to accommodate 18 passengers in two staterooms – at nine persons per cabin; conditions must have been rather close.

The former *Patricia K.* working cargo in Abaco as the mail freighter *Old Horse Eye* in Abaco. This 74-foot long, 19-foot wide vessel weighed 97 gross tons and was a hybrid of both sail and power, as she had both masts and rigging as well as a 165-horsepower motor. Built of wood as the *Patricia K.* in 1930 by T. Berlin Albury in Harbour Island, she mostly plied between Nassau and Miami, whilst also serving communities in North Eleuthera and Abaco. Her first owners were Kelly's Lumber Yard in Nassau and she was commissioned by Allan H. Kelly andnamed for his daughter. In 1940, she was sold to John Percy Sweeting, also of Nassau, and from 1956 Captain Percy Sweeting of Harbour Island owned her.

A rough montage of an old newspaper image of the *Isle of June* docked in Miami and taken from the rails of the *Monarch of Nassau*, which replaced her. This was an 83-foot long vessel with dual propulsion provided by two masts as well as a steam engine. She was built by Edward Roberts in Harbour Island in 1926 and spent most of her career shuttling between Nassau and Miami with freight, passengers and the mails. Her owners were the Kelly Lumber Co. of Nassau. Until 1927, when the *Ena K.* (same owners) joined the service, *Isle of June* was the only vessel on the route.

Priscilla, from the Wyannie Malone Historical Society, in Hope Town, Abaco. She was built under sail power alone in 1921 and then had a 115-horsepower Fairbanks Morse Diesel engine added. *Priscilla* was 100 feet long and served Abaco and its cays between 1923 and 1932. She replaced the home-grown schooner,*Albertine Adoue* on the mail route. At one point her Captain was Hartley Roberts, Mate Howard Lowe, and Cook Osgood Lowe, all from Green Turtle Cay. In 1932 a large hurricane blew her ashore and *Priscilla* was destroyed; despite having managed to find temporary anchorage off Green Turtle Cay.

Gary Roberts from *The Harbour Island Story* by Jim and Anne Lawlor. Like the *Noel Roberts* and the *Richard Campbell*, this vessel was named for one of Sir George W. K. Robert's sons. Fairly small for a passenger freighter, she was 66 feet long, 16.5 feet wide, 7.2 feet deep, and 59 gross tons. Built by Earl and Gerald Johnson in Harbour Island starting in 1940, she was launched in either 1941 or 1942. Her main route was to and from ports in Andros. Edgar L. Rolle of Lowe Sound, Andros is believed to have owned her for a time and kept the name. Craig Symonette's family shipyard had to dry-dock her and he found that the little ship suffered from a hogging keel (bending or sagging), which had a deleterious effect on the 24-foot propeller shaft as well as the boat's ability to avoid seepage from the shaft through-hulls. After being re-launched, they had to wait 24 hours for the boat to regain a healthy shape! *Gary Roberts* met its demise as a mailboat on the 5 October, 1978 from causes unknown.

The future Bahamas mailboat *Willaurie* as the *Willmary* loading cargo in the UK. This vessel was one of the early European coastwise ships to be imported to the Bahamas in the second, or in some cases, final phases of their lives, to replace the wooden or sailing mailboat fleet. A large ship of 138 feet length, 25 feet width, and 199 gross tons; she was designed to carry 376 tons of cargo but was vulnerable amidships as the ship low to the water when loaded and vulnerable to the high waves and swells of the open ocean that could be expected on trips to Inagua. The vessel did not have an illustrious career in the Bahamas, rather it spent most of its time as the red-headed stepchild which no-one wanted to take responsibility for. Built in the Netherlands in 1966, she traded to and from industrial bulk cargo ports in England. Then in 1980 *Lloyd's Register* stripped her of classification and she voyaged to the Bahamas and that flag of registry. Her duties in the Bahamas included the mail run to Rum Cay, San Salvador, and Cat Island. But in early August of that year the Royal Bahamas Defence Force (RBDF) had to evacuate passengers, due to engine troubles (presumably meaning engine failure). The *Willaurie* was sold by Antler Limited of London to W. B. Hart of Nassau. The ship is understood to have languished, abandoned, alongside Potter's Cay, taking up dock-front space for no good commercial purpose. The story does not improve.

Willmary trading coastwise in Europe with full cargo.

A forlorn and abandoned *Willaurie* aground off Clifton Bay, New Providence, having broken its tow to its sinking; a not uncommon occurance.

Willaurie wreck underwater as a dive site off Clifton, southwest New Providence.

Miss BJ under her former name, *Sambre*, in Europe. Another previous name for this European freighter was *Juleta*. Built of steel in the Netherlands in 1965, this vessel was 152 feet long, 24.9 feet wide, and 8.5 feet deep, weighing 330 gross tons. Known as the *Juleta* between 1990 and 1999, she was during that time owned by two Bahamas firms – Trans-Bahama Shipping Ltd. and M/V *Jeleta*[sic.] Mail & Ferry Services, M.V.B.S. While in the Bahamas, the ship was modified significantly, with the house extended forward across most of what had been cargo hatches, roughly tripling the passenger-carrying capacity. It is not known which name – *Miss BJ* or *Juleta*– came first, but the only photos of her are as the *Sambre* in Europe in the 1960s and in the 1990s at Prince George Dock as the *Miss BJ*. It is likely that *Miss BJ* was her final name, and in any event, she was scuttled off Atoll Island just outside Nassau Harbour on 22 June, 1999, as a dive site.

Miss BJ at Prince George Dock in downtown Nassau. Note the stack of a small Carnival cruise ship in the background.

Miranda, as the confiscated *Gilbert Sea*, being sunk off Florida. This ship began as the *Geulborg* (roughly translated as "gold deposit"), in 1966 when owner, Wagenborg, launched her in the Netherlands for the Black & White Line. In 1977 the Taylor Corporation and family bought the ship and had her delivered to the Bahamas, where it remained from 1977 to 1996. Up to 1996 the 176-foot long, 28.5-foot wide, and 399-ton ship was the *Miranda*. She traded from Miami to Turks, Caicos, Exumas, as well as Long Island. Captain Eddins Taylor said that the ship was sold to Haiti under its same name. Indeed, Haitians renamed it *Paradise Express* from 1996-99, then Honduran owners christened her *El Compa* for less than a year, and finally she was bequeathed the name *Gilbert Sea* up until 2002, when it was sunk. Whilst Honduran flagged, US Customs officials discovered 75 pounds of cocaine in a false bottom of a 55-gallon drum. It was decorated with murals, towed 1.5 miles from Palm Beach Inlet, anchored, and sunk.

The *Deborah K. II* in Europe as the *Klaas, Sawi,* or *Windhund*, earlier in its career.

In 1978, the *Deborah K. II*, a large, steel, Diesel-powered vessel took over the route from Nassau to Abaco carrying mail. The convention of naming mailboats to end with the letter 'K' for 'Kelly' family daughters (as in *Betty K., Ena K.*, and *Deborah K.*) was adapted by the owners of Kelly Lumber Corp. early on. Built in Hamburg as the *Windhund* in 1965, this vessel was 348 tons, could carry 474 tons. Though most Kelly ships plied to and from Florida with freight, *Deborah K. II* was for many years the primary domestic link between Marsh Harbour and Nassau, and is believed to have retired around 2000, and is listed as "dead ship." This photograph was taken by Captain Calum Legett in about 1993. Note both the rugged landscape of eastern Potter's Cay as well as the many lifeboats above the large cabin, and a large derrick that appears to be at least in part hand-operated.

The modern, Chinese-built Ro-Pax (roll-on roll-off passenger) ship, *Fiesta Mail*, serving Freeport, leaves Nassau Harbour under the competent hand of a third-generation captain, Limas Taylor. Photo taken from Fort Charlotte.

The storied ship-owning family of Captain Ernest A. Dean of Sandy Point built the *Mia Dean*. Up to March, 2014 she was serving Clarence Town, Long Island. After that date, presumably on a temporary basis, she was replaced by the *Sea Spirit*, which also called Long Cay, Acklins, and South Long Island. Like a cluster of other vessels, from seafood transporters to international freight carriers and mailboats, the vessel is docked at the Dean's special spot on Potter's Cay. Such spots are allocated by an unwritten pecking order and longstanding verbal arrangements, which are not made by, but tacitly acknowledged and condoned by the Dock Master. For example, if one company voluntarily steps in where the government won't, and finances the effective removal of wreckage, that firm will exercise exclusive and mutually respected domain over the dock space freed. In the summer of 2017 it was understood, however, that the *Mia Dean* has been out of service and laid up at this spot for many years, taking up space.

The ever-professional *Captain C.*, run by the Maycocks of Ragged Island, approaching Black Point, Exuma, as seen from the deck of another Bahamian mailboat, the *Lady Frances*. She symbolizes the adaptability of Bahamian mailboat owners and investors in a fluid environment and 100,000 miles of geographical, archipelagic terrain, which is unique in the western hemisphere, in North as well as South America.

Obstructions in action. This is a very telling image of what happens when wrecks ruin a percentage of the available commercial space at Potter's Cay. The Captain of the fishing vessel shown above naively believes that a large swathe of Potter's Cay between the bridges is available for his crew and him to tie up to after a long voyage. As he grimly discovers, the large abandoned wreck has completely obstructed this invaluable bit of real estate, which leads directly into Bahamas Ferries' warehouse. Word has it that Bahamas Ferries paid a salvor good money to remove it, and they began to do so in mid-2016. Then a hurricane came, and work was stopped. Into April, 2017 some of their equipment remained, but the rusted underwater hulk has not moved. The fisherman – and any other vessels trying to dock there – has been forced to move on.

The *Lady Mathilda* heading for its home–berth like a horse back to the barn.

Breakfast of grits and bacon, *Champion II*, 1991.

Captain Emmett the day she arrived from the Cook Islands in Polynesia to replace *Sherice M.*, July, 2019

Nassau, tug

Lisa J.

Lisa J. wheelhouse.

Lisa J. engine room

Lisa J. II

Endion or unnamed Government Dock Harbour Island, 1920s, Richard Malcolm.

Stede Bonnet, Abaco, 1950s, possibly Ancil Albury in cap.

Betty K. VII, unconfirmed.

Jenkins Roberts.

Unnamed mailboat, Potter's Cay, c.1972.

Betty K. at launch, Harbour Island.

Mailboat painting, 1960s, William Johnson, aka Uncle Bill.

Deborah K, or *New Day*, unconfirmed, 1988.

Lady Rosalind I

Isle of June

Betty K. IV 1990 Nassau at the Kelly Lumber Dock

Harley & Charley, Potter's Cay, 1989

Bimini Mack, Potter's Cay, 1989

Grand Master cabin, 1989

Signs showing Bahamian mailboat companies are open for business.

Wooden Boats, to the Present

There have been some 235 wooden-hulled sailing and power and sail with auxiliary-power vessels in the mailboat trades in the Bahamas. Identifying the make of a hull is not always precise, as until the 1950s it was largely assumed smaller sailing craft were wood, and these transitioned into moter vessels by cutting masts and adding engines. One boat still running, the *Current Pride* was made of wood in St. Augustine but later sheathed in fiberglass. So an educated assumption was made in some instances based on the years and location of build and service.

The wooden-hulled boats, sail, motor and steam, include the *Abaco Sloops, Admired, Air Pheasant, Air Swift, Albertine Adoue, Albury's, Alice Mabel, Aline, Alisada, Almeta Queen, Amelia Ann, Amie, Andros Trader, Arabella, Arawak, Arctic, Arena, Argosy, Arrow, Astonish, Attic, Bahama Land, Bahama Trader, Bahamas Daybreak 1st, Beluga, Bertie, Betty Ann, Bimini, Blanche Eva, Brontes, Brothers, Cape Hatteras, Captain Dean, Captain Dean II, Captain Dean III, Captain Dean IV, Captain Moxey 1st, Captain Roberts, Caribbean Queen, Carleton, Caroline, Castlereagh, Celeste, Central Andros Express, Charlotte, Child, Christina, Church Bay, Cicero, Clermont, Columbia, Content S., Content 1st, Coraline, Cruiser, Current Queen, Daily Gleaner, Dart, Dash, Defense, Dollymae, Dove, Eastern Isle, Eastern Prince, Eastern Queen, Eclipse, Edna M. R., Ego, Electric, Emerald, Emma, Emmie, Empress, Ena K., Endion, Estrella, Eugene, Evangeline, Experience, Experiment*, and *F.A. Marie*.

Then the *Frances E., Frecil, Gary Roberts, Gary & William, Gaskill Bros., Georgina, Ghost, Glynn, Go On, Graceful, H.J.C., Halcyon, Harley & Charley, Hattie Darling, Hattie H. Roberts, Hazel Dell, Herman, Hero, High Purchase, Huron, Increase, Indiana, Invincible, Ivy S., J.G. Converse, Jane, Jimmie, John Bull, Joyce Roberts, Julia, Julius, Kate Sturrup, Kim, Lady Baillou, Lady Blanche, Lady Dundas, Lady Eula, Lady Mathilda, Laura Louise, Lelia, Leon, Liberty, Lillian & Brothers, Linnet, M.E.B., Madam, Madam Elizabeth Rolle, Madam Queen, Magic, Marcella 1st, Margaret Rose, Maria Ellen, Marmaduke, Mary & Elizabeth, Mary & Susan, Mary Ella, Mary Jane, Mayaguana Queen, Mayflower, Maysie, Merle, Merlin M., Mia Dean, Midinette, Midwest, Miss Andros, Miss Beverly, ML 371, Monarch, Mountain King, Nassau Moonglow, Nassau 1st, Nassau 2nd, Nay Dean, Nellie, Nellie Leonora, New Plymouth, Noel Roberts, Nonesuch, Olga, Olivette, Ollie Ford*, and *Osborne*.

Paddy Helferty followed, and *Palestine, Paragon, Passing Jack, Patricia K., Patsy, Pearline, Pelican, Petrel, Pilgrim, Pleasant, Plymouth Queen, Ponce De Leon, President, Princess Montagu, Quankey, Quick, Raven, Rebecca, Renown, Repeat, Rescue, Resolve, Return, Richard Campbell, Right Arm, Rising Sun, River Queen, Rock Sound, Ruthie Melrose, S.C. Louise, Saale, Samana, San Cristobal, San Salvador, San Salvador Express 1st, Sappho, Sarah E. Douglass, Sea Bird, Sea Witch, Sea Wonder, Senela, Serene, Shamrock, Silver King, Siren, Skipper Bill, South Andros Express, South Andros Queen, Spanish Rose II, Spanish Sea Queen, Staniel Cay Express, Star of the Sea, Stede Bonnet,*

Sydue, Three Bays, Trackless, Tropic, Tryon, Union, Valiant, Vergemere IV (built on Whale Cay), *William & Charles, William H. Albury, Wisdom M., Wissagua, Wissama, Zelma Rose*, and *Zephyr* closes the list.

Aside from the nearly 100 steel-hulled craft, the motor vessel *Sealink*, which began service in 2000, is aluminum, as are several of the Bahamas Ferries vessels, *Priscilla* from 1885 was constructed of iron, and the *North Andros Princess I* from the 1984 timeframe was fiberglass, as the *Current Pride* became in 1998. There were only five steamships on the intra-island route, namely the *City of Nassau* in 1885, *Antila*, *Bahamian* (ex-*Firequeen* Lighthouse Tender, which was built in 1882), *Ballymena* built 1888, and mail packet ship *Corsica*.

There were three basic but distinct types of mailboats serving the Bahamas over 200 years: wooden, European, and modern, meaning purpose-built, steel, twin-screw vessels. For each epoch, we will look into the colourful histories of a half-dozen or so vessels. Here we cover wooden boats built between 1867 and 1977, many of them sail, some of the latter ones fitted with engines. Specifically let us take a look at nine summaries of the career histories of the *Dart* (c.1867), *Kate Sturrup* (1890), *Endion* (1898), *Arena* (c.1910), Content S. (1920), *Old Horse Eye* (1930), *Selma* [or *Zelma*] *Rose* (1947), *Spanish Rose* (1977), and *Current Pride* (c.1980).

Dart was built as a 35-foot harbour pilot boat in c.1867, for speed and agility in crossing the Nassau bar and placing and retrieving pilots aboard visiting ships. Sporting two masts, the schooner was enlarged twice. Believed to have been built in Harbour Island, she served that community and Spanish Wells, one time setting a record of eight hours for the passage. Owned by John Saunders Harris of Eleuthera, the *Dart* is credited with providing the first regular inter-island mail and freight service, as opposed to those vessels shuttling mail from steam-ship depots on Fortune Island (Long Cay) and Crooked Island to Nassau.

Dart won a number of racing regattas under the command of various members of the Harris family. According to the Taylors of Mayaguana, there was a "coloured deck hand" nicknamed Old Blarney who would fire a small cannon from the foredeck to announce her arrival at the Harris Wharf, at the foot of Pine Street in Dunmore Town. According to historians the cabins were reserved for white passengers. The historic little vessel served for over 55 years and is believed to have been lost in a hurricane in 1922.

The 51-ton schooner, *Kate Sturrup*, was likely built in Harbour Island in 1890. Two years later she briefly replaced the *Dart* on the Nassau – Harbour Island run for just a year. Henry William F. Sturrup owned her, and one of her later captains was Arnold Ingraham. The *Tribune* of 10 May, 1916, records that the *Kate Sturrup* served its civic duty in delivering members of the Third Bahamas Contingent on the first leg of their long journey to Europe to fight in the First World War.

The *Nassau Tribune* editor, Captain Dillet, followed the contingent as far as Jamaica, writing: "The Police Band discoursed a variety of music in fine style from the deck of the Colonia while she was towing the *Zellers* and the *Kate Sturrup*, and when a rag time item was on, many people, both on the boats and on the land, swayed themselves to the time thereof in rhythmic fashion. Those who witnessed the scene will not easily forget it, and many who would scorn to weep loudly found a strange choking sensation at the throat as this new body of soldiers left our shore ... Those of the contingent who sailed on the *Zellers* were under the care of Capt. Cole, while Capt. Dillet had the control of those who embarked on the *Kate Sturrup*." Forty years later *Kate Sturrup* left the Bahamas permanently for Jamaica.

The *Endion* was built in 1898 in Boston as a 103-foot private yacht, with an oil-burning engine and capacity for 18 passengers in two staterooms. After a stint as a US Navy vessel (USS *SP-707*) in WWI, she was purchased, in 1921, to replace the *Dart*, at auction by the Harbour Island Steamship Company (Albert Sweeting, Director, value set at US$7,000). After a refit in New York in October of that year, Captain E. B. Sweeting delivered *Endion* to the Bahamas, together with crew Gerald Johnson, Roy Sweeting, Percy Bethel, Frank Johnson, Nick Sawyer, and Albert Sweeting. Her other captains included Albert Sweeting and William G. Harris. The *Guardian* noted: "Every 10 days, for the price of 8 shillings cabin or 5 shillings steerage, tourists and locals could visit historic and picturesque Dunmore Town – the ideal health resort of the Bahamas."

The diminutive 50-foot sailing sloop *Arena* began its career as a humble sponger on the Bahama Banks in the late 1800s. With the demise of that industry in the 1920s, she was put to work by the indefatigable Captain Sherwin Archer of Abaco, as the last of the wind-driven mailboats serving that island from Nassau. In her classic photo-essay of the northern Bahamas entitled *Out Island Portraits*, Ruth Rodriguez described Archer as "Man-O-War's Sears Roebuck. He cheerfully entered each order in his notebook, whether it was a packet of needles or a new engine for a boat. His small miracle: everything delivered in good shape and – weather permitting – on time."

The motorized mailboats, *Stede Bonnet* and *Priscilla*, had been plying the trade from Nassau to Abaco; there was even an air service in the form of a 21-seat Catalina amphibious plane. Captain Archer and his son Bobby, the relief captain, supplemented the service. His sloop was to ply the traditional trade for a decade from 1940 to 1950. Then, it was upgraded and an engine was installed. Ultimately, *Arena* was supplanted by the motor vessel Tropical Trader– thus ended the days of sailing merchants between Abaco and the colony's capital. Archer went on to become a senator representing Abaco.

The mailboat *Content S.* began its career as the 110-foot wooden motor yacht *Percianna II* in Quincy, Massachusetts in 1920, where a researcher recently discovered the original slipway of the J. M. Densmore boatyard where she was built. For 16 years, the yacht served various owners, from a socialite member of the New York Yacht Club named Percy, then a Mr. Spaulding from inland Vermont, then she languished in Miami under the name *Content* until Carl Sawyer of R. W. Sawyer in Nassau found and purchased her in 1936, adding an "S" to her name, presumably for Sawyer.

Two of her Bahamian captains were Stanley Weatherford of Green Turtle Cay, and Roland Roberts of Eleuthera. Grover Theis – Waterfront Reporter for *The Miami News*, wrote on 27 March, 1940: "Now with a converted yacht in the service offering deluxe accommodations, it is not unlikely at all that lots of folks who hesitated about taking the "tramp" trip will slip off on the *Content* for a little vacation excursion and see for themselves what lies in our front yard." *Content S.* had accommodation for 12 passengers and she was originally put on the run from the northern Bahamas to Miami. According to "Papa" Floyd Lowe, patriarch of Green Turtle Cay, as well as Patrick J. Bethel, of Cherokee Sound, the vessel was more of a yacht than a cargo carrier and never did particularly well as the latter.

Underutilized in Nassau, the *Content S.* was chartered by HRH the Duke of Windsor to sail from Nassau first to Cross Harbour Abaco to rescue survivors of the Norwegian tanker *O. A. Knudsen* on the 8 March, 1942, then about a week later to Hope Town to rescue survivors of the British tanker *Athelqueen*. She dutifully carried these many passengers on deck to Nassau. One of them, Alan Heald, still living in Preston, England, was so impressed that he thought they were rescued by the royal yacht *Victoria and Albert*. Whilst serving as a banana boat in the West Indies she was rammed, sunk by the tug *Foundation Aranmore* off Cuba in 1946.

The mixed sail and power 87-footer *Old Horse Eye* began its career as the motor vessel *Patricia K.* in 1930, in the slipway of T. Berlin Albury at Dunmore Town, Harbour Island. It was almost 100 gross tons and the motor was 165 horsepower. The original owner was Kelly's Lumber Yard, and Allan H. Kelly named it for his daughter Patricia. After 1940, John Percy Sweeting of Harbour Island owned it. While she may not have strictly carried the mail contract, this colourful vessel with an unforgettable name nevertheless added to Bahamian maritime lore.

Author Dave Gale of Island Marine, Parrot Cay Abaco recorded in *Ready About: Voyages of Life* in the *Abaco Cays* that "in 1956 she was leading an equally hard life as an inter-island freighter, smelling of old wood, flaky paint, and diesel fuel. Her helmsman turned her wheel in the protection of a pilothouse, perched tugboat style, at her bow. She rolled, but she didn't heel. Her helmsman could not hear her bow wave because of the insistent diesel engine that plunged her headlong into each wave without a care for easing her over it, and its throb was felt as well as heard throughout her hull. The vibrations worked their way up through the helmsman's feet and occasionally set a wheelhouse window to sympathetic rattling... As a Bahamian boat, it was easy to assume she'd been named for the Horse Eye Jack. [She] had a charter with a hardware and lumber company to carry freight from Miami to Nassau."

The author, raconteur and long-time Abaco entrepreneur Dave Gale believes she got her second name – *Old Horse Eye* – after 1956 from a type of Jack fish popular in the Bahamas. Gale's prose bears repeating. He found the vessel leading a "hard life as an inter-island freighter, smelling of old wood, flaky paint, and diesel fuel. Her helmsman turned her wheel in the protection of a pilothouse, perched tugboat style, at her bow. She rolled, but she didn't heel. Her helmsman could not hear her bow wave because of the insistent diesel engine that plunged her headlong into each wave without a care for easing her over it, and its throb was felt as well as heard throughout her hull. The vibrations worked their way up through the helmsman's feet and occasionally set a wheelhouse window to sympathetic rattling."

Benjamin Roberts of Marsh Harbour writes that his father built the *Selma Rose* (also spelt *Zelma*), in 1947 in Abaco. She was a 30-ton wooden motor vessel under the command of Captain Edison Higgs. Though little is known about her early life, with the help of Mrs. Eldwith J. Roberts and the 6 June 1952 *St. Petersburg Times*, we know that six persons tragically drowned when at 2:50 a.m. on 1st June, 1952, whilst transporting passengers from Nassau to Spanish Wells, she was overwhelmed by 15-foot seas near Fleeming Channel. Among the dead were a 23-year-old nurse, Oona Newbold, her 18-year-old sister Carol, a 61-year-old Sunday school teacher from the UK, crew Welbourn Pinder and Ephraim from Andros, and Charles Algreen (44) of Current. The cargo of lumber, furniture, and canisters of gasoline shifted in the momentous seas and she capsized quickly. A sloop named *Sally* managed to rescue 17 survivors clinging to flotsam.

Remarkably an 18-month-old child named Terrance Lightbourn survived. His father Paul managed to find the infant in a submerged cabin and pull him out by a little foot. Nurse Oona Newbold directed the parents in successfully resuscitating the child, then she herself drowned shortly thereafter. The survivors then got by clinging to the wreck and a dinghy until some eight hours later, when the boat sank and rescue arrived. It was rumoured that Captain Higgs swam all the way to Current to summon help, however given that it was ten miles away, and rescue arrived in eight hours, this is unlikely. A folk song recounting the wreck of the *Zelma Rose* was released around 1954, popularizing awareness of the incident.

The 75-foot *Spanish Rose II* was built in 1977, most likely by shipwrights in her homeport of Spanish Wells. Her owners were the brothers Captains Gurney Elon and Stephen Pinder of that port. Her primary purpose was to replace the first *Spanish Rose* (from 1965), running frozen crawfish tails to Nassau so that they could be shipped to the US market in Florida. The boat was available to passengers, as evidenced by an article in the *Los Angeles Times* by Jerry Hulse on 12 May, 1985, reading in part: "If you're in no hurry, it's a bargain – only $18 for the five-hour ride, which includes a soft drink and a sandwich and a world of untroubled waters. Don't get me wrong, [*Spanish Rose II*] isn't the *Queen Elizabeth II*. Sometimes an errant chicken will run squawking along the deck in a flurry of feathers, a dog hot on its spurs. But there are compensations. If the seas are smooth, it's a pleasant journey, and occasionally someone will break out a guitar and strum calypso melodies."

In a 2013, in an article in *The Eleutheran*, Captain Gurney Elon Pinder relates in the laconic style characteristic of mariners, that sometime in 1997 "... Gil Pinder said to me, I have 26,000 pounds of lobster tails to go to Nassau ... I said no problem and loaded them with my wife and nephew ... We got into Nassau 8:30 a.m. – off loaded and left to return between 3:00 p.m. and 3:30 p.m. that afternoon. At 4 p.m. I had to put out a Mayday call – the boat was sinking and rapidly. We were in the ocean, and in the engine room the water was up four feet, but no lives were lost. We launched a lifeboat, paddled off, and we didn't even get wet."

Very little is known about the 88-ton motor mailboat *Current Pride*, except that she is still operating, and believed to be the last of her tree-derived breed plying the islands of the Bahamas on a commercial basis, carrying the mails as her brethren have for over 200 years. Her master is said to be Captain Patrick Neilly. For a relatively diminutive vessel, she has a busy schedule, connecting Nassau with the entire western and most of the northern coasts of 120-mile-long Eleuthera, from Upper and Lower Bogue, The Bluff, Current Island, and Gregory Town, to James Cistern and Hatchet Bay/Alice Town, a produce-exporting port which was blasted through the coast to provide a lagoon protected 350-degrees around.

For those that wish to ride this historic vessel, they can do so in a few days. She departs Nassau every Thursday at 7 a.m. and returns from Hatchet Bay on Tuesdays at 11 a.m. The voyage lasts for five hours and this unforgettable experience costs $30. Call the Potter's Cay Dock Master ahead of time to be sure! Through the *Current Pride* the tradition of transporting freight and passengers amongst the Bahamas aboard wooden boats enters its third century.

In 1922 the Harbour Island Steamship Co. Ltd. (directed by Captain Albert Sweeting, and presumably with the backing of Capt. William G. Harris and the District Commissioner, named McKinney who advocated transportation upgrades), purchased the *Endion* to replace the redoubtable but long-serving sailboat *Dart*. The delivery voyage began not from Boston but from nearby Miami, and she was intended to take up a run between Nassau, Harbour Island, and Miami. Her delivery crew was led by E. B. Sweeting, and included Gerald Johnson, Roy Sweeting, Percy Bethel, Frank Johnson, Nick Sawyer, and Albert Sweeting, a director of the owning firm and her captain for 20 years. In fact, her first voyages were carrying the mails, cargo, locals, and visitors alike between the capital and Spanish Wells and Harbour Island.

Ultimately, another Kelly vessel, the *Betty K.*, took over her route in 1938. She could carry 12 passengers. *Isle of June* had a colourful, if sometimes tragic, career. In early 1930, she helped rescue 20 survivors from the 35-foot sponger *Pretoria*, from which 17 drowned. In 1928, her master, Captain W. C. Wheeler was found aboard, dead from a self-inflicted gunshot wound after three years aboard her. He was replaced by Captain Frank Johnson. It was said that a Bahamian woman also killed herself by leaping off the gangplank. On a brighter note, Captain Richard H. Sweeting rode out a hurricane aboard in 1929 despite losing the rudder and having to construct a makeshift one. Two of her engineers were Leslie and Walter Albury.

European Boats, to the 1990's

There have been 18 boats either built in Europe or to Royal Navy designs and specifications in the Bahamas and Jamaica, which have entered the Bahamian mailboat industry and left an impression. They are, by year of construction, past (European) names, and place of build: *City of Nassau* Laura, formerly the *Granville* built in Whiteinch, Glasgow, Scotland, in 1885, the *Bahamian*, formerly the yacht *Candace*, HMS *Firequeen* (1920) Lighthouse Tender *Firebird*, built in Leith, England in 1882, and the *Monarch of Nassau*, aka *Sir Charles Orr* (1930-1936), built in Cheshire, England, in 1930. Then in 1935 the *Goldfinger II* was built, and variously named *Gold Finger, Jant Je Eppiena* (1935), *Alja-V* (1957), *Brigadoon II* (1970), from Delfzijl, in the Netherlands. A mine-layer named *ML 371* was built as HMS *ML371* at Belmont Dock, Kingston, Jamaica during World War II in 1940, as was *Stede Bonnet* built at HMS *MM 194* for the Royal Navy in Nassau, on Hog Island, in 1942.

Frecil was an ex-Royal Navy MTB, motor torpedo boat, built in the UK in 1942, and *Exuma Pride* began as HMS *LCG(M)192* before becoming *Hjelmeland Fjord* in Norway in 1949; she was built in Tees-Side, England in 1945. *Lisa J. II* was built as the *Schokland* (1952-1965), and later renamed the *Netty* (1965-1981), starting in Alphen ad Rijn, Netherlands in 1952. *Marcella II* was constructed in Busum, Germany in 1956, the *Marcella III* as the *Jade* in Wilhelmshaven, Germany in 1959, and *Lisa J.* as the *Ellen-Søby* (1960-1973), then *Runden* (1999-), and finally at Freeport Grand Bahama she sat on the seller's block as the *Lisa J. 3* in 2005. The vessel began in Marstal, Denmark in 1960 and ended up scrapped. The *Abilin* started as the *Emsstrom* (1977-1984), then *Dinslaken* (1962-1977), and was built in Duisburg, Germany in 1962.

Eleuthera Express 1st was the *Spiekeroog, Wischhafen*, and later the *Treasure Trader*, having like *Marcella II* been built in Wilhelmshaven, Germany, but three years later, in 1962. *Deborah K. II* began as the *Windhund* (1965), *Sawi I* (1977), and became *Klaas I* (1978), having been been fabricated in Hamburg, Germany in 1965. *Miranda* had previously been the *Geulborg* (1977), which was built in Delfzijl, Netherlands in 1966. *Willaurie* was named (or mis-named) the *Willmary* and *Will Mary*; she was built in Hoogezand, in the Netherlands in 1966. Finally the *Miss BJ*, possibly a sister ship to the mailboat *Jeleta*, was formerly named the *Sambre*, which was built in Wirdum, Netherlands, in 1965.

Broken down by six countries, with only German, Netherlands, UK and Denmark in Europe, the boats are: Bahamas: *Stede Bonnet*, Denmark: *Lisa J.*, Germany: *Beluga, Eleuthera Express 1st, Marcella II, Marcella III, Abilin,* and *Deborah K. II*, Jamaica: ML371, Netherlands: *Goldfinger II, Miranda, Willaurie, Lisa J. II,* and *Jeleta/Miss BJ*. UK: *City of Nassau, Bahamian, Monarch of Nassau/Sir Charles Orr, Frecil,* and *Exuma Pride*.

If we divide the Bahamian mailboat fleet into three parts, the wooden, the European, and the modern, this author finds the middle epoch to be the most colourful. Whereas at first the wooden vessels were drawn locally and wereoften hand-built, their lives for the most part began and ended in the islands, near where they were born, as it were. During phase three, the modern era, most mailboats are built in the US Gulf or Florida and are for the most part somewhat charmless to look at, with efficient twin-screw propulsion, square steel sterns, and utilitarian, but not graceful – cranes and ramps sticking out of their foreparts.

However, during the 1950s to 1980s there came to the Bahamas a dozen or more graceful European freighters, rescued from their careers, plodding along the stormy North Sea coasts and up British and European rivers with coal and other commodities, to serve the balance of their days in the sunshine, carrying mail and cargo for us. Perhaps I am drawn to them because my father, a Swede, took the same route. Though most of them lay their weary hulks to rest at the bottom of Bahamian waters, some of them have gone on to Central and South America, where they may still be operating. Sadly, to my knowledge, none of them are still active in our islands.

Few vessels in Bahamian history have had the kind of stories as the humble freighter *Bahamian*, the remains of which can still be found between Paradise Island and Blue Lagoon Cay. She was built as the racing yacht *Candace* in Leith England in 1882 apparently for an aristocratic British playboy. At 168 feet long, 24 feet wide, and 12 feet deep she was a substantial ship of 269 gross tons with a 500-horsepower engine. From the 1880s to 1930 or so she served the Royal Navy as HMS *Firequeen*, the flagship of an admiral. Then she was assigned to the Imperial Lighthouse Service in the Bahamas as a lighthouse tender named *Firebird*. In 1935, the *Firebird* Captain was W. Moxley, the Second Officer was H. Pinder, F. Pool was the Chief Engineer, and Cleveland Malone was radio officer. For the list of the crew and officers of the *Firebird*, see *The Early Settlers of the Bahamas and Colonists of North America,* by A. Talbot Bethell.

In 1941, the underwater photographer, J. Ernest Williamson, shot scenes about the *Firebird* for Paramount's famous film *Bahamas Passage*. Later she was the inter-island *freighter Bahamian* for eight years and Charles Munro of Nassau was her owner and likely the captain. Sometime in the 1950s, she was "reduced to a plain, general cargo ship, her stately masts were chopped off, while peeling paint and rust appeared on the hull . . . the failing derelict had one tune of glory yet to play. Tied to the wharf, waiting to be stripped of her engines and fittings, the dock master received a call that nearly 100 Bahamians were marooned on a small island, 20 miles away. They were awaiting rescue from a hurricane with raging winds heading their way, but none of their small boats available to him could hold more than a dozen people."

"The captain of the Bahamian was summoned and quickly assembled a crew, cranked up the engines and headed into rough seas hoping the old vessel would hold up for one more voyage. It was a rocky trip, but the seasoned craft made it safely to the island, loaded everyone aboard and made it safely back to port." Wrecked just west of Blue Lagoon Island (Salt Cay), north of Paradise Island (Hog Island), she is now known as the *Mahoney Wreck* in 25-45 feet of water.

How many countries can boast that a local entrepreneur re-purposed a World War II lifeboat into a mail and freight boat on a local route? That is exactly what was done by Captain Granville Bethel of Cherokee Sound, Abaco. His home port was shallow and required shuttling of small vessels to carry cargo and people ashore, so Captain Bethel devised an ingenious way to supply the similarly isolated community of Crossing Rocks to the south. He salvaged a lifeboat from a torpedoed Allied freighter that had washed up there. According to his son Patrick, the small craft was renamed *Beluga* and plied its route from 1945 or so into the 1950s fitted with a small engine. The boat could have come from the *O. A. Knudsen*, the *Athelqueen*, or the *Daytonian* – all sunk off Abaco by German and Italian submarines in March, 1942 – or from any of the 130 other ships sunk around the Bahamas in WWII.

The *Marcella II* was built in 1956 at Husumer Schiffswerft in Husum, Germany. Her predecessor was the Bahamian-built *Marcella* I, built in 1969 of wood, 90', burned in Salt Pond, Long Island in 1986. Eddins and Nathaniel Taylor had captained her, sons of the owner, from Pirate's Well, Mayaguana. *Marcella II* was 170' long, 298 gross tons, and built of steel. She presumably traded coastwise from Germany 1956-1980s when she served Freeport from Nassau. In around 1988 she was badly damaged in a storm and became an artificial reef off Long Island. Capt. Eddins Taylor of the Taylor Corporation, owner, said that this *Marcella II* was the first steel-hulled mailboat owned by black Bahamians.

The *Marcella III* has been trading in Europe, the Bahamas, and South America for 57 years under different names, and is believed to be still sailing today – in Bolivia. She was built as the *Jade*, with green colouring throughout, and delivered in Neue Jadewerft, Wilhelmshaven, Germany on 2 June, 1959. Because the yard shares a name with the ship, she was probably built on spec, or without a buyer lined up yet. About 130 feet long, the ship was 364 gross tons, 9.2 feet deep, and could carry 480 tons of cargo.

Purchased by the Taylor family in Germany in 1985, she motored across the Atlantic to her new home under Captains Limas and Eddins Taylor, then served Freeport from Nassau for many years, leaving Wednesdays at 4 p.m. *Marcella III* traded in the Bahamas for some 22 years, still under the original green colour scheme, before the Taylors sold her to Haitian buyers in 2007. Renamed *Miss Eva*, her new owners then sold her to Bolivian interests around 2009 and she motored south to that country, on the southeast coast of South America, where she is believed to be trading as the *Michelda*.

The Andros mailboat *Lisa J.* began its career shuttling school children and others between the islands of Denmark in the 1960s. This unique-looking ship was originally named *Ellen Soby* from 1960 to 1973, then *Runden* until 1999, then *Lisa J.* She is 123 feet long, 28 feet wide, and only 8.6' deep. Weighing 347 tons, her MaK-Diesel engine, pushed the ship at 12 knots with as many as 150 passengers and 25 personal cars. H. C. Christensen's Staalskibvaerft in Marstal, Denmark, built her where she served the communities of Soby and Faaborg, then Sejero and Havnsoe. From 1999 she was sold to the North Andros Shipping Co. Ltd. and sailed across the Atlantic in July. *Lisa J.* was on the route from Nassau to North Andros, namely Nicholl's Town, Mastic Point, and Morgan's Bluff, departing on Wednesday evenings.

Sometime after 2005 she was sold to Honduran owners, where she is today. It is interesting to know how history lives on in vessels: in 2009, I was working in Freeport at a mixed-use ship yard when a Danish yacht sailor said he couldn't believe his eyes, but there was the ferry that took him to school as a child! It was the *Runden*, or *Lisa J.*, with its original name! Scottish maritime consultant, Capt. Calum Legett, kindly provided rare photos of her at work.

The German MAN GHH Dock & Schiffbau in Duisburg built the *Abilin* in 1962. Her tonnage was 430. Very little else is known about this striking looking coastwise vessel, except that in the 1980s she was purchased by Bahamian owners and voyaged to the Bahamas on her own hull. Thereafter she served ports of Long Island until around 1998, when she is listed as "detained." It is believed that in 2007 she was sunk either "on" or "as" a reef in the Bahamas.

There have been two vessels of this name, however the older, European version was built as the *Spiekeroog* in Neue Jadewerft Wilhelmshaven, Germany, the same yard that produced the *Marcella III*. She has also been named *Wischhafen* (1974-1978), and *Treasure Trader* (1978-1979), whilst trading in Europe. The ship is 250 tons, with 400 tons of cargo capacity. She served in the Harbour Island, Spanish Wells, Rock Sound, and Governor's Harbour from 1979 to the late 1980s. In the early 1980s, she is believed to have been sold to owners in Miami, who renamed her. Capt. Junior Pinder is the master of the present, newer *Eleuthera Express*. He informed one of the ship's original owners, Capt. Jan Rautawaara of Finland that the original ship sank between Cuba and Haiti in the late 1980s or early 1990s.

The enigmatic Dutch freighter *Miss BJ* was launched as the *Sambre* in 1965 at the Apol A., Scheepswerf C.V., the shipyard in Wirdum, Netherlands. She was 152' long by 24.9' wide by 8.5' deep, and roughly 330 gross tons. She served European coastal ports and rivers from 1965 to 1973 under the ownership of Kamp's Scheepvaart En Handelsmaatschappij, N.V., of Groningen, Netherlands. Then between 1990 and 1999 she was named *Juleta* and owned by Trans-Bahama Shipping Ltd., possibly also M/V *Jeleta* [sic.] Mail & Ferry Services, M.V.B.S. After lying unclaimed for a time at Prince George Dock, the ship was deliberately scuttled off Nassau on 22 June, 1999. According to *What's On Bahamas* this is now a dive site off the coast of Atoll Cay northeast of Nassau.

The mailboat *Willaurie* was built in 1966 as the *Willmary* at Hoogezand, Netherlands. She was 138' long by 25' wide, and 199 gross tons. Her single German 290 horsepower engine pushed her along at 8.5 knots. In the 1960s, she was sold from Netherlands to a firm named Antler Ltd. of London, UK, and was used for coastal trades to ports like Goole, Charlestown, Hartlepool, and Fulham. In 1980 her classification by Lloyds Register was withdrawn and her flag changed from UK to Nassau, where W. B. Hart owned her. While in the Bahamas she served Rum Cay, San Salvador, and Cat Island in the south-eastern Bahamas, presumably from 1980-1988.

This is another vessel whose demise is at least as interesting as her career, as she continues to attract tourists – divers – to our islands. According to a dive website, whilst carrying passengers and freight among the Bahama Islands on the 2 August, 1980, *Willaurie* experienced engine trouble and passengers were taken aboard Royal Bahamas Defence Force vessel/s. Apparently, the ship was berthed at Potter's Cay for years, for in 1988 it was reported foundered, or at least partially sunk, there. Then it was raised and was being towed west when, in heavy seas, the towline parted. The towing vessel managed to get the *Willaurie* to Clifton Pier, southwest New Providence, where it sank. Then the local dive operator, Stuart Cove, patched her enough to be towed several miles west to a point Southeast of Goulding Cay, where he sank her as a diving attraction the day after Christmas in 1988.

The vessel had a very low freeboard, suitable for coastal waters but less so for open ocean passages to places like the southern Bahamas. I recall as a child and teen seeing her at Potter's Cay. To me the vessel epitomized the romantic, tramp steamer, and 'rust bucket' image of the mailboat fleet – a grand old lady waiting to die. At the same time, her European lineage was clear, giving her an exotic air. In the early 1980s the Ministry of Transport & Aviation has entries for both "Proposed mailboat M/V *Will Mary*[sic.]" and "Contract mail service *Will Laurie*[sic.] Vol. 2". Today she sits defiantly upright, atop a reef. In the nearly 28 years since she was sunk, the *Willaurie* has become a premier dive site, and images of her have graced the photo collections of divers in all corners of the globe, a fitting tribute to her international provenance.

The *Miranda* has been owned not only by the Taylor mailboat dynasty (12 ships) of Mayaguana, but by Dutch, American, and Honduran investors as well. Sander Gebroeders in Delfzijl, Netherlands built her as the *Geulborg* in 1966. Wagenborg Shipping owned her until 1977, when the Taylors purchased it, delivered it to the Bahamas, and she traded from Miami to Turks & Caicos and Exumas as well as Long Island. One of her captains in the Bahamas was Bob Garraway from St. Vincent. Her dimensions were 176' long, 28.5' wide, 9.2' deep, 399 gross tons, and a 450-horsepower engine propelled her at 9.5 knots.

In 1996, the Taylors sold her to Haitian owners and renamed the *Paradise Express* until 1999, when a Honduran company purchased her, with the name *El Compa*. From 1999 she was known as the *Gilbert Sea*, owned by the Gilbert Shipping Corp. of San

Lorenzo, Honduras. However, she seems to have rotted away in the Miami River. The website divespots.com adds, "She was seized by the US Customs Department – 74 pounds of cocaine were found hidden inside the false bottom of a 55-gallon drum – as part of Operation Riverwalk and is now part of Governor's Riverwalk Reef. The front portion of the wheelhouse was painted with murals [and she] was sunk in 90' of water just 1.5 miles from the Palm Beach Inlet and is quickly becoming a haven for tropical and game fish."

The *Betty K VIII* continues a 130-plus-year tradition of European-built vessels, supplementing the fleet providing mail and freight services amongst and to and from the Bahama Islands. Though built in 1984 by Lurssen-Werft, Bremen, Germany, and connecting Florida and beyond with the Bahamas, she is flagged to the tiny port of Avatiu, Rarotonga, Cook Islands (where, coincidentally, the author has sailed to and obtained a driver's license from). The ship is a general cargo ship of 2,191 gross tons, capable of carrying about 1,500 tons of cargo. Since May, 2014 she has been plying the cargo route between Miami, Nassau, and Abaco under the ownership of the *Betty K*. Line of Nassau.

This Bahamian owner, though not strictly a mail carrier, deserves mention. According to their website, they have been serving The Bahamas since 1920 and grown to be full service shipping company operating between Miami, Nassau, and Abaco. *Betty K.* was named after the daughter of the founder, the Late Mr. C. Trevor Kelly. A fully owned Bahamian company was born out of an idea from the owner, who saw the need to purchase a boat to take care of their personal needs. The boat, then nicknamed the "Potato and Onion", would transport lumber for the Kelly families."

The original *Betty K.* and the smaller Kelly vessel *Ena K.* provided an indispensable service, connecting the colony to the US during the war, when larger Canadian ships were withdrawn to their homeland. These little ships returned hundreds of Allied sailors to the mainland after German and Italian submarines had sunk their ships off the Bahamas in 1942. Canadian historian and author Kevin Griffin adds, "The 164-ton *Betty K.* was built in 1938. The "motor boats", as the Duchess [of Windsor, Wallis Simpson, wife of the Governor, formerly King Edward VIII] called them, offered sailings every Sunday, Tuesday, and Thursday in each direction between Nassau and Miami. Before the war, they had sailed from Miami at noon and from Nassau at 2 p.m. but [during World War II in the early 1940s] they moved back and forth as cargo offered. More than eighty years later, Betty K Agencies Ltd of Nassau would introduce the sixth and seventh ships of that name, the 1,457-ton *Betty K VI* in 2004 and 2,028-ton *Betty K VII*.

As happens with abandoned property, particularly the waterborne variety, it sank at the berth. Salvors managed to raise it sufficiently for the ship to be towed out of Nassau Harbour in boisterous winter weather. The pair (towing and towed) made it as far as the oil jetty at Clifton Pier before the tow line parted and the *Willaurie* wrecked upon the rocks at the base of a cliff. It was the third and final time the vessel was distressed in Bahamian waters. No one seemed to know what to do until enterprising dive instructor Stuart Cove showed his mettle. On the day after Christmas, in 1988, he and some friends and colleagues managed to pry the hulk of the *Willaurie* and tow it to a suitable depth where she was sunk as a lasting underwater attraction which appeals to divers and aquatic life alike.

Modern Boats, 1990's to the Present

The third and final general category of mailboat is the modern type, defined as having at least one engine, being built of steel fairly recently in the US Gulf or Florida, and having cargo derricks or cranes on the forward decks, or roll-on / roll-off (ro-ro) capabilities for vehicles. There are numerous advantages of the modern type over its predecessors, the wooden and the European type. Wooden vessels were generally sail-powered, subject to the vagaries of wind, waves, and current to the degree that motor ships overcame those obstacles. Any wooden boat leaks, and wooden boats fitted with cantankerous machinery tended to leak a lot more. Also, wood is a lot less resitant to rot and reefs than steel is. Planks tend to break and it only takes a few of them to cause a sinking.

As for the European ships, they were designed for the rivers, canals, and coasts of northern Europe, and as a result very long and thin, and tended to be deeper in draft than required for the Bahamas. They also had low deck-lines between the wheelhouseaft and the bow, which could be swamped in the open waters of the southern Bahamas, damaging cargo and harming passengers. Finally, they tended to be single-engine, meaning that if something went wrong with one engine, the ship would be disabled. Single engine vessels are also more difficult to control in port and whilst docking.

The modern mailboat design can be traced to the mid-1980s to vessels like the *North Cat Island Special* and the *Champion II*, where were small, stout little ships, custom-built for the Bahamas mail, passenger and cargo trade. Roughly 75 feet long and only six feet deep, they were built of steel, were less than 100 tons, and powered as a general rule by twin diesel engines. *Champion II*'s builder, Capt. Ernest Dean, admitted he built her small to get into the US market with less paperwork. Vessels like the *Grand Master* were built exclusively for the Bahamas market at almost twice the size – 214 tons, longer, wider, stronger and capable of withstanding bigger seas. For over 30 years this design has predominated, and makes up roughly half of the present fleet, although there were decades of change in the 1970s to 1990s during which all manner of craft – repurposed ferries, fishing vessels, offshore supply boats, landing craft, etc. were used.

Why is the modern mailboat so popular? It is strong, seaworthy, shallow, maneuvrable, stable and thus comfortable, can work its own cargo, get into and out of hard-to-reach shallow docks, and if it goes aground on a reef, chances are (and many instances have proven) the steel hull will remain intact and the relatively flat bottom will keep it upright until the seas subside, the tide turns, the boat can kedge-anchor (crawl) its way to safety, or it can be salvaged. The only disadvantage is that unlike the ro-ro variety, modern mailboats cannot simply motor nose-first to the shore – they require some kind of dock or at least another vessel to offload onto.

I thought this second-to-last feature would be one of the easiest to write – identify and describe some 20 vessels still sailing – but it is not. If you search online for a mailboat schedule (it is called the "inter-insular mail-boat schedule" in government parlance), the most recent one, on a government website, is a decade old and lists several vessels (*Lady D.*, sank in 2014 and *United Star* sold to Honduras after a collision, and *Bimini Mack*, replaced by the *Sherice M.*) that are no longer operating in the Bahamas.

Amazingly in this era of instant information, if one is planning a voyage on a mailboat, the best way to prepare is to visit the friendly dock master on Potter's Cay Dock – at the eastern end. The team there will cheerfully photocopy that week's actual schedule for you, for free. Armed with that information you should be able to locate the vessel/s of interest and if the boat is in, wander down to ask a few questions about schedules directly with the officers or crew. That way you are less likely to be disappointed by arriving long before a departure, or worse, after the boat has left.

Even after riding mailboats for some 40 years (my siblings and their children recently returned in 2016 from Ragged Island on the *Captain C.*, in 2017 the), and studying these sturdy craft from afar for the past decade or so, there is a vessel operating today that I know nothing about: *Lady Katheirina*. I cannot find a single image of her, and only gather that she has served Mangrove Cay, Moxey Town, and Lisbon Creek, Andros for over a decade, and that the trip takes six hours and costs $45. Captain Tom Hanna has snookered me again, introducing another new vessel (after the *New G.* and the *VI Nais*), named after his beloved daughter, recently passed, whose name will live on in maritime history.

Overall, there are nearly 50 ports in the archipelago, situated on some 20 of the larger islands, which a fleet of around 20 mailboats serves today. From Bimini and Grand Bahama in the north to the many ports of Eluethera, Chub and Farmer's cays, and Bullock's Harbour in the Berry Islands, several ports in Abaco, including Hard Bargain, Staniel Cay, Black Point, and other settlements in Exuma as well as Georgetown; each can expect a weekly or at least monthly mailboat call. Then Rum Cay and San Salvador, Abraham's Bay Mayaguana, the length of Long Island, Crooked and Acklins islands as well as Long or Fortune Cay between them, and Matthew Town, Inagua – are all covered, as is Duncan Town, Ragged Island.

The 20 or so work horses which accomplish the logistics of delivering people, goods, vehicles, vessels, and creatures to and from the islands are similar but, of course, like their hybrid wooden and European predecessors, not the same. Almost half, or nine of these vessels are the modern ro-ro type popularized by landing craft in World War II and well suited to the shallow islands of the Bahamas due to their low draft and ability to dock, discharge, and load with minimum shore-side infrastructure; often a simple bull-dozed mound or earth would suffice for a ramp (as an additional advantage, the hull, or draft forward is about half as deep as the stern, which carries the engine and fuel and is thus a lot heavier).

The names of some of the new generation of ro-ro ships are *Fiesta Mail* (China-built and unique), *Sea Spirit II* (ex-*United Spirit*), *Island Link*, *Lady Rosalind II*, *K.C.T.* and her substitute *VI Nais*, *East Wind*, and *New G.* The latter vessel was delivered to Bahamas for Capt. Tom Hanna in early 2015. The oldest in the present fleet is also the only holdover from wooden mailboats: *Current Pride*. Though we have many photos of this vessel, I don't know when, where, or by whom she was built – presumably in north Eleuthera or Abaco in the 1960s or 1970s.

Are mailboats as essential and vibrant today as they have been for over 200 years? As vibrant as ever! To illustrate the point, if you were to spend a week "mailboat spotting" at Potter's Cay – the only place in the Bahamas where more than two congregate at a time - you would not be disappointed. On Monday, you would see the *Bahamas Daybreak III* sail for North Eleuthera, then the (New) *Eleuthera Express* heading out for South Eleuthera, followed by the *Captain Moxey* that evening, serving South Andros. The *Fiesta Mail* would set off for Freeport at dusk, and before midnight the *K.C.T.* or *VI Nais* will push off for a long voyage to Acklins and Crooked islands.

On Tuesdays mid-day the *Lady Rosalind* heads for northern Andros, then *Grand Master*, under Captain Lance, does what his father did – takes off for Georgetown mid-afternoon as well, followed soon after by either *Captain Emmett* or *Island Link*, for northern Long Island (Seymour's, Deadman's Cay, Salt Pond). That very day *Legacy* takes an overnight passage to Abaco's capital and Hope Town and Green Turtle Cay. *Captain C.* heads for Ragged Island via several Exuma cays, and *Captain Gurth Dean* heads into the night for the Abaco islands via the Berries. The *Lady Frances* heads for San Salvador and Rum Cay, and *Lady Mathilda* for Mayaguana and Inagua. *Lady Emerald* sails for Smiths Bay Cay Island as well as San Sal and Rum Cay.

On Wednesdays, the *Bahamas Daybreak* has returned from south Eleuthera and heads for the northern portion of the island. The *Fiesta Mail* has likewise returned to Nassau and goes back to Freeport, as she will thrice weekly. *Lady Rosalind* heads west for north Andros later in the afternoon. The following evening – Thursdays – she is off again, this time for northern Cat Island – Arthur's Town, Dumfries, Orange Creek, and Bennett's Harbour. That evening the *Sherice M.* heads for Bimini via Cat Cay and Chub Cay in the Berry Islands. *Current Pride* makes for Hatchet Bay and the Bluff, Eleuthera, and the (New) *Eleuthera Express* under Captain Junior Pinder heads for nearby Spanish Wells and Harbour Island. Early – at 2 a.m. – the *Lady Katheirina* heads for Mangrove Cay, Moxey Town, and Lisbon Creek, Andros, arriving at dawn.

Fridays and the weekends things cool down on the docks as vessels come back to roost at base. At 10 a.m. the *Fiesta Mail* returns to Freeport for the Taylor family of Mayaguana, often with a Bahamian band to entertain weekend passengers. That evening the *Captain C.* returns, followed by the *Captain Gurth Dean* and 12 hours after she left the *Fiesta* again. *Lady Frances* folds its wings Friday morning, right after the *Legacy* returns from Abaco. On Saturday, *Lady Emerald* returns from the southern islands, followed by the *Lady Mathilda* from even further afield in Inagua. The *Daybreak* comes back Sunday at 4 p.m., preceded that morning by the *Sherice M.* from Bimini. The (new) *Eleuthera Express* comes back just after noon, then the *Fiesta*. Finally, *Lady Rosalind* returns from Cat Island.

One defining feature of these myriad voyages is that you can rely on comfortable, if by no means luxurious, accommodation, running water, shared plumbing, three meals a day, good company, and by pretty much, by any standard, very reasonable rates of between $25 (*Current Pride*) and $90 (*Lady Mathilda*) per passage – not bad considering the distances travelled. But remember, don't rely on the internet, or even the papers to figure out mailboats: the real experts are the men and women operating them, and the real experience begins right under our noses – on Potter's Cay or the nearest government dock in the community you live in.

Roundup: Mailboats as a Living Bahamian Tradition

Bahamians are justifiably proud of their fleet of dozens of mailboats that connect the islands. Well they should be. Since the inception of inter-island mail delivery, it has been a locally sponsored and a locally developed trade. In 1804, world powers such as the United Kingdom, France, Germany, and the United States sent their mail and freight to the colony via a then cosmopolitan, now nearly abandoned Fortune Island, or Long Cay, in the Crooked Island District. Larger, foreign-owned vessels generally brought mail and goods to Nassau from there and from ports in the US, Europe, Central and South America, and Caribbean.

But then something new happened, locally built wooden sailing crafts began carrying the mails and goods first between Fortune Island and the capital in Nassau (a considerable voyage), but then to nearby communities in North Eleuthera, Abaco, and so on. Soon farmers and fishermen came to rely upon this service to bring goods to market and return with the essential materials to enable them to expand their communities. As Fortune Island's demise has shown, without efficient trade, communities die off: they lose their most important commodity – people – first. Imagine homecoming celebrations nowadays without mailboats to provide happy, affordable, and sociable platforms for folks to go back to their roots?

In order to sustain the communities where their voting constituents resided and owned land, politicians and civil servants set about stabilizing trade with Nassau, which thus connected them with the wider world, its markets and transportation hubs. They agreed to subsidize the carriage of mail and permitted the investors and owners of mailboats (many of them "mom and pop" business with the owner or his sons as captains), to profit from carriage of extra freight and passengers. The government also oversaw licencing and certification of vessels and officers and the allocation of routes and vessels to serve those routes. Given the inherent dangers of maritime navigation, the age of some of the vessels, and the costs in terms of time and capital of replacing mailboats, there has always been an informal system of standby, or replacement vessels to fill in. That system is illustrative of the interdependence and cooperation of mariners in this particular market.

The Bahama Islands require a well-adapted and large fleet of vessels to serve its many communities, particularly because the islands rank as one of the top archipelagos in the world. Bahamas is, according to Wikipedia, roughly in the top-ten, with some 3,000 cays or islands, behind Indonesia, Philippines, clusters of islands in Scandinavia, the UK, etc. The Bahamas were recently granted formal archipelagic status by the United Nations and are the largest such cluster of islands north of the Caribbean on this side of the Atlantic, as far as the Arctic. Our islands stand out from space (astronaut Gordon Cooper is still mesmerized by them). And to keep the roughly 35 districts together the commonwealth has devised a system of mailboats to supplant flights by calling at some 50 communities on over 20 islands.

Since some of those communities have no regular air service, having a mailboat call, even every two weeks is essential. After all, just having an airstrip isn't enough: on San Salvador, I inquired why the only airplane on the runway had a wing missing and was told the owner was so tired of folks demanding the use of his plane that he removed a wing and took it home – the rough equivalent of a wheel clamp.

These boats provide reliable contact, more or less weekly, with the capital, in a hub-and-spoke system. Importantly, mailboats are not exclusive – other freighters can ply their trade on unscheduled or private routes as they please. It is not a perfect system, in as much as everything must go through the capital, and islanders have historically complained that merchants in Nassau can be rapacious and impose usurious fees, etc. However, folks from far-flung districts have also developed their own channels of trade, accommodation, and supply based on familial and long-standing relationships. Having mailboat owners and captains originate in the communities they serve has reinforced this tradition.

So, mailboats have survived for over 200 years, the readers might say, but will they continue to survive? In my opinion, backed by nearly 30 years of seagoing or commercial maritime experience, yes, mailboats are here to stay. To put it simply, until they can fly petroleum in bulk lots, or ripe vegetables, and concrete, the world will still need the reliable old freighters. We need only look a dozen years back, at the *United Star* versus *Sea Hauler* to realize that accidents will continue to happen. That case was particularly egregious because the officers had tools to avoid it – radar and radios. Nowadays the tools for collision avoidance are even better, however, they are useless without a well-rested, trained, and an alert person operating them. Some 15 years ago I thought it was charming to be woken up by a mailboat's erratic motion, to wander into the bridge to find it abandoned, then voluntary take the helm, one captain to another, until the skipper returned from repairing machinery. As we all know now, there is nothing charming about a vessel without a lookout slamming into another one also steaming blind in the night.

As for the fall-out from the *Sea Hauler* and *United Star* collision, in which four Bahamians were killed and 25 injured, including an amputee, let's leave aside the contentious facts and look at the perception. To this day the official report is not readily available. Victims were left in the dark for months, then years. It is during times like those that citizens rely on their government for decisive, compassionate action. Yet families felt compelled to protest in the streets. The perception given was that authorities were hiding information and dragging their feet to compensate victim's families. And yet admiralty law is for the most part very settled and straightforward, is based on British Common Law, where virtually every kind of maritime casualty has been adjudicated. On top of which all the evidence needed made it back to the dock to undergo scrutiny. The handing of this case illustrates how much we all stand to learn from the humble mailboat.

Let's look at the fallout from the deadliest merchant marine accident in the Bahamas in living memory another away: In April of 2021 it will soon be 18 years since the accident, and there is still no official report published. Here is the latest update from the casualty section of the Bahamas Maritime Authority:

> A marine casualty investigation was conducted by Senior Justice Joseph Strachen (retired Supreme Court Judge) who was appointed by the Minister responsible for Maritime Affairs. The Minister ordered an inquiry in the form of a formal investigation as required by section 243 of the Merchant Shipping Act, Chapter 268 by appointment of a Wreck Commissioner. The BMA did not conduct the investigation (email, May 5, 2020).

We can also learn from how the sinking of the *El Faro* in Bahamian waters was handled: again, despite the many facts which appeared to weigh against them, the ship owners and government regulators were immediately out in front of the media, settling quickly with family members, keeping the ball moving and the public informed. In today's multi-media information-driven world, where what the disempowered say online can be empowering, perception is extremely important.

As for the future, it is virtually certain that other maritime fatalities will strike the mailboat fleet again; particularly if mariners and the public are not afforded the opportunity to learn what caused recent ones. If we could outlaw shipwrecks, or car accidents, it would have been done. From casualties (often) flow changes: after the cruise liner *Yarmouth Castle* caught fire *en route* to Nassau in November, 1965 and 90 people perished, the Safety of Life at Sea (SOLAS) regulations were overhauled. As a leading flag state provider; seventh in the world with 1,512 ships in 2019, the Bahamas has an especially high duty towards its small domestic fleet, and has the specialized resources at its disposal to investigate and transparently report on casualties.

Put another way; how will the Bahamas have authority over foreign-owned ship casualty investigations if it never releases its findings on the deadliest domestic accident in its own back-yard, 18 years later, and, realistically, forever. By contrast, when the mailboat *Sherice M.* burned and was a lost on 16 June, 2018 the maritime authorities published their 22-page, illustrated casualty investigation eight months later, on 25 February, 2019. That's the way the system is *supposed* to work. The report was online, requiring no log-on to access it, and there weren't injuries aboard *Sherice M.* The Spanish government's mishandling of the $5 billion Bahamas-flagged *Prestige* oil spill beginning in 2002 cost them their jobs. A similar tanker spill from the oil terminals on New Providence or Grand Bahamas could be highly disruptive to tourism, fisheries, and the environment. When Hurricane Joaquin washed the *Emerald Express* far ashore on Acklins in October, 2015, there was fortunately no loss of life.

Maritime crises are inevitable in a geographically delicate island nation through which major sea-lanes pass, connecting oceans and continents via the Old Bahama Channel, the Providence channels, Straits of Florida, Windward Passage and many through the southern Bahamas. With the Panama Canal expansion complete, seaborne traffic will likely only increase, placing even greater emphasis on the maintenance of navigational aids. Captains not only have radar but AIS, enabling them to know the names, sizes, speeds, courses, destinations and other details of most of the ships around them. But the equipment is only useful when utilized. A vessel making headway with no one operating the wheel, standing watch, and using all the wonderful collision-avoidance equipment is considered "not under command," even if there is a person present if they are incapacitated by lack of sleep or inebriated.

What are the lessons that we can learn from mailboats in the Bahamas? That adaptability to the local environment is key, that grafting foreign equipment to a new purpose in different lands can sometimes work quite well, but that ultimately the home-grown solutions prevail. It is fascinating to read comments like these from a commissioner on Andros, in 1912, regarding the importance of local knowledge as well as derring-do:

> It must be admitted that there are a few very dangerous channels along our shore to contend with, and when a strong north easterly breeze disturbs them, they send forth such breakers that the master of any vessel who broaches them must draw pictures as fanciful about his service as about his life. After all, some daring is necessary and the master who is void of it will never successfully convey the Andros Island mails. The vessel is a good one and fully suites the purpose, and with a little more courage and ability infused into the master and crew, we will have very good mail service.

In 1913 he continued: "....perhaps as the captain gets better acquainted with the shore, things will continue to improve. But there are two essentials to this (a) the mail vessel should have an efficient mate, as it is impossible for the captain to see after things on board, and on shore the same time. (b) Some measures should be taken to see that she leaves Nassau on time."

Mailboats have not always been popular; due to inadequate boats, management, weather delays, dangerous ports which were bypassed in certain weather, overland and waterborne alternatives having to be made – and from the 1950s via airlines as well, and then, during all of its history but particularly during the US Prohibition from 1920 to 1933, when wild amounts of money could be made particularly at West End

Grand Bahama and Bimini, the age-old scourge of the sailor showed it's head. Not all relatives of families involved in the mailboat industry over a century ago will be pleased to read these reviews made by island commissioners, some of whom, perhaps Oxbridge-educated, honed their acerbic wits for the most damning portrayals, including these gems:

"The elements joined forces with the people in pouring forth complaints about her" the poor little *Linnet*, a small sponging sloop yanked from the shallows to fill in for *Arawak*, which filled in to for the *Nellie Leonora*, wrecked on Rum Cay in 1916.

"She outlived her usefulness, the zinc pail which is called a privy is very untidy, and nauseous." The *Columbia* in 1925; she traded from Abaco to Inagua from 1901 to September 17, 1926, when in a hurricane at Simms, Long Island, she was beached. This description certainly explains the reluctance of some passengers to be becalmed on a sailing vessel with no motor for days on end between Inagua and the capital.

The *Emerald* served Grand Bahama, making 12 trips, to cover for the motor boat *Cruiser*, sloop *Sydue*, and motorboat *Christina*, from 1924 to 1926. The commissioner observed that the "captain and crew are very unreliable and discourteous," suggesting that they were much more concerned with loading liquor for West End, rather than humdrum cargo or mail, which was of course a lot less profitable.

In 1923 the Commissioner covering North Andros reported a new captain, on the *Repeat*, thus: "The irregularity of trips is excused by captain and crew under the plea of 'weather conditions;' very often these conditions come from the inside of bottles."

Fortunately not all feedback was negative, and indeed commissioners are often frank in distributing blame to including subsidizing the wrong vessel, providing docks which were inadequately protected, sometimes for an entire winter, giving the boats too many ports, not providing enough deck space for livestock to make the voyage without shrinking or dying, and so on. The *Petrel,* owned by Charles R. Arteaga in 1907, earned these accolades; "Nothing can be said against the present vessel and its crew. She is clean and comfortable, and her master is ready and obliging."

1919: Nicholl's Town; "...the boat was so leaky that it was dangerous to make a trip across the ocean in her. The trips were so irregular that freight to and from Nassau was carried by boats running direct from each settlement;" in other words local communities simply went around the mailboat system and did it themselves. Yet again, there were bright spots as well, as when the Resident Justices Office at Mangrove Cay in 1907 reported "I am pleased to see that the suggestion made in my last report for the extension of the mail service to the Southern part of the island has been acted upon.... The mail made her first call at Kemp's Bay Settlement. This now gives us a service all along the shore, as well as with Nassau." (Edward Bailey Proud, *The Postal History of the Bahamas*, UK, 2000, p.282-285)

When the system is tweaked, then, for example the men and women who have stooped, and continue to stoop to the ground to scrape some bark off the cascarilla plant, bag the strips in sacks, soak them to soften it, and then export the sacks by mailboat to ultimately reach the Compari distillery in Italy where the Bahamian herb gives the world-renown aperitif some of its unique flavor: those persons can profit from a cash crop, such as the wire cages of live crabs that are often caught the night before the mail leaves, so that they remain fresh for market at Potter's Cay Causeway and beyond.

Even commissioners, owners, captains, mates, crew, passengers, shippers and other customers cannot control such vagaries as weather, including hurricanes, accidents, including engine seizures or overhauls, crane breakages, crew walk-offs, vessel inspections for insurance and financing, refueling, provisioning, and so many other moving parts. That's why there's always a margin of some 20% substitute mailboats for when – not if – things go sideways.

A mailboat chokepoint: the north side of Potter's Cay Dock, looking west towards the Prince George Docks, cruise ships, and Nassau and NP. This is between the bridges, from the original Paradise Island Bridge. In the left foreground are mostly Haitian trading and fishing boats. But then the gap before the light green mailboat is rendered unusable by any craft by virtue of the abandoned mailboat hulk reaching to the surface. This should be removed or covered over to provide a usable waterfront, it is too valuable not to do so. Use of the cargo bays and sheds would permit direct contact, sheltered from sun and rain, between truck chassis and vessels. For years it has simply obstructed commerce and still does, despite several efforts to remove it.

Potter's Cay Dock and the Future

From looking at the press and applying other models, some basic truths seem to emerge about financing a sector like mailboats. As Captain Ernest Dean's early experience shows, insurance is very important – and expensive – as boats catch fire and sink, and sometimes persons are killed aboard them. They can also cause environmental damage far beyond their economic value. Any shipping or maritime endeavour is cyclical. While the government has sought to stabilize critical national infrastructure such as mailboats, it is impossible to iron out all the troughs and peaks in a global economy ruled by supply and demand.

That government and private investors can work together, so long as neither smothers the other. Entrepreneurialism and capitalism backed by government guarantees instils confidence by investors and captains in their vessels and businesses, and the local communities that are the end-users and beneficiaries. Wouldn't it be wonderful to develop a Bahamas-class vessel, based on what the owners and captains have learned? Even better, to have them manufactured, say at the Grand Bahama Shipyard, and exported? Another example is fuel subsidies: neither the owners nor the sponsoring government will always be happy, with one side (say, the owners) claiming it is not enough, and the other (government) claiming at times it is too much – which at times like this with low fuel prices, can be true. But without a fuel subsidy, communities like Duncan Town Ragged Island or Port Nelson, Ragged Island, which don't have regular air service, would be effectively cut off.

Even if the owners operate a route at a loss (not good for anyone in the long term), they still need subsidies to call on those ports. Without them, they might go out of business. One technique is to peg the subsidy to a set price: fuel goes above that price and the government compensates on a percentage basis. Below that price, no subsidy is offered. As for freight and passenger rates, it is my understanding that these are also set by the government and standardized, enabling even those of modest means the opportunity to conduct business, obtain medical care, and see family and friends in Nassau and on the islands where they have people. If I were asked whether I would change the fuel subsidies or tariffs for cargo and passengers, I would suggest just leaving them alone.

Risk may be managed, not eliminated. The mailboat market place already has a high barrier to entry. The US is the preferred builder, and financing new vessels requires considerable up-front investment and risk. Because of their own subsidies, US shipyards tend to be very expensive when compared globally. The Bahamian investors who take those risks deserve to be rewarded. And the administrative burden of keeping vessels, crew, safety equipment and certifications up-to-date grows every year.

In conclusion, if there is one item this author and Nassuvian would advocate for, it would be wreck removal. It's not the kind of ribbon-cutting, photo-opportunity which politicians tend to prefer, when compared with the colourful vessels and ports, however it is nonetheless a critical one. We've talked about 200 or more vessels, but without a place to tie up in the capital, their cargo and people could not get ashore. I knew someone who abandoned an old car in the bush out west, only to be called by the police weeks later and politely asked to move it. But the same does not happen with vessels. Owners and their insurers may wrangle for so long that it costs more to remove a wreck than to abandon it. Then it becomes the government's problem, to attempt to adjudicate, to order removal, and in remove the wreck. On 28 July, 2014, ZNS aired footage of the *Lady D.*, a fairly modern (22-year-old) mailboat serving seven communities in Andros, sinking at its berth just east of the old Paradise Island Bridge. The channel is fairly shallow there, so most of the vessel is still above water and clearly visible. It has also blocked this invaluable bit of real estate for nearly two years. No one can claim ignorance of this blemish on our national image and trade.

In 2009, a Bahamian salvage company in Freeport that I worked for at the time raised a similar-sized vessel, which was completely submerged, also at a busy dock-face, in four to six hours. When the casualty occurred, I fail to understand how there were not sufficient crash pumps from other vessels or on shore. The fact is that if someone in authority puts their mind to it, they could have the *Lady D.*'s hull temporarily sealed, the water pumped out long enough for her to be towed to a nearby boat yard, where she could be hauled out of the water and out of the way of other mailboats, and the millions of tourists who see her annually from the bridges. Yes, the *Lady D.*'s removal cost money. But the owners and insurers can be easily ascertained, and while they sort out those details, the boats would be out of harm's way on shore – perhaps sold to offset costs? Do it first and bill them later.

Potter's Cay is indisputably the capital of mailboats nationally – the only place they consistently congregate. Though it lies beneath bridges heavily trafficked by tourists and is passed hundreds of times a day by various vessels, many of them filled with tourists. Locals and tourists alike drive parallel to it in droves daily. Probably all Bahamians have at some point eaten seafood landed at Potter's Cay. Yet as a society, the island and its vital business is virtually invisible to many of us, perhaps even more so the younger generation.

Potter's Cay is .75 miles long and only 75 yards wide. Starting at the western end, there are the ro-ro mailboats and open-market ramp-style vessels, some of them owned and operated by Bahamas Ferries, serving most of the islands. Then the *Fiesta Mail* docks on the northwest tip, and beneath the Sir Sidney Poitier (western) Bridge cluster a number of mid-sized to large fishing boats. Then we have a travesty: a ship was abandoned right between the two bridges, taking up a huge area of roughly an acre which could easily be occupied by half a dozen other vessels, but it is now rendered useless. If Potter's Cay is to remain vibrant, relevant and picturesque, the hulk needs to be removed. Recycling of the steel could offset the cost.

East of the wreck, also littered by the hulks of *Lady Tasha* and other boats, lies a small fleet of what appear to be Haitian cargo boats. It seems these are what is left of the sailboat fleet that used to utilize the southeast corner of Arawak Cay. They are loaded to the gills with bicycles, mattresses, and other miscellaneous cargo, some of which litters the dockside. Recently the free access to walk around the island has been cut off by a fence erected by one of the warehouse operators. As a result, more junk is likely to clutter this area unless something is done. Moving east and out from under the original PI bridge, the wharf is dominated by mailboats of the modern type, lining the north pier to the northeast corner, which is home to a number of large, long, ro-ro type ramp boats. These also dominate the eastern jetty, which is hemmed in by a current-ripped reef marked by a rusting pole.

To the southeast of Potter's Cay, a number of conventional modern mailboats line the wharf, then the wooden *Current Pride*, then an assortment of mid-size to small fishing vessels. The channel they must use, between private yacht slips to the south and the cay itself, is very narrow, sufficient but only barely. If a large yacht is berthed on the outside slip and two or more mailboats are docked side by side on the cay, passage is effectively blocked. The problem can be remedied by removing one of the yacht jetties, or by prohibiting yachts from tying at the end, or from mailboats from double docking. On the other side of the causeway are more smallish fishing vessels, a number of them appearing to be no longer actively fishing. These lead to the dock where the *Bo Hengy II* and others dock.

This brings us to the land-side of the cay: there are two clusters of seemingly derelict containers, a larger one at the western end, between the new bridge and the ocean (I saw Capt. Tom Hanna and his team clearing some of these in March) – they take up parking spaces, and some are used for office and storage purposes. The others are scattered lightly in front of the fort at the eastern end, and owners, too, use some of them, for storage and office space. Probably this space could be put to better use, and unused equipment cleared away to provide more parking for the many passengers on the dozens of vessels. Finally, there are the buildings: a dozen or so mailboat and passenger companies have set up make-shift retail offices in old containers and trailers, the largest of which is the cluster of trailers belonging to Bahamas Ferries. These facilities all offer critical services to passengers regarding tickets, scheduling, luggage, and freight.

The yellow government building to the east is a warehouse that seems to be clean and well run and sells farm seed during the day. There are fences separating some of the waterfront from the causeway, but I am not aware of when the fences are closed, as mailboats leave at all hours. To the east are more parking spaces, neatly laid out, a cluster of semi-abandoned containers, then Bladen's Battery, built in the late 1780's and restored in 1949 and again in 1990, and largely eclipsed by commercial activity. Behind the large dock master's building is an enclosure on land containing dozens of small vessels, including regatta sloops.

Leaving aside the question of the condition and hygiene of the seafood stalls on the causeway (the acres of conch shells prevalent in the 1970's and 1980's have been removed, and a good deal of the conch shack business has moved to Arawak Cay, along with container traffic), there arises the final issue of utilization of the buildings between the bridges. Most of them appear to have very active tenants: rats. In the early 1990s my brothers and friends would stop in Big Daddy's daiquiri bar there in the evenings and entertain ourselves by trying to scare the rats with empty bottles. In the afternoons, it was a nice place to meet the mailboat skippers. At one point the Taiwanese government tried to farm shrimp there, and before that I recall seeing sea turtles splayed out, upside down, for sale. But nowadays, aside from some basic warehousing the buildings are mostly derelict and abandoned. Though forklifts busily inject some life, the overwhelming prospect of the area is of abandonment.

Potter's Cay is a major economic engine for locally grown produce, from frozen lobster tails from Spanish Wells and beyond to farmed goods, and unique Bahamian products like cascarilla from Acklins and Crooked. For the small and important few who remain behind on the home islands, raising families, crops, and maintaining churches, schools, post offices, and clinics for future generations, not to mention manning the ballot boxes, it would seem to be in the government's best interests to invest in this incubator of progress. Errant vessel owners and their insurers should not be allowed to dump old steel in the waters of our nation's finest harbour, any more than the government permit a truck to be abandoned in Rawson's Square.

At either end of Potter's Cay, while imperfectly maintained, exudes the crisp pace of inter-island trade and travel being conducted fairly and efficiently. Not so the middle sector. Without adequate dock-front and a hygienic, safe platform for operators and passengers, this important commercial hub will remain handicapped. Certainly, tourists won't be attracted to it, which is a pity because Potter's Cay offers some of the most authentically Bahamian experiences – visually, historically, edible, and in terms of hands-on travel.

Potter's Cay should be the commonwealth's pride and joy, connecting the capital and its banking high-rises with Paradise Island, the cradle of our all-important tourism product. Like Prince George's Dock extending into the western harbour to accommodate cruise ships, Potter's Cay is home and haven for our island family and the captains and sailors who bring them to and from their communities. Yet a very slovenly core of Potter's Cay greets new arrivals – one that could be invested in, reinvigorated, and turned around with a combination of capital and innovation. After all, Potter's Cay is not only situated in the centre of the capital but serves as the hub and spoke – the economic as well as social heart of the nation. We need to ensure it keeps pumping, keeping the furthest spokes on the hub connected with the capital. While commerce by mailboat remains vibrant, we cannot allow distance from our nautical heritage to grow. Mailboats are more than a lively topic of historical interest – every few hours they sally forth with the government's steadying hand, to connect the people and islands of the Bahamas not just with each other, but the world economy.

After much on-site sleuthing, this author understands that the miscreant vessel is the original *Lady Rosalind*, which was built in 1979 in the US and brought to the Bahamas in 1987. She is reliably said to have struck a rock somewhere undisclosed, and damaged beyond repair in 1997-1998. That would fit in with the first *Lady Rosalind*, who was damaged late in 1997 and finally lost (sank) in 1998. According to reliable local source, the vessel submerged at Potter's Cay was being cut up for scrap, and the workers had made it from the superstructure (wheel house, cabins etc.) down to the deck level when they made a series of mistakes which resulted in the ship sinking to the bottom. Yet, because of its size and the depth, the wreck remains partially above water – you can climb on top of it at low tide. This has made it impossible for any vessel, whatever their draft (short of a hover craft) to utilize the space. That was almost twenty years ago.

Finally, please remember that for every mailboat listed herein there were probably two or more candidates who were turned away either because only one source described them as mailboats, or no matter how wonderful their stories they simply were never subsidized and tasked with carrying the government's mail and cargos.

Being featured on the final list of national mailboats should be considered, at least in this author's estimation, joining a place of honor in the tableau of maritime history of the Bahamas, along with those who invested in, rode upon, and operated them; everyone took a chance on those boats and gave a bit of themselves to keeping they, and their memory alive, in exchange for being taken across the bar and to their destinations, most of the time. Remember the old adage: we must treat our horse, right, and our horse will treat us right.

Note at April, 2021: *Lady D.* has since been removed, as has *Lady Tasha*. The wreck between the bridges was being pumped and sealed for raising when a hurricane interrupted salvage. Though this author witnessed how tantalizing close they came to removing the wreck, it still hasn't happened, with the north wall of Potter's Cay between the bridges largely underutilized by mailboats do to inadequate wreck removal and fragmented usage which seems to suggest at least a measure of Darwinism. After years of study this author still doesn't know whether mailboat dock allocation is self-policing, government-decreed, or most likely a hybrid. There is always a degree of mysticism to the trade which has perhaps enabled it, along with constant adaptation and improvisation, to survive.

Historic Post Offices, by Edward B. Proud

Causeway, Cupid's Bay, Governor's Harbour, Eleuthera.

Post Office, Pine Ridge, Grand Bahama, 1946, Postmaster C. V. Albury at left.

Post Office and Postmaster, Williams Town, Little Exuma.

Spanish Wells, later 1960's, with Mailboat Alongside.

Post Office, Rolletown, Exuma, Mrs. I. R. Rolle residence.

Post Office, Rose Long Island, B. L. D'Arville, Postmaster, June, 1973.

Post Office, Spanish Wells, St. George Cay, Eleuthera, and Postmaster.

Post Office, Steventon, Exuma, Postmaster, 1969.

Matthew Town, Inagua Communications.

Post Office United Estates, San Salvador, Postmaster Jerome Hunt, 1970.

Post Office, Eight Mile Rock, Grand Bahama.

Post Office, Forbes Hill, Exuma, 1969, Postmaster W. C. Ferguson.

Post Office, Georgetown Exuma, 1969.

Post Office, Green Turtle Cay, Abaco, and Postmaster at Left.

Crooked Island - said to have been the Bahamas' first post office.

Post Office, Long Cay, Fortune Island, Crooked Island District.

Photos are by philatelist Edward B. Proud, in *The Postal History of Bahamas*, Proud-Bailey Co., Ltd., Heathfield, East Sussex, UK, 2000, Chapter 4: "Post Offices and Postmarks," pp.135-260. This author is deeply indebted to Mr. Proud's meticulous gathering and artful sharing of the movements of most of the early mailboat fleet.

Ports

Lady Frances in Exuma, 2018.

Air Swift, Government Dock, Harbour Island, 1954, Richard Malcolm.

Lady Frances, Rum Cay.

Lady Mathilda, Inagua.

Lady Rosalind, Inagua.

Great Harbour Cay, Berry Islands.

Capt. Gurth Dean in Abaco.

Abraham's Bay, Mayaguanua, former US Navy jetty.

Fire on Potter's Cay.

Accident getting cargo onto a mailboat, Potter's Cay.

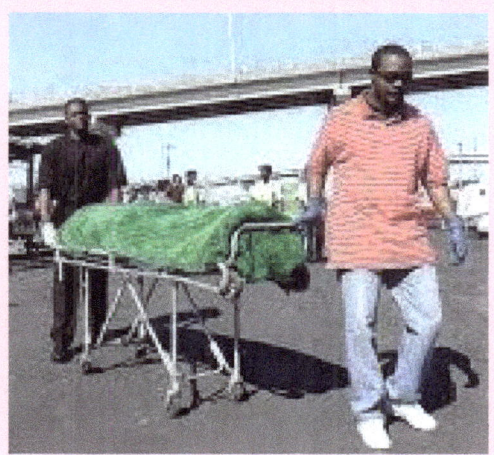

Cadaver across Potter's Cay.

Sign outlining mailboat mooring area, South Andros, 1970s.

Cargo

Protecting the mail and bank strong box, Harbour Island, 1960s, Dick Malcolm.

Lady Frances, washer dryers on deck, San Salvador voyage.

Lady Frances discharges San Salvador.

Forklift operators serving *K.C.T.* and *Fiesta Mail*.

Strong moon over cargo, *New G.*, Cat Island, 2018.

Lifeboat aboard *New G.*, entering Bennett's Harbour, Cat Island.

Passengers, most precious cargo, *New G.* cabin, southbound.

Portraits

Michael Mardon, journalist

Owners

Sir Roland Symonette, owner, builder

Alisada, Jack Farrington, 1960

Builders

James Jenkins Roberts

Andros Queen builder, 1970's

Victor Percy Cleare, Hatchet Bay Eleuthera

Photos of Mailboat Voyages, 1984 – 2019

President Taylor *Voyage, Nassau to Inagua, Mayaguana, 2018*

Cousins horsing around on *President Taylor* before departure for Inagua

Dads, brothers at Shanya's Matthew Town Inagua.

Trans Cargo II with Egyptian name in Arabic.

Officers and crew engage teenage passengers in friendly games of dominoes.

Abraham's Bay, Mayaguana.

Abandoned aircraft at largely abandoned airfield, Mayaguana.

President Taylor interior.

Capt. David Hyde.

A close fit for *President Taylor* at Inagua.

Passenger and cook hail another mailboat – *Lady Frances* – east of Exumas on the high seas.

New G. in Bennett's Harbour, Cat Island, 2019

The abandoned mailboat wreck between the bridges at Potter's Cay.

Former *Marcella II* lifeboat near *Lady Rosalind II*, eastern Potter's Cay

Munson Shipping dock office; believed to be a blend of the Munroe & Sons business from Ragged Island.

Grand Master II

M/V Deborah K II *Family Voyage Nassau To Abaco, 20-21 August, 1984*

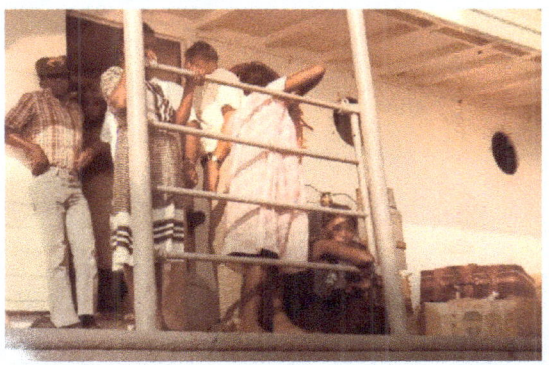

A hand-hewn resort in the Abaco Cays has sent a small boat to collect passengers and their luggage, as the dock cannot accommodate the *Deborah K. II*. Photos by Mrs. Jane Wiberg.

Mailboat Voyages Over 40 Years

ISLAND	DESTINATION/ROUTE	MILEAGE	PORT	# OF VOYAGES	ISLANDS CLOCKWISE
1	Abaco: Hope Town, Marsh Harbour, Green Turtle Cay, Sandy Point, Coopers Town	1500	6	10	2
2	Acklins: Landrail Point, Long Cay	500	2	2	9
3	Andros: Nichols Town, Andros Town, Morgans Bluff, Driggs Hill, Lisbon Creek	300	4	5	15
4	Berry Islands: Bullock's Harbor	100	1	1	16
5	Bimini: Alice Town	300	1	3	17
6	Cat Island: Bennett's Harbor, Smith's Bay, Dumfries, Orange Bay, Fernandez	700	4	2	4
7	Crooked Island: Spring Point	500	1	1	8
8	Eleuthera North: The Current, The Bluff, Upper Bogue, Spanish Wells, Harbor Islands	2500	4	15	3
9	Eleuthera South: Hatchet Bay, Rock Sound, Governors Harbor	550	3	4	4
10	Freeport, GB: Mclean's Town/East End (to Crown Haven Abaco)	50	1	1	1
11	Long Island: no ports	0	0	0	7(0)
12	Mayaguana: Betsy Bay	600	2	1	11
13	Exuma: Black Point, George Town, Highbourne Cay, Staniel Cay	750	6	8	14
14	Inagua: Matthew Town	600	1	2	12
15	Nassau NP: Potter's cay (system hub)	0	1	0	18
16	Ragged Island: Duncan Town	450	1	1	13
17	Rum Cay: Nelsons Bay	300	1	1	6
18	San Salvador: Cockburn Town	300	1	2	5
18	SUMMARY: 40 years=avg. 250miles/year, 20 persons, 170m/trip, 600 miles/island, c.30 mailboats	10,000	40	59	17 called

Fleet Overview, Over 200 Years

The period of highest activity in the 1800s were the 13 boats joining the fleet in 13 years from 1865 to 1878 reacting to a trade boom during the US Civil War. And in the twentieth century the 1970s and 1980s were a time of unprecedented growth, with 46 boats from all over – Europe, the US, the Bahamas – joining the fleet at an average rate of nearly three year, or one every five months. Not all of them lasted for very long.

Since 2000, the mailboat fleet growth has been characterized by consolidation of larger (but fewer) vessels, larger (but fewer) owners, and greater vessel homogeneity, with many ships able to land on coasts with almost no infrastructure using ramps, and to load vehicles without cranes and accommodate passengers with luxuries such as air conditioning and refrigeration and freezers for foodstuffs as well as commercial cargo.

While there are holdouts like *Current Pride* (which is old-school wood with modern fibre-glass overlay to protect it), and the Dean fleet, most mailboats in 2020 conform to two basic patterns: square-stern, steel boats over 100 feet with deck cranes forward and a wheelhouse and passenger accommodation aft, or the Ro-Ro-type ramp-loading, longer vehicles with passenger accommodation and wheelhouse aft.

Both of these types, but particularly the latter, which were conceived to serve the offshore oil and gas industry in the Gulf of Mexico, are generally built in the US, and more of them are being built to order, with Bahamian capitalists commissioning them and owning them the majority of their commercial lives.

Over 216 years 198 mailboats that equates to roughly a *new mailboat entering the Bahamas service every year*, possibly more often as this study is unlikely to account for every substitute mailboat or even every vessel that entered the fleet. Historical public records are kept on a boats' ownership and dimensions but not necessarily on its employ, or on government subsidies received.

Mailboats by Dates of Service Entry, by Decade

To 1810: *Mary & Susan* and *Nassau 1st*

To 1820: *John Bull*

1820s: *Dash* and *Paragon*

1830s: *Rising Sun*

1840s: *Palestine*

1850s: *Experiment, Union,* and *President*

1860s: *Corsica, Electric, Eugenie, Georgina, Amelia Ann, Brothers,* and *Mary Jane*

1870s: *Jane, Quick, Arabella, Jimmie, Admired, Cicero,* and *Dart*

1880s: *Argosy, Carleton, Osborne, Rebecca,* and *Arctic*

1890s: *Kate Sturrup, Hattie Darling, Hattie H. Roberts, Pelican, Star of the Sea, Trackless, Eastern Queen, Experience, Raven, Return, Sappho, Antila, Tropic, Glynn, Siren, M.E.B., Pilgrim,* and *Albertine Adoue*

To 1910: *Columbia, Renown, Right Arm, J.G. Converse, Maria Ellen, Senela, Emma, Herman, Zephyr, Estrella, Julius, Olivette, Petrel, Valiant, Sarah E. Douglass, Ponce de Leon, Celeste, Increase, H.J C., Mary & Ella,* and *Nellie Leonora*

To 1920: *Ghost, Arawak, San Salvador, Frances E., Defense, Mountain King, Linnet, Pearline, Bertie, Charlotte, Sea Witch,* and *Julia*

1920s: *Amie, Coraline, Eclipse, Edna M. R., Endion, Hazel Dell, Kim, Magic, Princess Montagu, Resolve, Tryon, Brontes, Content 1st, Empress, Indiana, Invincible, Mayflower, Maysie, Ballymena, Caroline, City of Nassau, Alice Mabel, Priscilla, Repeat, Emerald, Serene, William H. Albury, Wisdom M., Blanche Eva, Christina, Cruiser, Graceful, Halcyon, Hero, Nonesuch, Sydue, Alisada, Lady Cordeaux, Laura & Louise, Quankey, Saale, William & Charles, Gaskill Bros., Sea Bird, Skipper Bill, F. A. Marie, Huron, Madam, Nellie, Olga,* and *Ollie Ford*

1930s: *Dove, Ivy S., Patricia K., Sir Charles Orr, Bimini, Castlereagh, Ruthie Melrose, Bahamian, Content S., S.C. Louise, Arrow, Go On, Lelia, Madam Queen, Rescue, Emmie, Lillian & Brothers, Patsy, Marmaduke, Midwest, Monarch, Monarch of Nassau, Paddy Helferty, Richard Campbell, Sea Wonder, Albury's Child, Gary & William, High Purchase, Merlin M.,* and *Midinette*

1940s: *Arena, DollyMae, Lady Dundas, Merle, Samana, Shamrock, Three Bays, Beluga, New Plymouth, Stede Bonnet, Ego, Liberty, Noel Roberts, Gary Roberts, Vergemere IV, Captain Roberts, Caribbean Queen, ML 371, Betty Ann, Evangeline, Joyce Roberts, Zelma Rose, Air Pheasant, Air Swift,* and *Ena K.*

1950s: *Lady Baillou, South Andros Express, Tropical Trader II, Captain Dean, Frecil, Church Bay, Passing Jack, San Cristobal, Margaret Rose, Bahamas Daybreak 1st, Silver King, Drake, Almeta Queen, Aline, Madam Elizabeth Rolle,* and *Wissama*

1960s: *Eastern Prince, Mayaguana Queen, Abaco Sloops, Cape Hatteras, Clermont, River Queen, Andros Trader, Captain Dean II, Lillian, Wissaugua, Astonish, Bimini Gal, Current Queen, Spanish Rose II, Spanish Sea Queen, Bahama Land, Daily Gleaner, New Day, Bahama Trader, Marcella 1st, Staniel Cay Express, Captain Dean III, Harley & Charley,* and *Plymouth Queen*

1970s: *Eastern Isle, Lady Tasha, Miz Desa, Pleasant, Andros Express, Deborah K., Delmar L., Gleaner Express, Goldfinger II, Johnette Walker, Marcella II, Miss Andros, Nassau Moonglow, New Day II, San Salvador Express 1st, San Salvador Express 2nd, Sea Salvor, Captain Dean IV, Lady Blanche, Lisa J., Offshore, South Andros Queen, Lady Moore, Commonwealth, Miss Beverly, Captain Dean V, Bahamas Daybreak II, Exuma Pride, Lady Eula, Miranda,* and *Eleuthera Express 1st.*

1980s: *Current Pride, Willaurie, Bimini Mack, Marcella III, Treasure Lady, Bahamas Daybreak III, Captain Moxey 1st, Lady D., Abilin, Deborah K. II, North Andros Princess I, Bahama Sky, Big Yard Express, Lady Gloria, Lisa J. II, Miss Juanita, Nay Dean, Champion II, Lady Rosalind 1st, North Cat Island Special 1st, Central Andros Express, Andros Express, Mangrove Cay Express, Maxine, Windward Express, Lady Eddina, Lady Frances, Lady Mathilda 1st, Mal Jack,* and *Sea Hauler*

1990s: *Captain C., Jeleta, Mia Dean, Miss BJ, Grand Master 1st, Captain Fox, Lady Margo II, Sherice M., Eleuthera Express 2nd, Alma B., Captain Moxey 2nd, Emmett & Cephas, Lady Mathilda 2nd, Captain Gurth Dean, Sea Spirit II, United Spirit,* and *United Star*

To 2010: *Sealink, Fiesta Mail, Lady Rosalind I, Legacy, Lady Emerald, North Cat Island Special II, Seawind, Lady Kathreina, Lady Rosalind II, Legend II, East Wind,* and *VI Nais*

To 2020: *Sea Spirit, K.C.T., Island Link, Trans Cargo II, New G., Inagua Spray, Cape Mail, President Taylor, Tolyn, Daybreak, Grand Master II,* and *Captain Emmett*

Mailboat Names

Abilin
Admired
Air Pheasant
Air Swift
Albertine Adoue
Alicada
Alice Mabel
Alma B.
Almeta Queen
Amelia Ann
Andros Express
Andros Trader
Arabella
Arctic
Arena
Argosy
Atabasha
Bahama Land
Bahama Trader
Bahamas Daybreak
Bahamas Daybreak II
Bahamas Daybreak III
Bahamian
Bahamas Sky
Beluga
Betty Ann
Big Yard Express
Bimini Gal
Bimini Mack
Brontes
Brother
Brothers
Cape Hatteras
Cape Mail
Captain C.
Captain Dean
Captain Dean II
Captain Dean III

Captain Dean IV
Captain Dean V
Captain Emmett
Captain Fox
Captain Gurth Dean
Captain Moxey
Captain Roberts
Caribbean Queen
Carleton
Central Andros Express
Champion II
Church Bay
Cicero
City of Nassau
Clermont
Columbia
Commonwealth
Content S.
Current Pride
Current Queen
Dart
Dash
Daybreak
Deborah K.
Deborah K. II
Defense
Delmar L.
Dollymae
Drake
East Wind
Eastern Isle
Eastern Prince
Edna M. R.
Ego
Electric
Eleuthera Express
Emmett Cephas
Endion

Eugene
Experiment
Exuma Pride
Feziel
Fiesta Mail
Frecil
Gary Roberts
Georgina
Gleaner Express
Goldfinger II
Grand Master
Harley & Charley
Hazel Dell
Hero
Inagua Spray
Island Link
Jane
Jeleta
Jimmie
John Bull
Johnette Walker
K.C.T.
Kate Sturrup
Lady Blanche
Lady Cordeaux
Lady D.
Lady Dundas
Lady Eddina
Lady Emerald
Lady Eula
Lady Frances
Lady Gloria
Lady Kathreina
Lady Margo II
Lady Mathilda
Lady Montagu
Lady Moore
Lady Rosalind

Lady Rosalind I
Lady Rosalind II
Lady Tasha
Legacy
Legend II
Liberty
Lillian
Lisa J.
Lisa J. II
Madam Elizabeth Rolle
Magic
Mal Jack
Mangrove Cay Express
Marcella
Marcella II
Marcella III
Margaret Rose
Mary & Susan
Mary Jane
Maxine
Mayaguana Queen
Mayflower
Mia Dean
Miranda
Miss Andros
Miss Beverly
Miss BJ
Miss Juanita
Miz Desa

ML 371
Monarch of Nassau
Mountain King
Nassau
Nassau Moonglow
Nay Dean
New Day
New G.
Noel Roberts
Nonesuch
North Andros Princess I
North Cat Island Special
North Cat Island Special II
Offshore
Osborne
Palestine
Paragon
Passing Jack
Patricia K.
President
President Taylor
Priscilla
Quanky
Quick
Rebecca
Richard Campbell
Rising Sun
River Queen

Samana
San Cristobal
San Salvador Express
Sea Hauler
Sea Spirit
Sea Spirit II
Sealink
Seawind
Sherice M.
Silver King
South Andros Express
South Andros Queen
Spanish Rose II
Staniel Cay Express
Stede Bonnet
Tolyn
Trans Cargo II
Treasure Lady
Tropical Trader II
Union
United Spirit
United Star
VI Nais
Willaurie
Windward Express
Wissama
Wissaugua
Zelma Rose

Owners, Part-Owners

Adderly, Eunice (or Louise)
Albury, Carlysle
Albury, Hilton C.
Albury, John
Anderson, J.
Andrews, John aka Jack
Archer, Family
Archer, Sherwin
Bethel, A.
Bethel, Family, Nassau
Bethel, Granville
Bethel, Sarah M.
Black, Fred (Fed)
Black, Mary Jane (Mrs. Fred)
Bowleg, Carlton
Bowleg, Mr.
Brown, Family
Brown, Jeffrey
Brozogzog, Family
Brozogzog, Lance
Bullard, Francis
Burnside, Ellis H.
Cleare, John
Collie, Alfred
Collie, Cornelius
Collie, Rev. Samuel Albert
Curry, Sox
Dean, Ernest Alexander
Dean, Jonathan
Deleveaux, F. G.
Demeritte, Thomas
Edgecombe, William H.
Elden, Family
Elden, Gerald
Elden, Reynold
Farrington, John aka Jack
Farrington, Reginald
Forde, Oliver, aka Ollie
Gray, Rolly
Griffin, Robert
Hanna, Thomas, aka Tom
Harris, John Saunders, aka Run Joe
Hart, W. B.
Higgins, Mr.
Higgs, George
Johnson, A.
Johnson, Ivan
Johnson, Mott
Johnson, Oscar
Kelly, C. Trevor
Kelly, Godfrey
Kelly, Robert Austin
King, Rev. Herbert
Levarity, John A.
Levy, Austin
Lowe, David
Macarthy, Felix
Maloney, Dr.
Maycock, Etienne Sr.
Maycock, Family
Maycock, William
McKinney, George
Missick, Mr.
Moxey, Family
Munroe, Emmett
Munroe, Family
Munroe, Jed
Munroe, Shawn
Neilly, Patrick
Newton, John
Patton, G. Maureen
Percentie, Humphry
Pinder, Albert
Pinder, Gurney Elon
Pinder, Junior
Pinder, Stephen
Robert, Benjamin
Roberts, Harvey
Roberts, Henry L.
Roberts, Noel
Roberts, Richard, aka Dickie
Roberts, Sir George William Kelly
Roberts, William Augustus
Rolle, Edgar L.
Russell, Allan
Russell, D.
Russell, R.
Saunders, John
Saunders, Uriah
Sawyer, Betram
Sawyer, Carl
Sawyer, Quincy
Sawyer, Richard W.
Sawyer, Robert H.
Simms, Harley
Smith, John
Smith, Rev. James
Stuart, Gerald
Stuart, Theopholous
Sturrup, Henry William F.
Sweeting, Albert
Sweeting, John P.
Sweeting, Percy
Sweeting, Rupert
Symonette, Burton
Symonette, Donald
Symonette, J. H.
Symonette, Julius

Symonette, Sir Roland Theodore
Taylor, Eddins B.
Taylor, Elvin
Taylor, Limas
Taylor, Nathaniel Bruce
Thompson, Leonard
Weech, Osborne
Weech, William Ferris
Weeks, William A.
Williamson, Louis
Woodside, Family
Young, James R. C

Other Participants and Contributors

Archer, Beechen, Percy's uncle, owned a boat named *Exceed*
Archer, Capt. Robert, owned sponge fishing fleet
Archer, Everett, Abaco politician
Archer, Percy, owner of Ambassador Inn, Abaco
Bain, Frederick, believed to be maternal grandfather to PM L. Pindling, captain of *Alicada*, 1920s, 1940s, read Euclid
Bosfield, N. E., Commissioner of San Salvador 1961
Burrows, D. H., Chief Out Island Commissioner, 1961
Cadoret, Brita French photographer, Exumas, Ragged Island, 2018
Chisholm, Hermis government minister, co-ordinator, Mailboat services
Curtis, Craig, past dockmaster, Potter's Cay,
Diedrick, Amanda, author, Little House by the Ferry blog,
Dillett Capt. Stephen Albert, postmaster and defender of Bahamas in WWI
Duncanson, Edwin, Capt., master, inter-island Esso tanker Inagua Cay, 1950s-60
Forbes-Berry, Delores, Executive Officer, Dockmaster's Office, Potter's Cay Dock
Grant, Martin Lee, hosted mailboat talk, Harbour Island, 2018
Gray, Frederick, Nassau Port Authority, related to captains Rolly Gray and Lenny Brozozog, Exuma
Heraty, Margaret, hired by IDB 1979 as transportation expert, study transport
Jennings, Rev. D. supporter of exhibit on wooden boats
King-Burns, Kimberly, of Harbour Island, Expats Bahamas
Lockhart, Edward, on Buena Vista Cay, Ragged Island alone for Hurricane Irma, 2017
Lowe, Alton, Green Turtle Cay artist, Albert Lowe Museum (his father)
Mather, Reswell, aka Prince, Harbour Island mariner
Roberts, E. Dawson, son of Jenkins
Williams, James Carter, business owner, operator on San Salvador since 1980s

Builders, Bahamian

Albury, Johny, Abaco
Albury, T. Berlin, Abaco
Albury, William H., aka Uncle Will, Man-O-War Cay, Abaco
Cleare, Victor, Hatchet Bay, Eleuthera
Collie, Cornelius Acklins, Mayaguana
Curry, Joseph, Abaco
Dean, Ernest Alexander, Sandy Point, Abaco
Demeritte, Thomas
Gates, Matthew, Green Turtle Cay, Abaco
Hatcher, Walter, Abaco
Johnson, Earl & Gerald, Harbour Island, Eleuthera
Maycock, William M.
Roberts, James Jenkins, Abaco & Nassau
Roberts, Walter H.
Roberts, William A., Spanish & Green Turtle Cay, Abaco
Saunders, Uriah
Smith, Rev. James
Williamson, Louis, Mayaguana

Builders, Overseas

Aitken & Mansel
Alphen and Rijn, Netherlands
Apol A., Scheepswerf C.V.
Bollinger Shipyards
Husumer Schiffswerft (HSW)
Candies Shipbuilders, LLC
Chu-Chu Perez, No. 1 Boat Manufacturing
DeJong, Lebet
Deutsche Werft AG
F. B. Walker & Sons
George Lawley & Son, Boston
Gurlivesti
H.C. Christensen Steelworks
Halter Marine
His Majesty's Royal Navy
J. Crighton & Co. Ltd.
J. M. Densmore, Quincy (Boston)
Jerry Thompson, St. Augustine Trawler Co.
John Petrudis
Luders Marine
MAN GHH Dock & Schiffbau
Master Marine
Mickon Shipbuilders
Neue Jadewerft
New Jersey Shipbuilding
P. K. Trawlers
Robinson Marine Construction
Rodriguez Coden
Russell Portier Shipyard, aka Portier Shipyard
San Sebastian Marine
Sander Gebroeders
Scheepswerf Gebr. van Niestern & Co.
Scully Bros. Boat Builders
SFsea
South Pacific Marine Construction
Spiekeroog
St. Augustine Marine Trawlers
St. Augustine Shipbuilding
Stadium Boat Works
Tees-Side Bridge & Engine Works, UK
Thomas Knutson Shipbuilding Corp., NY, US
VT Halter Marine
Walker Marine
Walter E. Abrams Shipyards, NY, US
Xinhe Shipbuilding

Yards Large Enough to Both Build and Repair

Archer & Albury, aka the (Walter) Archer Boat Yard, near Land & Surveys Dept., East Bay Street, later landing dock for *Mile 52* and Hatchet Bay Plantations vessels importing produce in 1950s

Bradford Marine, Freeport, Grand Bahama, since 1997

Grand Bahama Shipyards, Freeport, Grand Bahama, since 2000

Higgs Boat Works, East Bay Street, Nassau, active 1981

Nassau Boat Works, aka A. E. Bethel Shipyard, on Hog Island, 1905

Nassau Shipyard, aka Symonette Shipyard, managed by Jenkins Roberts, moved from Hog Island to East Bay Street in 1960s

Mailboat Captains, 1804 to 2020

Albury, Ancil
Albury, Leland
Albury, Lloyd
Archer, Garnett
Archer, Robert, aka Bobby
Archer, Sherwin
Bain, 1850
Bain, Elliston
Bain, Frederick
Barnett, Richard, aka Ricky
Bethel, Archibald, aka Archie
Bethel, Granville
Bethel, Michael, aka Mike
Black, V. H.
Brown, Spence
Brozozog, Lance
Brozozog, Leonard H., aka Lenny

Carey, John
Carroll, Clifford, aka Cliff
Cartwright, Jason
Cunningham, 1850
Davis, Nigel
Dean, Ernest Jr.
Dean, James
Dean, Jonathan, aka John
Faquharson, Alrington E.
Faquharson, Nevis
Ferguson, Leroy Fisher
Fulford, William G.
Garroway, Robert, aka Bob
Gibson, Daniel
Gibson, James Edgecombe
Gray, Rolly

Grey, D.
Griffin, Carlton
Hanna, Thomas, aka Tom
Harris, William G.
Harris, William James
Higgs, Edison
Hyde, David
Ingraham, Arnold
Johnson, Alfonso
Johnson, Gifford
Johnson, Ivan
King
Knowles, Christopher, aka Chris
Lockhart, Anton
Lockhart, Roy Oral
Lowe
Malone, Cleveland
Maycock, Etienne Jr.
Maycock, Etienne Sr.
McKie

Miller, Rodney
Moss, (*Daybreak*)
Moxey, Boycel Jr.
Moxey, Kevin
Moxey, Ralph
Moxley, W.
Munro, Charles
Munroe, Emmett
Munroe, Jed
Munroe, Shawn
Munroe, Spellman
Neilly, Patrick
Newman
Newton, John
Nielly, Whitford, RBDF
Patton
Pinder, Gurney Elon
Pinder, Stephen
Rahming, F.
Roberts, Everett
Roberts, Hartley
Roberts, Jenkins
Roberts, Leland
Roberts, Osbourne
Roberts, Roland
Roberts, William Augustus, or A. W.
Rolle, Napoleon
Russell, Allan, Sr.
Russell, Robley
Saunders, Uriah
Sawyer, Quincy
Sayers, Richard, aka Richie
Simms, Harley
Smith, Roy William
Storr, Claudius
Stuart, Ashok
Stuart, Jack
Styles, W. P.
Sweeting, Albert
Sweeting, E. E.
Sweeting, Percy
Taylor, Eddins Bruce
Taylor, Elvin
Taylor, Limas
Taylor, Nathaniel Bruce
Wallace, Leonard
Watkins, Michael, aka Mike
Weech, William Ferris
Weech, *Osborne*
Williams, 1851
Williams, William, aka Bill
Wilson, William, aka Willy
Woodside, Joseph
Woodside, Ulric

Crew, Mates, Cooks, Engineers

Adderley, cook, *Lisa J.*
Albury, David, crew
Albury, Raymond, aka Ray, crew
Bastian B.
Bastian, P.
Bethel, William, mate
Bowleg, Kirkwood, crew, *Lisa J.*
Burrows, Errold, crew
Campbell, K.
Cash, Thomas, aka Tommy, crew
Cleare, Victor, crew
Curry, C., mate
Curry, Stanford
Delancey, D.
Demeritte, T.
Donnie, mate with Archers
Johnson, A., crew
Kemp, Stanley, crew
Maitland, crew
Mather, Reswell, aka Prince, crew
Mather, William, aka Willy, crew
Munroe, Prince, crew
Pinder, Welbourn, crew, *Zelma Rose*, drowned on duty
Sawyer, Calvin, engineer
Sawyer, Fred, port engineer
Sawyer, Henry, aka Brother, Bo Hengy
Sawyer-Beasley, Benhilde, crew
Shippee, Albert, crew
Stevens, Herbert, crew
Sweeting, A., mate

Charts

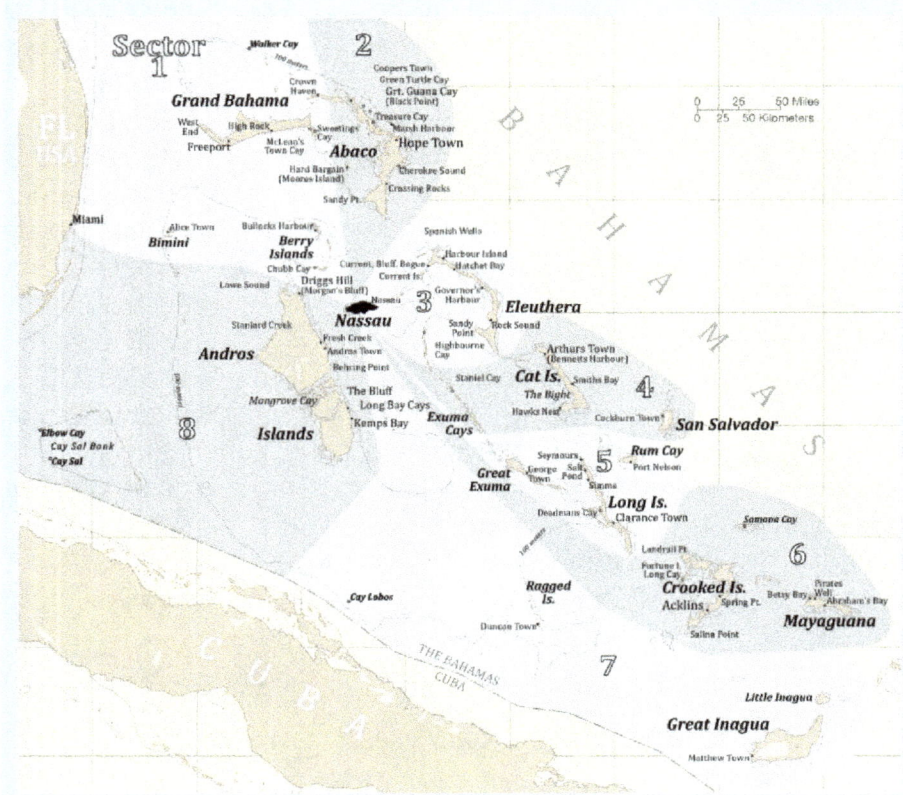

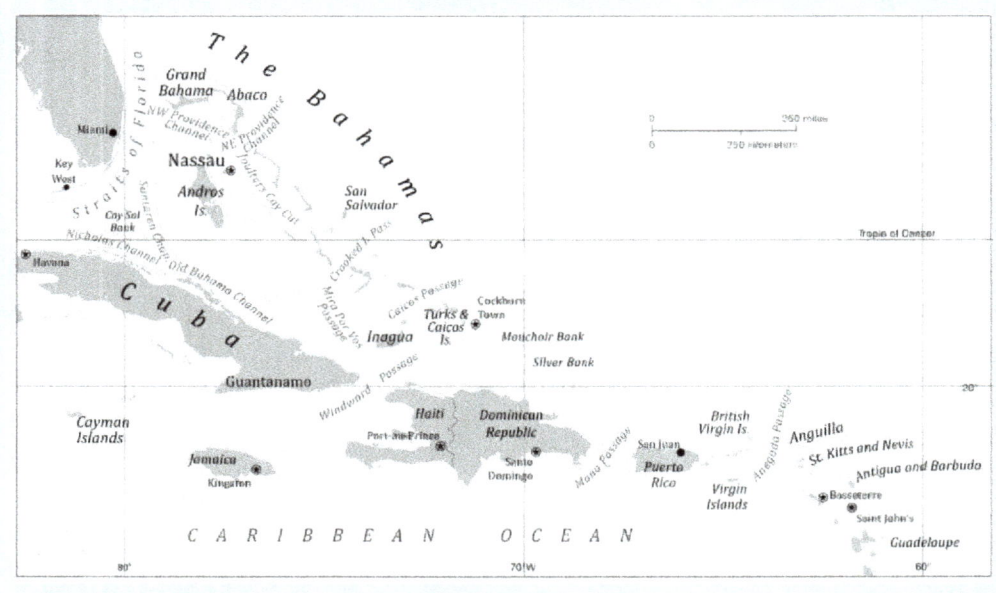

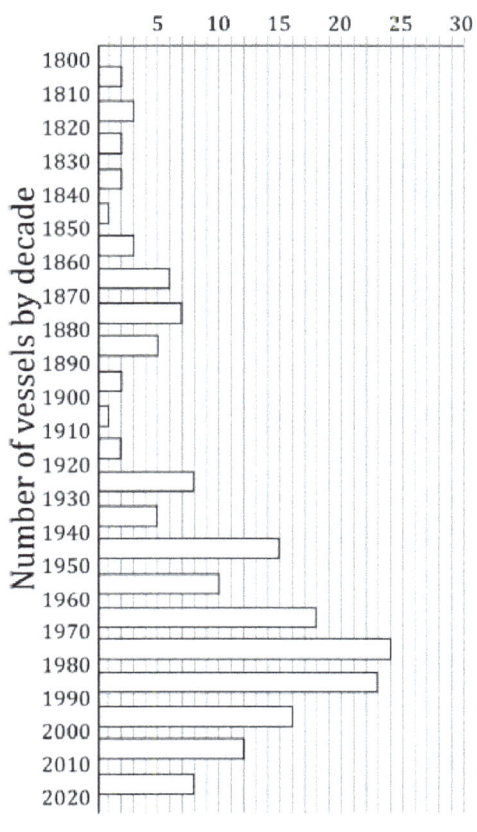

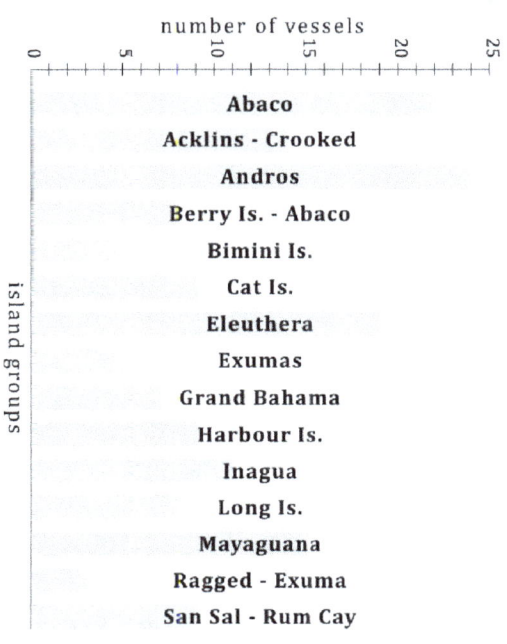

Further Reading

- Adderley, Augustus John, *Fisheries of the Bahamas*, International Fisheries Exhibition, London, 1883, ISHA Books, Gyan Books, New Delhi, India, 2013
- Albury, K. Alison, *Life on A Rock*, 2008, POD Amazon, US
- Albury, Haziel L., *Man-O-War My Island Home*, 1977, Holly Press, Cowan, US
- Albury, Paul, *The Story of the Bahamas*, Macmillan Caribbean, London, UK, 1975
- Aranha, Paul C., *Island Airman and His Bahama Islands Home*, 2006, Media Enterprises Ltd., Bahamas
- Bahamas Government Information Services, Cabinet Office, *Bahama Islands: Report for the Years 1966 and 1967*, Rawson Square, Nassau, N.P., Bahamas, 1968
- Baker, Christopher P., *Bahamas Turks & Caicos: Lonely Planet Guide*, 2001, *Lonely Planet* Publications, US
- Barnette, Michael C., *Encyclopedia of Florida Shipwrecks Vol.1: Atlantic*, Association of Underwater Explorers, US, 2010
- Barratt, Peter, *Bahama Saga: The Epic Story of Bahama Islands*, 2004, 1stBooks, Author House (POD), US
- Barry, Tracy, Kinkead, Cookie, photographer, *Island Rhythm, the Way We Live*, The Landing, Harbour Island, Bahamas, 2017
- Berg, Daniel & Berg, Denise, *Tropical Shipwrecks: A Vacationing Diver's Guide to the Bahamas and Caribbean*, Aqua Explorers, USA, 1989
- Bethell, A. Talbot, *Early Settlers of Bahamas and Colonists*, 1937, Heritage Books Inc., US, 2008
- Black Frost, Katie, Coeffic, Marc, & Paungger, Harry, Eleuthera, *Capturing Magic*, Clever Dolphin, LLC, Atlanta, GA, US, 2015
- Blake, Dave, *Bahamas by Mailboat, Through My Lens*, Dave Blake Photography, MyPublisher, US, 2018
- Bloch, Michael, *The Duke of Windsor's War*, 1983, Coward-McCann Inc., US
- Boyd-Malone, Shelley, & Campbell-Roberts, Richard, *Nostalgic Nassau Picture Postcards 1900-1940*, 1991, Nassau Nostalgia, Bahamas
- Braman, Frederik A., Capt., USN (Ret.), *Cruising by Mailboat, History, Culture and Adventure in the Bahama Islands,* Dave Blake, photographer, paintings by Randy Curry, DiggyPod Jacksonville, FL, US, 2021
- Burns Higgs, Helen, *Presenting Nassau*, The Pryor Press, Chicago, IL, US, 1936

- Carr, J. Revell, *All Brave Sailors: The Sinking of the Anglo-Saxon*, August 21, 1940, Simon & Schuster, New York, NY, US, 2004
- Charters, Samuel, *The Day is So Long and the Wages So Small*, Marion Boyars, New York, 2003
- Cirillo, Christopher L., *Spanish Wells, Bahamas, The Island, The People, The Allure*, Author House, Bloomington, IN, 2010
- Cottman, Evans W., *Out-Island Doctor*, 1963, Hodder & Stoughton, UK
- Craton, Michael, *History of the Bahamas*, 1986, San Salvador Press, Canada
- Craton, Michael, *A-Z of Bahamas Heritage*, Macmillan Caribbean A-Z Series, Macmillan Education, Oxford, UK, 2007
- Culmer Jenkins, Olga, *Bahamian Memories, Island Voices of the Twentieth Century*, University Press of Florida, Gainesville, FL, US, 2000
- Davis, Betty J., *Adventures in the Bahamas, Books 1 and 2*, America Star Books, US, 2007
- Dean, Ernest Alexander & Woodcock, Gary W., *Island Captain*: An Autobiography of a Mail Boat Captain, White Sound Press, US, 1997
- De Marigny, Alfred, *Conspiracy of Crowns*, Crown Publishers, US, 1990.
- Defries, Amelia Dorothy, *In a Forgotten Colony, Being Some Studies in Nassau and at Grand Bahama During 1916*, with numerous illustrations by Armbrister, Sands, Saunders together with photographs of pictures by visiting artists, The Nassau Guardian, Nassau, N.P., Bahamas, 1917
- Del Lorraine, Adela, *Letters from the Bahama Islands*, Written in 1823-4, H. C. Carey and I. Lea, copyright holders, Mifflin & Parry, printers, Philadelphia, PA, 1827
- Dodge, Steve, *Abaco History of an Out Island and Its Cays*, 1984, White Sound Press, US
- Dodge, Steve, and Collingwood, Dean W., Eds., *Modern Bahamian Society*, Caribbean Books, Parkersburg, IA, 1989
- Dupuch, Sir Etienne, *A Salute to Friend and Foe*, The *Nassau Tribune*, Dupuch Publications, Nassau, NP Bahamas, 1982
- Forbes, Rosita, *Islands in the Sun*, Evans Brothers Limited, London, UK, 1949
- Ford, Jack, *Reminiscences of an Island Teacher*, White Sound Press, US, Decatur, IL, 1992
- Fodor's, Miller, French, Knight, Eds., *Fodor's The Bahamas*, New York, NY, US, 1998

- Gale, David, *Below Another Sky: A Bahama Memoir,* Caribe Communications, Raleigh, NC, US, 2011
- Gale, David, *Ready About, Voyages of Life in the Abaco Cays*, Caribe Communications, Raleigh, NC, US, 2002
- Gardiner, Robert, ed., *The Advent of Steam: The Merchant Steamship Before 1900, Conway's History of the Ship,* Conway Maritime Press, London, UK, p.36, 1993
- Gisburn, Harold G. D., *Postage Stamps & Postal History of the Bahamas*, Stanley Gibbons, Ltd., London, UK, 1950
- Griffin, Kevin, *St. Lawrence Saga: The Clarke Steamship Story,* The Cruise People, London, UK, 2014
- Griffiths, Geraint, *Into the Blue Diary of RAF Bahamas 1943-45*, lulu.com POD, US, 2009.
- Hanington, Felicity, & Kelly, Percy A., *Lady Boats Canada's West Indies Merchant Fleet*, Dalhousie University, Canada, 1980
- Hannau, Hans W., *Bahama Islands in Full Color*, Argos Books, US, 1970
- Hannau, Hans W., *Nassau in the Bahamas*, Wilhelm Andermann Verlag, Germany, 1962
- Hardcastle-Taylor, Jean D., *The Windsors I Knew: A Secretary's Memoir 1940-1944*, Saint Michael's Press Book, US, *2016*
- Helleberg Fields, Meredith, Ed., *Yachtsman's Guide to the Bahamas*, Tropic Isle Publishers, Inc., Miami, FL, US, 1998 et. al.
- Her Majesty's Stationery Office, *Colonial Reports, 1952 and 1953: Bahamas,* Colonial Office Report on The Bahamas for the Years 1952 and 1953, London, UK, 1955
- Her Majesty's Stationary Office, Registrar General of Shipping and Seamen, London, UK, *Mercantile Navy List and Maritime Directory*, in print: 1868, 1875, 1876, 1879, 1880, 1882, 1891, 1892, 1896, 1899, 1904, 1907, 1911, 1913, 1914, 1918, 1919, 1921, 1923, 1924, 1925-1940, 1947, 1949, 1951, 1953, 1955, 1957-1965, 1968, 1973, also on microfiche 1857-1864, 1866-1908, 1910-1914, 1916-1920, 1922, Memorial University Maritime History Archive, Digital Archive, Newfoundland, Canada, collections.mun.ca, also Crew List Index Project, or CLIP, at crewlist.org.uk
- Hill, J. R. & Ranft, Bryan, *The Oxford Illustrated History of the Royal Navy*, Oxford University Press, UK, 1995

- Hintz, Martin, *The Bahamas, Enchantment of the World Second Series*, Children's Press, Scholastic, Inc., New York, NY, US, 2013
- Johnson, William R. Jr., *Bahama Tales, With Illustrations* by the Author, Lubbers Quarters, Abaco, Bahamas, 2019
- Johnston, Randolph W., *Artist on his Island, A Study in Self Reliance*, Noyes Press, US, 1975
- Jones, Roger M. & Jones, Peggy (illustrator), *PT Boat Episodes: PT-163 in the Pacific*, Merriam Press, US, 2000
- Klingel, Gilbert, Inagua, *An Island Sojourn*, Lyons & Burford, Guilford, CT, US, 1940, 1997
- Knowles, Sir Durward, as told to Cox, Albert E., Jr., *Captain of Industry, A Commentary on My Life in Perspective*, Sea Wolf, US, 2014
- Lawlor, Anne, Lawlor, Jim, *The Harbour Island Story*, 2008, MacMillan Education, UK
- Lawlor, Jim, Paul Albury: *A Man and His Writings*, 2013, Media Enterprises Ltd., Bahamas
- Lester, George, *In Sunny Isles: Chapters Treating Chiefly of the Bahama Islands and Cuba*, Charles H. Kelly, London, UK, 1897, Forgotten Books, London, UK, 2015
- Lightbourn, Ronald G., *Reminiscing: Photographs of Old Nassau* Vol. II, 2005, Ronald G. Lightbourn, US
- Lloyd, Jane, *History of the I.O.D.E. in the Bahamas*, 1901-2005, 2016, Media Enterprises Ltd., Bahamas
- Lloyd's Register of Shipping, *Lloyd's Register of American Yachts; A List of the Sailing and Power Yachts, Yacht Clubs and Yacht Owners of the United States and the Dominion of Canada*, New York, NY, US, 1933
- Lloyd's Register of Shipping, *Lloyd's Register of American Yachts*, New York, NY, US, 1969
- Lonsdale, Adrian L. & Kaplan, H. R., *Guide to Sunken Ships in American Waters*, Compass Publications, US, 1964.
- Lowe, Jack, *My Life: The Abaco Boy Story*, The Abaco Print Shop, Marsh Harbour, Bahamas, 2005
- Ludington, Morris Hoadley, *Bahamas Early Mail Services and Postal Markings*, Alpha Philatelic Printing & Publishing, Washington, DC, US, 1982
- Lurry-Wright, Jerome Wendell, *Custom and Conflict on a Bahamian Out-Island*, University Press of America, Inc., Lanham, MD, US, 1987

- Lyon, David, *The Sail and Steam Navy List: All the Ships of the Royal Navy*, 1815-1889, Chatham Publishing, London, UK, p.286, 2004
- Maclachan Bell, Major H., *Bahamas – Isles of June*, with a Foreword by His Excellency the Governor, Sir Bede Clifford, Robert M. McBride, New York, NY, US, 1934 (Ingram, Lightning Source, Milton Keyes, UK, 2018)
- Malcolm, Richard, *The Way We Were: Harbour Island in 50's and 60's*, 2011, Richard Malcolm, Harbour Island, Bahamas, 2011
- Malcolm, Richard, *Island Secrets, People, Places and Events, Then and Now, Including North Eleuthera, Current Island, Harbour Island, Spanish Wells*, Richard Malcolm, Harbour Island, Bahamas, 2015
- Maples, Don, *The Making of the Bahamas*, Longman Caribbean History, Hodder Education, London, UK, 2015.
- Marx, Robert F., *Shipwrecks in the Americas*, Bonanza, Crown, US, 1983.
- McCartney, Donald M., *Bahamian Culture and Factors Which Impact Upon It, a Compilation of Two Essays*, Dorrance Publishing Co., Pittsburgh, PA, US, 2004
- McCulla, Patricia E., *Bahamas, Major World Nations series, Chelsea House Publishers*, Philadelphia, PA, US, 1999
- Mills, Carlton, *History of the Turks & Caicos Islands*, MacMillan Publications, UK, 2008.
- Moseley-Moss, Valeria, *Reminiscing: Memories of Old Nassau*, 1999, Ronald G. Lightbourn, Bahamas
- Mueller, Edward A., *Savannah Line Ocean Steamship Co.*, Steamship Historical Society of America, US, 2001
- Munnings, Harold Alexander Jr. (MD), *Healthcare in the Bahamas*, 2014, Media Enterprises Ltd., Bahamas
- Munnings, Harold Alexander Jr., *Westward Walk of a Bahamian Doctor*, Xlibris, US, 2009.
- Nautical Publications, *Central Bahamas Andros to Exuma Eleuthera*, Maptech Inc., US, 2003.
- Nautical, Publications, *Northwest Bahamas Bimini & Berry Abaco*, Nautical Publications GmbH, Germany, 2004.
- Neely, Wayne, *The Major Hurricanes to Affect the Bahamas: Personal Recollections of Some of the Greatest Storms to Affect the Bahamas*, Authorhouse, Bahamas, 2006.

- Neely, Wayne, *Great Bahamian Hurricanes of 1926, The Story of Three of the Greatest Hurricanes to Ever Affect the Bahamas,* iUniverse, Bloomington, IN, US, 2009
- Neely, Wayne, *Great Bahamian Hurricanes of 1899 and 1932, The Story of Two of the Greatest and Deadliest Hurricanes to Impact the Bahamas,* iUniverse, Bloomington, IN, US, 2012
- Neely, Wayne, *The Great Bahamas Hurricane of 1929, the Story of the Greatest Bahamian Hurricane of the Twentieth Century,* iUniverse, Bloomington, IN, US, 2013
- Northcroft, George J. H., *Sketches of Summerland, Giving Some Account of Nassau and the Bahama Islands,* by the author of 'Sonnets of the Bahamas,' *The Nassau Guardian,* Nassau, N.P., Bahamas, 1900
- Parker, Philip M., *Bahamas: Webster's Timeline History 1492-2007,* ICON Group International, US, 2009
- Pearce-Jones, Guy, *Two Survived: 70 Days at Sea in Open Boat,* Lyons/Globe Pequot, US, 1940, (1976)
- Peggs, Deans A., PhD., *A Short History of the Bahamas,* The *Deans Peggs* Research Fund, *The Nassau Tribune,* Nassau, N.P., Bahamas, and The Crown Agents, London, UK, 1951
- Phillips, Michael J., Publisher, *Destination Commonwealth of Bahamas,* 2005, International Review, Review Publishing Co., Ltd. Channel Islands, UK, c.2010
- Popov, Nicolas & Dragan, *Children of the Sea: Exploring Diversity in the Bahamas, 1988-2000,* MacMillan Education Ltd., UK, 2000
- Powles, Louis Diston, *Land of the Pink Pearl: Recollections of the Bahamas,* 1996, Media Publishing Ltd., Bahamas
- Proud, Edward B., *The Postal History of Bahamas,* Proud-Bailey Co. Ltd., Heathfield, East Sussex, UK, 2000
- Pye, Michael, *King Over the Water: the Windsors War Years,* Holt Rinehart & Winston, US, 1981
- Ray, John R., *My Bahama Islands*; Vignettes, Omni PublishXpress, Nashville, TN, US, 2006
- Rigg, J. Linton, *Bahama Islands,* D. Van Norstrand Co., Inc., New York, NY, US, 1949
- Riley, Sandra, *Homeward Bound: A History of the Bahama Islands to 1850,* Island Research, Venture Press, US, 2000

- Roberts, Richard Campbell, & Malone, Shelley Boyd, *Nostalgic Nassau, Picture Postcards, 1900-1940*, Nassau Nostalgia, Nassau, N.P., Bahamas, 1991
- Rodriguez, Ruth, *Out Island Portraits, 1946-1956*, 1978, Out Island Press, US
- Russell, Joe, *Last Schoonerman: The Life of Captain Lou Kenedy*, 2006, Nautical Publishing, Far Horizons, US
- Schmidt, Roy, *Living the Harbour Island Dream*, 4 Square Books, Stillwater, MN, 2013
- Saunders, Gail & Craton, Michael, *Islanders in the Stream: A History of the Bahamian People: Volume Two: From the Ending of Slavery to the Twenty-First Century Vol. 2 End of Slavery-2000*, University of Georgia Press, US, 2000.
- Saunders, Gail, PhD., *Bahamas, A Family of Islands*, 2000, Macmillan Education, Oxford, UK, 2000
- Saunders, Gail & Huber, Linda M., *Nassau's Historic Landmarks*, MacMillan Education Publishers, UK, 2001
- Saunders, Gail, PhD., *Gambier Village, A Brief History, Gambier Community Development*, Nassau, N.P., Bahamas, 2007
- Saunders, Gail, PhD., *Historic Bahamas*, Lulu, US, 2010
- Saunders, Gail, PhD., *Bahamian Society After Emancipation, Essays in Nineteenth and early Twentieth Century Bahamian History*, Nassau, N.P., Bahamas, 1990
- Saunders, Gail & Cartwright, Donald, *Historic Nassau*, MacMillan Education, UK, 1979.
- Sherwood, Martyn, *Voyage of the Tai-Mo-Shan*, Rupert Hart-Davis, UK, 1957
- Simpson, Wallis, *The Heart Has Its Reasons*, David McKay, Van Rees Press, US, 1956
- Sliz, John, *Paradise Found and Lost: The History of the First All-Inclusive Resort in the Caribbean*, Travelogue 219, Canada, 2016
- Stark, James H., *Stark's History and Guide to the Bahama Islands: Guide to the Islands, Containing a Description of Everything on or About the Bahama Islands of Which the Visitor or Resident May Desire Information, Including Their History, Inhabitants, Climate, Agriculture, Geology, Government and Resources*, James H. Stark, Boston, MA, US, 1891, Forgotten books reprint, US, 2012 (Harvard College Library and Plimpton Press, MA, US)
- Summerscale, Kate, *The Queen of Whale Cay*, 2008, Bloomsbury, Viking, Penguin, UK
- Thompson, Anthony A., *An Economic History of the Bahamas*, Commonwealth Publications (1979) Limited, Nassau, N.P., Bahamas, 1979

- Thompson, R. Chester, *The Long Day Wanes: A Memoir of Love and War*, 2006, White Sound Press, US
- Toogood, Michael A., with Smith, Larry, *The Bahamas: Portrait of an Archipelago*, 2004, Macmillan Education, Oxford, UK, 2004
- Townsend, P. S. Anon, *Nassau Bahamas 1923-1924: Diary of Physician*, 1968, Bahamas Historical Society, Bahamas
- Turnquest, Orville, *What Manner of Man is This?*, Grant's Town Press, Bahamas, 2016
- Vincent-Barwood, Aileen, Vincent-Barwood, Allen, illustrator, *This Sweet Place, Island Living and Other Adventures*, Media Publishing Ltd., Nassau, N.P., Bahamas, 1998
- Waters, Sydney D., *Ordeal by Sea: New Zealand Shipping Company*, New Zealand Shipping Co. Ltd., New Zealand, 1949
- Wells, Geoffrey, & Wells, Victoria, *Elusive Beaches of Eleuthera Bahamas*, Gregory Town, Eleuthera, Bahamas, 2001
- Wiberg, Eric, *U-Boats in the Bahamas*, Bricktower Press, US, 2016
- Wiberg, Eric, *Swan Sinks, SS Cygnet Sunk by Italian Submarine Enrico Tazzoli, San Salvador, Bahamas in World War II*, Island Books, New York, NY, US, 2017
- Williams, Darius D., *Rail & Locomotive History of the Bahamas*, White Sound Press, US, 200
- Willoughby, Malcolm F., *The Rum War at Sea*, 1964, United States Government Printing Office.
- Wynne, Lewis N., *Florida at War*, Saint Leo College Press, US, 1993
- Young, Everild, *Eleuthera: An Island Called Freedom*, 1966, Regency Press, UK

Magazines, Booklets, & Pamphlets

Bahamas Handbook, Dupuch Publications, Nassau, N.P., Bahamas. Various years: an Index to articles relating to Mailboats, was created by Paul C. Aranha for the Bahamas Historical Society and generously shared.

1960	"Yachting on Blue-Water Superhighways," p.92
1960	"Sir Roland Symonette," Bahamian Knights series, p.136
1970	"Mailboats,".251, 256, 430, 489
1971-72	"Mailboats, 42, 365
1973	"Mailboats, 104, 511
1974-75	"Mailboats, 107, 111, 112, 115, 118, 121, 122, 127, 132-133 134, 136, 138, 140, 142, 410
1975-76	"Mailboats," 290, 505
1992	"Mailboats," 148, 160, 429
1997	"Mailboats," 571
1998	"Mailboats," 428, 488-489
1999	"Mailboats," 445, 505
2000	"Mailboats," 538
2001	"Mailboats," 506
2002	"Mailboats," 505-506
2003	"Mailboats," 505
2004	"Mail-boats," 451
2005	"Mail-boats," 432
2006	"Mail-Boats," 151-153, 412-416
2007	"Mailboats, 417
2008	"Mailboats, see also Transportation," 115-116, 128, 411
2009	"Mailboats," 111, 345-346
2010	"Mailboats," 159
2011	"Mailboats," 333-334
2015	Wiberg, Eric, "Bahamian Blockade Runner Turns Tables," p.87

Bahamas Historical Society:
- Pullinger, Diana, artist, Lawlor Jim, text, and Lightbourne, Ronald G., *The History of the Bahamas in Pictures*, Media Enterprises, Ltd., Nassau, N.P., 2012
- Nassau, Bahamas, 1823-4, *The Diary of a Physician from the United States visiting the Island of New Providence*, Her Majesty's Printers, London, UK, 1968
- Bowen, John, *Modeller's Draught, MV Sir Charles Orr, Model Shipwright* Number 90, Dec. 1994, p57, Conway Maritime Press, UK

- Braman, Fred, (Capt., USN-Ret.):
    - *Cruising by Mailboat, History, Culture and Adventure in the Bahama Islands*, with Photographs by Dave Blake and Paintings by Randy Curry, Jacksonville, FL, USA, March, 2021
    - "Bahamas by Mailboat," *Southwinds* News & Views for Southern Sailors, Sarasota, FL, US, Dec. 2017, p.52
    - "Bahamas by Mailboat Part II," *Southwinds*, Sarasota, FL, US, Jan. 2018, p.38
    - "Bahamas by Mailboat Part III," *Southwinds*, Sarasota, FL, US, Feb. 2018, p.36
- Department of Archives, Ministry of Education and Culture, *The Boat-Building Industry of the Bahamas*, Department of Archives Exhibition, 1981, Nassau, N.P., Bahamas
- Department of Archives, Ministry of Education and Culture, *Bahamas During The World Wars: 1914-18, 1939-45*, Department of Archives Exhibition, Nassau, N.P., Bahamas, 1985
- Dupuch, Publications, *Bahamas Handbook* and Businessman's Annual, 1992, various years, Bahamas Historical Society, National Archives have Paul Aranha's Index of all *Bahamas Handbook* articles
- IDB, International Development Bank, East Bay Street across from Brown's Boat Basin, generously shared a portfolio of photographs and captions regarding Potter's Cay and mailboats, particularly those from the Margaret Hegarty audit which the IDB funded
- Johnson, William R. Jr., *Seapath Bahama Notes & Other Stories*, 2003, Tortuga Productions, Bahamas
- Ludington, M. H. & Osborn, Geoffrey, *The Royal Mail Steam Packets to Bermuda and the Bahamas, 1842-1859*, Robson Lowe, Ltd., London, 1971
- Nielsen, Jon & Nielsen, Kay, *The Bahama Book, A History of the Bahamas from Columbus to the Present* (pamphlet), Voyager Press, Dobbs Ferry, NY, US, 1966
- Popov, Nicolas & Popov, Dragan:
    - *Island Expedition: Central, Southern Bahamas*, Nassau, N.P., Bahamas, 1988
    - *Island Expedition: School at Sea,* Nassau, N.P., Bahamas, 1997
    - *Island Expedition: School at Sea Experience,* Nassau, N.P., Bahamas, 1994
- *Scribner's Monthly* for November, 1877, Nassau, Island of New Providence, Bahamas, *A Guide to the Sanitarium of the Western Hemisphere, its Attractions and How to Get There*, with Illustrations… Including "An *Isle of June*. ….Issued by the New York, Nassau, and West India Mail Steamship Line, Savannah;

Nassau and Havana Mail Steamship Line, and the Royal Victoria Hotel of Nassau, N.P." Agents for the Steamship Lines, Murray, Ferris & Co., New York, NY, US, 1877 (Scholar Select, imprint of Andesite Press, US, 2018)
- Shukman, Henry, with Abramowicz, William, photographer, A Slow Boat to Cat Island, Condé Nast Traveler, New York, NY, Vol. 31, Issue 4, April, 1996, p.119
- Wiberg, Eric, "A History of Bahamian Mailboats, 1804 to Present," Powerships, The Magazine of Engine-Power Vessels, Steamship Historical Society of America, Warwick, RI, US, Fall, 2016, p.36
- Wiberg, Eric:
  - "U-Boats in the Bahamas," Journal of the Bahamas Historical Society, Vol. 31, Oct. 2009, p.65
  - *Drifting to Duchess,* Potlatch *Carstairs*, Bahamas Historical Society Journal, 2015
- Wylly, William, *A Short Account of the Bahama Islands, their climate, productions, some strictures upon their relative and political situation, the defect of their present government, By a barrister at law, late His Majesty's Solicitor General,* Reproduction form Harvard University Houghton Library, London, UK, 1789

Newspaper Articles

- *Abaconian*, numerous mailboat-related articles, e.g. the Sherwin Archer and Garnett Archer mailboat legacy.
- "Abaco Saw Brief Snow Flurries in 1977," 1996
- Bacon, Edgar Mayhew, *Notes of a Sub Tropic* Study, 1889, post-emancipation southern Bahamas by *Bahamian*
- The Bahamas Maritime Authority, *M/V* Sherice M*., Report of the Marine Safety Investigation Into a Fire on a General Cargo Vessel on Jun. 16, 2018*, London, UK, Aug. 31, 2018
- *The Bahamas Weekly*, Nassau, N.P., Bahamas
- Campbell, Kathryn, "Mailboat Owners and Operators Accept Government's Offer," Bahamas Information Service Update, May 12, 2012
- *Becker, Truman,* Mail Boats: Tourist's Special Delivery, *Christian Science Monitor*, Wisconsin paper, 1979
- Blackerby, Cheryl, *Cruise News,* "The Bahamas: Taking a Tropical Island Hob by Mailboat," Cox News Service, *The Orange County Register*, Los Angeles, CA, US, Nov. 6, 1994

- Dockmaster's Office, *Inter-Island Mailboat Weekly Schedule for the Period*, Potter's Cay, Nassau, N.P., Bahamas, various from 1988 to 2020, author's collection
- *The Eleutheran* Newspaper, articles and obituaries on Pinders, Weeches, Kellys, Symonettes, mailboat owners, crew, investors over the years:
    - ~ An *Eleutheran* Profile, Mr. Gurney Elon Pinder (70), Eleuthera, Bahamas, Local, p.14, Sep./Oct. 2013
- Emerald Ridge Mortuary, Obituary for Capt. Roy Oral Lockhart, Nassau, N.P., Bahamas, Mar. 16, 2002
- Fox, Porter, "Off the Tourist Grid in the Bahamas," *The New York Times*, New York, NY, Jan. 30, 2013
- Fred Mitchell Uncensored, "Bimini Mailboat Goes Down – Two Dead," Mar. 25, 2000
- Keller, Allan, He Said: "Tourists Never Take The Mail Boat' - That Clinched It," *The New York Times*, New York, NY, May 24, 1970
- Kleinberg, Eliot, "In the Bahamas, Long Island is Wild, Wonderful, Wide Open," Cox News Service, *Sunday Travel*, Sept. 17, 1989
- Gaudet, Larry, Mailboat Isle-Hop Not for the Fussy
- *The Kingston Gleaner*, Jamaica, "Storm Causes Widespread Destruction of Property in Nassau," Aug. 6, 1926 (from *The Nassau Guardian* of July, 1926)
- *The London Express*, Mails for the Bahamas, Dec. 31, 1867
- Lutcherath, Hugo Carl, "Land gangs fartoyene som ble Fjordabater; The Landing Craft that Became Passenger Boats" *Exuma Pride*, Stavanger, Norway, 2019
- *The Nassau Guardian*, Nassau, N.P., Bahamas:
- Knowles, Rachel, "Garbage Abounds at Potter's Cay Dock," Aug. 2, 2019
- Mailboat Broadcasts, to the Editor, Re: The M. V. *Drake*, the People of this Island Deeply Regret, 1964
- M/V *Drake* Crewman Jumps into Ocean, Missing at Sea, *Guardian* Staff Reporter, 1960s
- Notice to the Public, The Andros Island Mail Boat *Wissama*, Jan. 4, 1961
- Shipping, Expected Arrivals, the SS *Bahama* start from Miami, the M/V *Wissama*, Captain Roberts to Exuma
- Obituary for Capt. Arlington E. Farqhuarson, June 26, 2014
- Shipping Movements, In Port Arriving in Nassau Yesterday Were the M/V *Air Pheasant*
- Spanish Wells Loses Distinguished Citizen, Businessman, Albert Pinder, Jan. 20, 1960

- Welfare Doctor at Long Island, Welfare Doctor Left for Long Island by the Mail Boat *Gary Roberts*, "due at Simms," *The Nassau Tribune*, Nassau, N.P., Bahamas
- Brown, Geoffrey, Andros Farm: Mailboat System Overhaul Needed, July 22, 2014
- Classified section, "For Sale, Former Navy Mine sweeper MSC 194, ex-King Bird," Jun. 30, 1973
- Government Notices, Ministry of Transport and Aviation, Port Department, Boat License Applicants, Feb. 11, 2005
- Lawlor, Jim, Chapter 6 Continued: Hurricane Betsy, 1965, from *Paul Albury: A Man and his Writings*, part 29, Aug. 31, 2013
- Ministry of Transport & Aviation *Review of Mail Boat Operations*, p.3B July 4, 2005
- Ministry of Education and Culture Co-ordinated a Summer Youth Programme, caption, c.1975, *Air Swift*
- Press Tour with Esso, to See Big Out Island Project, p.5, columns 1-5, June 9, 1960
- Renewal Boat License, Family Island, Feb. 10, 2006
- Smith, Larry, *Tough Call: How the Old Man Came to the Sea at Bimini*, Feb. 11, 2013
- *St. Petersburg* Times, "Six Lives Lost When Excursion Sinks 40 Miles Northeast of Nassau," St. Petersburg, FL, US, June 5, 1952 (from Richard Malcolm, Island Secrets, p.146, 2015)
- "Two Known Victims Perish Near Nassau: Four Believed Dead: Seventeen Survive Sea Tragedy of MV *Zelma Rose*, June, 1952" (from Richard Malcolm, Island Secrets, p.150, 2015)
- Wiberg, Eric;
    - "Mailboats: Introduction, Background, Motives," March 24, 2016
    - "History of Mailboats from 1804," April 1, 2016
    - "Mailboats of and to Abaco Islands," April 8, 2016
    - "Mailboat of and to Eleuthera Islands," April 15, 2016
    - "Mailboats to Northern Islands," April 22, 2016
    - "Mailboats to Southern Islands," April 29, 2016
    - "Roberts Family Mailboat Dynasty," May 6, 2016
    - "Taylor Family Mailboat Dynasty," May 13, 2016
    - "Dean Family Mailboat Dynasty," May 20, 2016
    - "Hanna Family Mailboat Dynasty," May 27, 2016
    - "Wooden Mailboats (to the 1960s)" June 10, 2016
    - "European Mailboats (to the 1990s)" June 17, 2016
    - "Modern Mailboats (from the 1990s)" June 24, 2016

- ~ "Roundup, Mailboats as a Living Tradition," July 1, 2016
- ~ "Conclusion, Potter's Cay Dock, the Future," July 8, 2016
- *The Nautical Standard*, The Royal Mail Steam-ship *Conway*, Sept. 18, 1852
- Pleasants, Julian, ..."Or a Mailboat Can Take You to Endless Islands, Chicago," IL, US, 1983
- Rosenblatt, Leon, "Slow Boat to Abaco," *South Florida Sun-Sentinel*, Apr. 29, 1990
- Savage, Nancy, "Captain Lou Kenedy's Boat for Out Island Trade," Nova Scotia, Canada, 1960s
- Scheller, William G., Wolff, Tom, photographer; "In Search of Columbus, in Which, Almost 500 Years Later, Our Man in the Bahamas Finds Parts of the New World That Still Haven't Been Discovered," Leisure Magazine, Oct. 15, 1989, Washington Post and Getty Images
- Selkirk Enterprise, "Bahamas Mailboat Ride Different Way to Travel," WI, US, Sep. 3, 1975
- Soeren, "Danish-Bahamas Ferry Ellen-Soeby, Lisa J: Project Dropped When Owner of the Ferry Dies," Maritime Editor, Fyns Amts Avis, aka The Seaside, FAA.dk, Denmark, 2015
- Stratton, Mark, "Bahamas by Mailboat: Can this Unique Tradition Survive?," CNN, Atlanta, GA, US, May 7, 2014 "Take Slow Mailboat to Bahama Out Isles,' Utica, New York, Travel, p.4E, Mar. 7, 1975
- Strozier, Fred, "The US has found one of their hemisphere defense bases in the remote Bahamian island of Mayaguana," Somerset, PA, US, Dec. 4, 1940
- Talty, Alexandra, "On Board the Everything Boat," Roads and Kingdoms.com, Travel, Mar. 4, 2016
- UPI, United Press International, "Cubans Shoot at Bahama Boat to 'Reserve' Lobster Grounds," 1964
- Weitzel, Tony, "Out Island Hopping is Fun, Reasonable," Naples Daily News Travel Editor, Travel – Entertainment, Naples, FL, US, p.1D Feb. 11, 1973

Online Resources

1. 7seavessels.com
2. Abacoforum.com
3. Amver.com (Automated Mutual Assistance Rescue logs)
4. Ancestry.com
5. Bahamas.com
6. Bahamasb2b.com
7. Bahamasbeachfrontvilla.com
8. Bahamas4u.com/bahamasmailboat

9. Bahamasferries.com
10. Bahamasforvisitors.com
11. Bahamas-guide.info
12. Bahamashandbook.com
13. Bahamasguru.com
14. Bahamashistoricalsociety.com (and journal)
15. Bahamaslocal.com
16. Bahamasnationalarchives.bs
17. Bahamaspress.com
18. Bahamasspectator.com
19. Bahamasuncensored.com
20. Blog.writewellter.com (*Sea Hauler* op.-ed.)
21. Books.google.com (access to *Mercantile Navy Lists*)
22. Bradford-marine.com
23. Briland.com
24. Caselaw.findlaw.com
25. Choosingthebetterlife.com
26. Collections.mun.ca/PDFs/mha_merchant/MercantileNavyList
27. Crewlist.org.uk
28. Deanshipping.com
29. Deviantart.com
30. Discover-eleuthera-bahamas.com
31. Divespots.com
32. Ericwiberg.com
33. Equasis.org
34. Escapefromamerica.com
35. Facebook.com (groups, travel blogs, etc.)
36. Faergelejet.dk
37. Fleetmon.com
38. Forms.bahamas.gov.bs (legal bases for mailboat subsidies)
39. Fultonhistory.com
40. Geographia.com/Bahamas/trabetween
41. Grosstonnage.com
42. Interferry.com
43. Issuu.com/abacojournal/docs (*Abaco Journal*)
44. Islandmag.com
45. Jabezcorner.com/grand_bahama/golden1 (older news)
46. Knutsonmarine.com
47. Law.justia.com (for legal cases in US courts)
48. Littlehousebytheferry.com (Green Turtle Cay blog by Amanda Diedrick)

49. Mailboatbahamas.com
50. Marinelike.com
51. Marinetraffic.com
52. Maritime-connector.com
53. Mtaintranet.weebly.com/uploads/1/5/6/6/15660628/mailboats.pdf
54. Myharbourisland.com
55. Nationalfamiyislandregatta.com
56. Nassaucontainerport.com
57. Nassauparadiseisland.com/4-famous-historical-shipwrecks-in-the-bahamas-2
58. Nationsonline.org/oneworld/island-countries (Bahamas as #25)
59. Navsource.org
60. Navypedia.org
61. Newspaperarchive.com
62. Oldbahamas.com
63. Oxfordinklings1942.com/2013/11/01/island-wreck-dishes-recipe-for-adventure (*Firequeen*)
64. Pbase.com/twolanetommy/mailboatbahamas2017 (Dave Blake photos)
65. Photoship.co.uk
66. Research.mysticseaport.org/collections (Mystic Seaport, CT)
67. Roroshippingcompany.com
68. Seshippingnews.typepad.com
69. Shipbuildinghistory.com
69. Shipscribe.com
70. Shipindex.org
71. Shipspotters.nl
72. Shipspotting.com
73. Shipwreckexpo.com
74. Sshsa.org (Steamship Historical Society of America)
75. St.nmfs.noaa.gov (database of all US vessels)
76. Stampauctionnetwork.com
77. Stamplibrary.org
78. Stamps.org
79. Thebahamasweekly.com
80. Thefreeportnews.com
81. Thenassauguardian.com
82. Therumelier.com (historic photos)
83. Theshipslist.com
84. Tribune242.com (*Nassau Tribune*)
85. Ufdc.ufl.edu (Univ. of Florida Bahamian news free digital archive)

86. Ufdcimages.uflib.ufl.eduWhatshipru.com
87. Whatsonbahamas.com
88. Wikileaks.org
89. Wikipedia.org
90. Wikitree.com
91. Woodenyachts.com
92. Worldnavalships.com
93. Wrecksite.eu
94. Yachtaide.blogspot.com (many yacht blogs have useful photos)
95. flickr.com/photos/rstehn/24386245874/in/photostream, Rüdiger Stehn
96. whitehouse2002.co.uk/cuttings2.html, M/V *Frecil* story, photos
97. classicboatmuseum.com/carstairs, Marion Carstairs' yachts
98. offshoreleaks.icij.org/nodes/30021971; *Panama Papers,* reveals corporate layers

Government Resources

- Annual governmental reports; obtained a small sampling of Archives in Nassau, Washington, DC, and London
- Bahamas Maritime Authority's London office produces excellent casualty reports
- Ministry of Transport and Local Government; contacted all island administrators by email
- Nassau Harbour Pilots Association, Freeport Harbour Pilots, not so relevant to mailboats
- Nassau Port Authority; visited since early 1990s, not much contact
- Potter's Cay Dockmaster; frequent and sustained contact; in person, phone, email

Filmography

vimeo.com/265552444# = , *Abentur Leben Taglich*, by Hans-Otto Film in Berlin, Germany, with *Sherice M.* and its captain Sean Munroe, before the June 16, 2018 fire at Alice Town which decimated the vessel, causing replacement *Emmett Cephas* to be sailed by Bahamians from Cook Islands, Pacific, to Nassau, arriving end July, 2019. Film shot early 2018, author's brother James Wiberg helped the film crew coordinate connecting with *Sherice M.* and *Captain C.* Tagline is "We accompanied a mailboat in the Bahamas and visited the most modern DHL parcel center in Germany."

youtube.com/watch?v=pwKPOLrfHD4, Tim Reeves Video, Dec. 2015, informative short film of *Lady Rosalind II* at Morgan's Bluff, includes interviews with dockmaster, Ms. Kaydra Storr, vessel crew, customers, etc.

youtube.com/watch?v=FuId_wKqZZE, Mailboat Operators Resume Operations, after Hurricane Matthew, ZNS, *The Bahamas Tonight*, by Fern Carey, with Capt. Jed Munroe, Island Link, Capt. Eddins Taylor, *Lady Rosalind II*, ZNS Network, Nassau, Oct. 14, 2016

youtube.com/watch?v=VKU_7w21ZI4, Bahamas Ferries, *Grand Master II*, a narrated voyage from Potter's Cay to Exumas with good access to the bridge just as the boat was delivered, by Adrienn Moncur and team, June. 17. 2018.

youtube.com/watch?v=scL-kYLTjqE, *The Unique Boats of Nassau*, Jun. 8, 2018, an informative tour of mailboats in the harbour and other ships from the dinghy of an American yachtie couple with dog. Blog *Tula's Endless Summer*, at tulasendlesssummer.com; Caption "Nassau Harbour is a big busy commercial port in the Bahamas. You see every kind of boat and ship from commercial fishing boats to mail boats to mega yachts. We take a quick dinghy ride around Nassau Harbour."

youtube.com/watch?v=6pMb4EMeer8, "Mailboat Company Withstands Strong Storm Surge," Elizabeth Russell, marketing VP for The Mailboat Company shows ZNS TV damage and repairs underway at Arawak Cay, Nassau Harbour, ZNS Network, Nassau, May 5, 2018.

youtube.com/watch?v=6pMb4EMeer8, "Mailboat Operators on Tropical Wave," various mailboats; *Lady Frances, Lady Rosalind*, at Potter's Cay, Capt. Eddins Taylor, *Lady Mathilda*, interview with Silvin Brown, mate of *Lady Frances* about whether they could make it south and back before tropical storm. ZNS Network, Nassau, Aug. 24, 2016.

Interviews

1. Andrew Albury, Bahamian-American Assoc. President, New York City
2. Paul C. Aranha, pilot, author, historian, mentor
3. Mrs. Sybil Archer, widow of Capt. & Senator Sherwin Archer, nearly a centarian
4. Captain Lance & Lenny Brozozog
5. Kendal S. Butler, expert on wooden boats in Bahamas
6. Carl Campbell, Rev., United Methodist
7. Robert I. Carey, MD, PhD and John Carey, MD
8. Delores Forbes-Berry at Dockmaster's Office
9. Capt. Willard Matthew Fox, M/V *Offshore*, M/V *Captain Fox*, via email, 2017
10. Rod Freundt, AUTEC Kids facebook site, served in US Navy
11. Thomas Hanna, owner
12. Mr. Higgins, Pirate's Well (for Louis Williamson)
13. Jim Hood, for Calum Legett
14. William (Bill) Johnson (chronicler of Bahamian fishing smacks)
15. Kimberly King-Burns, Expats Bahamas
16. Ronald G. Lightbourn, author, historian, photographer
17. Captain Calum Legett, maritime consultant to government for mailboats
18. Capt. Lockhart of Ragged Island, briefly ran Emmett & Cephas
19. Pericles Maillis, lawyer, historian
20. Marcus Mitchell, salvage master, pilot
21. Mrs. Kimberley McPhee, niece of Mrs. Archer, assisted interview and emailing
22. Mrs. Rosemary Moss Williams, niece of Sherwin Williams, sister of Donald Moss
23. Capt. Joseph Moxey of Mango Creek, Andros, worked 15 mailboats till blinded
24. Percentie (via phone, first name unknown, re: fate of *Air Swift*)
25. Eldyth Roberts, relative of Abaconian shipbuilders and captains
26. Florence Roberts, relative of Jenkins
27. Niel Sealy, Media Enterprises
28. Larry Smith, journalist, publisher (RIP)
29. Eddie Spargur, AUTEC Kids Facebook page
30. Mike Stafford, Bradford Marine, Freeport
31. R. Craig Symonette, mentor, expert at vessels built, operated Bahamas, post-war
32. Taylors: Eddins, Limas, Elvin, & managers, officers, on shore, dock, on vessels
33. Robert Turnquest
34. Jacob Wilson, Ragged Island

Note: Most "interviews" were just short, informal but informative exchanges on docks and mailboats. Potter's Cay Docks and commercial ships in general are busy places with many moving parts where everyone is constantly engaged in one activity or another, and long conversations are a challenge.

Illustration Credits

The author took most photographs, or permission was granted (via email) to use them on his 230-vessel blog, searchable at ericwiberg.com, starting in 2012. If a reader notices an oversight, error, or omission the author sincerely apologizes. Errata can be emailed to eric@ericwiberg.com. The author takes full responsibility for any and all errors and omissions. It is hoped that, even where full credit was not properly given, someone else documenting these same unique craft and their workaday lives will be a kindred spirit and be willing to forgive. Furthermore, since many readers will not have had the chance to ride aboard a mailboat, the illustrations in this text are obviously both integral and indispensable. I would like to thank every individual who ever snapped, shared, painted, tattooed or drew an image of a mailboat and shared it.

- P.2, bottom right: *Bimini Gal,* 1965, Dave Gale, *Below Another Sky*, p.281
- P.3, bottom left: *Captain Dean II*, 1963, *Island Captain, The Autobiography of Mail Boat Captain,* Ernest Dean of Sandy Point, Abaco, Bahamas, with Gary W. Woodcock, White Sound Press, Decatur Illinois, 1997 p.106
- P.8, top left: Peter and Tracy Roberts, Bahamas.
- P.10, middle left: *Legend,* 2005, Photo of the Legend in cargo operations in the Bahamas, by bloggers Dave & Carol of New Horizon at http://intoanewhorizon.blogspot.com/2010_11_01_archive.html
- P.13, middle left: *Patricia K.,* 1930, Dave Gale, *Ready About*, page, 168
- P.13, middle right: *Queen, Athelqueen* lifeboat, 1942
- P.27: Map of Bahamian archipelago, Capt. Paul C. Aranha, *Mail Day*, painting by Bill Gillies, in Dave Gale's *Ready About*, page 52, and *Below Another Sky*, p.165.
- P.28, top: *Liberty* in Spanish Wells, North Eleuthera, Ronald G. Lightbourn
- P.28, bottom: *Liberty* entering Fresh Creek, Andros, Eddie Spargur.
- P.35, top: Modern Potter's Cay Dock. copyright Google Earth
- P.56: *Dart* on voyage to or from Harbour Island and North Eleuthera, Harvey G. Oppmann, *Harbour Island: Yesterday and Today, A Memoir* (2009)
- P.57, top: Original *City of Nassau,* communes.com/basse-normandie/manche/Granville_50400/cartes-postales-anciennes.htm
- P.57, bottom: 1926 chart of the Bahamas, Captain Paul C. Aranha
- P.67: Reconstructed sailing mailboat *Albertine Adoue,* Evan Lowe, OutIslandBoy.wordpress.com

- P.77: *Bimini Mack*, leaving Alice Town, North Bimini, virtualtourist.com/travel/Caribbean_and_Central_America/The_Bahamas/Bimini_District/Transportation-Bimini_District-TG-C-1
- P.132, top: *Marcella III* at Prince George's Dock, Nassau, The Taylor Corporation
- P.132, bottom: Captain Eddins Taylor purchasing *Jade*, The Taylor Corporation
- P. 143: Captain of *Legend* working in the wheelhouse with guest, Carol and Dave bloggers at intoanewhorizon.blogspot.com/2010_11_01_archive
- P.145, bottom: A captain casually chatting in Exuma, Bob and Brenda. bloggers at sailpandora.com/? p=1862
- P.146, bottom: Captain Fed. Black, The Taylor Corporation
- P.147, top: Sir George William Kelly Roberts, The Sir George W. K. Roberts Memorial Library, Harbour Island, Bahamas. wikitree.com/photo/jpg/Roberts-10989
- P.151, top: Sailors aboard *Bahamas Daybreak* waiting for word to push off. suedkurier.de/tipps/reise/traumziele/Entspannter-Urlaub-auf-den-Out-Islands-d er-Bahamas;art502,3186468: Kubisch/dpa/tmn
- P.152, top: Crewmen using a large boulder in place of a bollard to hold their mailboat in place, Chris. blogger at travelswithpolarpacer.blogspot.com/2010/05/george-town-exuma
- P.153, top: Cephas Maycock, First Mate of the *Captain C.*, leaving the Exumas for Ragged Island, Roads & Kingdoms blog. globelivenews.com/on-board-the-everything-boat/
- P.156, top: *Lady Rosalind II* discharging stern-to in tight quarters at Matthew Town, Inagua, Max Dornbush, JB, and Christian. thejourneyoftheseeker.blogspot.com/2012/01/photos-from-egg-island-eleuthera-to
- P.157, bottom: *Captain Gurth Dean* discharging and loading cargo to and from Abaco at Potter's Cay, Peter Pateman. deviantart.com/morelikethis/artists/290629856? view_mode=2
- P.160, bottom: *Lady Frances* making a private delivery of construction materials to Exuma. anon. blogger
- P.161, top: *Lady Mathilda* arrives in Matthew Town, Inagua, Amy Jordan and Roger Block. bloggers at svshango.com/March%20Pictures.htm
- P.162, top: *Trans Cargo II* discharging *Fred Miller II* shipspotting.com/gallery/photo.php? lid=1770611
- P.162, bottom: *Legacy* loading at western tip of Potter's Cay, Jeremy Lavender Photography. redbubble.com/people/242digital/works/9341058-cargo-boat-

- at-potters-cay-loading-freight-to-deliver-in-the-family-island-nassau-the-bahamas
- P.163, top: *United Star* coming in to dock, rubbing and churning sand behind it. She is arriving in Exuma with decks filled with racing sloops ready to duke it out in the highly-contested regatta there. distantshores.ca/news_files/category-bahamas.html
- P.164, top: *Marcella III* utilizing service of a truck-mounted crane to load or discharge cargo from its forward hold, Capt. Calum Legget, Capt. James Hood.
- P.164, bottom: *Grand Master* discharging at Normans Cay, Exuma, *Kayak Guide*. kayakguide.com/Bah-Exuma.htm
- P.165, bottom: *Lady Frances* preparing to load Red Cross emergency supplies to a family island following a hurricane, the bahamas weekly. Thebahamasweekly.com/publish/bis-news-updates/Hurricane_Irene_Disaster_Relief_in_High_Gear17576
- P.169, bottom: *Captain Moxey* transferring passengers off Little Farmers Cay, Exuma, Ted and Ginnie. sailfirecracker.com/? p=494
- P.174, bottom: Rare photograph showing little tugboat BA 2 towing *Noel Roberts* from Harbour Island to Nassau on its maiden voyage, Mrs. Susan Roberts, corroborated by Craig Symonette
- P.175, bottom: Bahamian artist Chan Pratt painting the *AutoGo* in Abaco, *The Abaconian,* February. 15, 2004. ufdcimages.uflib.ufl.edu/UF/00/09/37/13/00348/02-15-2004.pdf
- P.176, top: Model of *Almeta Queen* at Lowe Museum of Art in Abaco, by Capt. Vertrum Lowe, Green Turtle Cay Abaco. uncommoncaribbean.com/2012/09/12/uncommon-buy-vertrum-lowes-bahamian-model-ships/
- P.176, bottom: First edition cover of *Abaco – The History of an Out Island and its Cays* by Steve Dodge and Laurie Jones, White Sound Press, (1987 2005).
- P.177, top: Fictional mailboat, *Lady Marguerite*, at passenger exit from Nassau International Airport, artist unknown, Bahamas Civil Aviation Authority. bcaa.gov.bs
- P.177, bottom: Watercolour of *Noel Roberts* given to Noel Roberts - shared by his widow, Mrs. Susan Roberts.
- P.179: Watercolour of *Lady Dundas*, given to Noel Roberts, Mrs. Susan Roberts.
- P.180, top: *Lady Gloria* run aground and abandoned in Andros, Aaron Gilson. hiveminer.com/Tags/freshcreek/Recent
- P.180, bottom: *Lady Mathilda* aground on a reef and being helped by small boat, The Taylor Corporation.

- P.181, top: Collision of *Sea Hauler* with *United Star*, Tim Aylen, copyright Associated Press.
- P.181, middle: Untangling wreckage of the fatal *Sea Hauler* crane collapse. bahamasuncensored.com/august03.htm
- P.181, bottom: A mailboat aground, semi-submerged, and rusting away off Cat Island, Jad Davenport, *National Geographic.* gettyimages.com/detail/photo/freightter-wreck-on-the-atlantic-coast-off-high-res-
- P.182, bottom: Rotting *Lady Tasha* at Arawak Cay, the other end of Nassau Harbour, Consul John Wiberg.
- P.183, bottom: *Island Hauler*, wrecked on the reefs off Long Island, Capt. John Wampler. yachtaide.blogspot.com/2012/02/st-thomas-usvi-to-fort-lauderdale.html (another personal friend)
- P.184, top: *Legacy* aground in the North Bar Channel, *The Nassau Tribune,* 9 November, 2011. myabaco.net/mv-legacy-is-pushed-up-on-rocks-at-the-north-bar-channel-in-abaco-bahamas
- P.184, bottom: *Grand Master* aground in Conch Cut off Georgetown, Great Exuma. exumaproperties.files.wordpress.com/2010/03/grand-master.jpg
- P.185: *Exuma Pride* aground off Crab Cay, Exuma, Greg and Duwan. bloggers at makelikeanapeman.com/2013/03/12/georgetowncrab-cay/
- P.186: *Church Bay* on fire at Potter's Cay, Nassau, The *Nassau Tribune*, 11 January, 1973 George A. Smathers Libraries. – Front Page, ufdc.ufl.edu/UF000 84249/03243, c/o George A. Smathers Libraries, University of Florida, Caribbean Newspaper Digital Library
- P.187, top: Sunlit cabin with bunks aboard *Captain C.*, sailblogs. sailblogs.com/member/finelion/? xjMsgID=303722
- P.187, bottom: Galley aboard the *Captain C.*, sailblogs. sailblogs.com/member/finelion/? xjMsgID=303722
- P.189, top: Bunk beds aboard *Captain C.*, sailblogs. sailblogs.com/member/finelion/? xjMsgID=303722
- P.207, top: *The Harbour Island Story*, Jim & Anne Lawlor, MacMillan Caribbean, Oxford, UK (2008).
- P.207, bottom: *Old Horse Eye* working cargo in Abaco, Dave Gale, *Below Another Sun*, Caribe Communications (2011), of Island Marine, Abaco. She later became the Abaco mailboat *Patricia K.*
- P.208, top: Rough montage of an old newspaper image of *Isle of June* docked in Miami, The *Miami News*, August 28, 1938.

news.google.com/newspapers?nid=2206&dat=19380828&id=2AUtAAAAIBAJ&sjid=QNQFAAAAIBAJ&pg=4596,4335568
- P.208, bottom: *Priscilla*, from the Wyannie Malone Historical Society, Hope Town, Abaco, also, Evan Lowe, *Out Island Boy*. blog, April, 2014, outislandboy.wordpress.com/
- P.209: *Gary Roberts* from *The Harbour Island Story* by Jim and Anne Lawlor. page 52, MacMillan Caribbean, Oxford, UK (2008)
- P.210: *Willaurie* as the *Willmary* loading cargo in the UK, 1960's, Rick Cox collection. 7seasvessels.com/?s=willmary
- P.211, top: *Willmary* trading coastwise in Europe with full cargo, © Charlie Hill of Swinefleet near Goole Passing Swinefleet inward for Goole. Coasters & Other Ships Revived. 7seasvessels.com/?s=willmary
- P.211, bottom: *Willaurie* ex-*Willmary* aground off Clifton Bay, New Providence, Steve Fink. shipwreckexpo.com/tsbahamanewprovidenceshipwrecks.htm
- P.212, top *Willaurie* wreck underwater as a dive site off Clifton, southwest New Providence. i.ytimg.com/vi/xV7Z2YNC-Cc/maxresdefault.jpg
- P.212, bottom: *Miss BJ* under her former name, *Sambre*, in Europe. wrecksite.eu/wreck.aspx?218991
- P.213, top *Miss BJ* at Prince George Dock in downtown Nassau. photoship.co.uk/JAlbum%20Ships/Old%20Ships%20M/slides/Miss%20BJ-01.jpg
- P.213, bottom: *Miranda*, as confiscated *Gilbert Sea*, being sunk off Florida. wrecksite.eu/wreck.aspx?139583
- P.214, top *Deborah K. II* in Europe as the *Klaas*, *Savi*, or *Windhund*, earlier in its career, Baltic Shipping. balticshipping.com/vessel/imo/6515631
- P.245: Dave Blake Photography, by kind permission
- P.304: Author Photo by *The Nassau Tribune*, Nassau, Bahamas, 2016, by kind permission.

About the Author

Captain Eric Wiberg few up as part of a large Swedish-American-Bahamian family in Cable Beach, outside of Nassau. His family first moved to the Bahamas from Sweden in 1952 where his parents operated Cable Beach Manor and his father and then brother represented Sweden in the Commonwealth. Since taking command of a large wooden sailboat that he met in Nassau to New Zealand, he has operated over 100 yachts more than 75,000 nautical miles, many of them as captain. A licensed master since 1995, he is qualified as a maritime lawyer and earned a Masters in Marine Affairs degree covering oceans policy and marine transportation and logistics. He commercially operated nine tankers from Singapore for three years for the family who once owned the Royal Victoria Hotel in Nassau, and worked briefly for two salvage firms, one in Freeport. For half a decade he served as broker and agent for over 100 mariners through Echo Yacht Delivery. He studied at six universities in three countries, including at Oxford and in Boston, Lisbon, Rhode Island, and New York City.

Eric has published several books of nautical non-fiction, three of them covering World War II in the Bahamas, and three covering institutions there. He has been publishing on nautical themes in *The Bahamas Handbook, What's On*, and the *Journal of the Bahamas Historical Society The Nassau Tribune* starting in 1989, and spoken in numerous venues in Nassau and North Eleuthera. Additionally, he has published nearly 1,000 articles and blog posts, some 15 books, and over three million words.

Eric's writing has been translated into Norwegian, Spanish, Portuguese, and French, and he has appeared in French, Norwegian, and Spanish documentaries. His work has been used by writers for *Rolling Stone, Vanity Fair*, and the *Boston Globe*, with the fourth-largest paper in the US, the *New York Post* recognizing his book *U-Boats in New England*, as a *Book of the Week*. His research lead to the discovery of several persons KIA in World War II, and resulted in the United States Congress and US Navy correcting the records for the sinking of U-84 northeast of the Bahamas, and the award of a Distinguished Flying Cross to the pilot.

Since the mid-1970's Eric has voyaged or flown to all of the major Bahamian islands except Long Island and Ragged Island. He has a special affinity for north Eleuthera, and southern Abaco, particularly Sandy Point, where he and a team found the grave a World War II Norwegian merchant sailor and affectionately named the area around the old Cornwall lumber dock at Cross Harbour, *Olaus Beach*. Eric lives and writes in Boston near son and co-author, whose middle name is Dunmore: Felix.

www.ingramcontent.com/pod-product-compliance
Lightning Source LLC
Chambersburg PA
CBHW051118110526
44589CB00026B/2972